FLASH MX APPLICATION & INTERFACE DESIGN

Data delivery, navigation, and fun in Flash MX, XML, and PHP

Pete Aylward
Ken Jokol
Jamie Macdonald
Paul Prudence
Glen Rhodes
Robbie Shepherd
Todd Yard

friendsof

DESIGNER TO DESIGNER

FLASH MX APPLICATION & INTERFACE DESIGN

First Printed October 2002

Trademark Acknowledgements

friends of ED has endeavored to provide trademark information about all the companies and products mentioned in this book by the appropriate use of capitals. However, friends of ED cannot guarantee the accuracy of this information.

Published by friends of ED
30 -32 Lincoln Road, Olton, Birmingham.
B27 6PA. UK.
Printed in USA

ISBN 1-904344-07-0

Credits

Authors
Pete Aylward
Ken Jokol
Jamie Macdonald
Paul Prudence
Glen Rhodes
Robbie Shepherd
Todd Yard

Additional Material
Peter Fletcher

Reviewers
Jason Anderson
Kristian Besley
Kim Christensen
Steve McCormick
Jon Steer
Michael Walston

Proof Readers
Jon Bounds
Simon Collins
Richard Harrison
Chris Matterface
Fiona Murray
Catherine O'Flynn
Gavin Wray

Commissioning Editor
Jim Hannah

Technical Editor
Julie Closs

Project Manager
Richard Harrison

Designer
Katy Freer

Indexer
Fiona Murray

contents

Ken Jokol

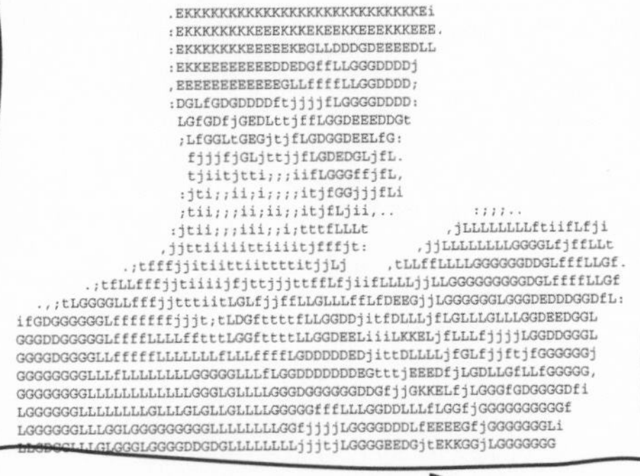

Since the last book (flash math creativity), the company I worked for got bought out by a larger corporation and I decided to go freelance instead of sitting in a big office block. So if you require any freelance work, contact me at kenj@pinderkaas.com.

I recently tuned my guitar (breaking a string in the process), and am now thinking of joining a band. Failing that, I'm open to offers of making music via email. Start by sending me a music file. Midi files also accepted.

jamie macdonald

I describe myself as a multi-disciplinary designer, which basically means I am a jack of all trades but master of none. My time is split between teaching undergraduate design students and looking after a well known publishers website. This leaves little time for actually getting any content up at hypeteila.com but I will do, one day.

Thanks to Peter Fletcher for throwing some funky karate moves.

pete aylward

jamie lives and works in london. when he finds time he updates his site www.nooflat.nu

I'm an artist. I used to paint & draw complex repetitive organic forms such as radiolarians and I've always considered these forms to be very beautiful. Since discovering Flash I've found little time to paint and now I cultivate simple actionscript routines to make configurable screen 'paintings', a few of these can be found at transphormetic.com. When not inside Flash I earn a living doing web design and creative development. Hopefully sometime soon I'll get around to finishing my online portfolio of this kind of work at slightspace.com.

paul prudence

glen rhodes

robbie Shepherd

I started my mind going early in life when I was about 4 years old. At that age, I began playing the piano, which was sitting unused in our house. I've been playing ever since then. Later, in 1997, I co-wrote a full-length musical called Chrystanthia. Somewhere along the way, I picked up game programming as a hobby, and eventually ended up making games professionally for home console systems. Then, in 1998, I discovered how I could take all my experiences and combine them when I discovered Flash. The rest is history. I share my ideas on my website, www.glenrhodes.com.

Robbie Shepherd is a self-taught designer/programmer who came into the IT industry at a fairly late age compared to most, a career choice which resulted in much hair loss (while learning Flash) and tears (victim of several dot com crashes) but which has ultimately provided the greatest satisfaction out of all the careers he's had. Despite Robbie's constant reiteration that he is a "Flash programmer", his parents insist on telling everyone they meet that their son is "a Flasher".

In his spare time Robbie makes things in Flash that he likes to call "Flash things". When he's not doing this he is either getting tattooed or watching Leeds stomp Newcastle in the Premier League, neither of which can happen often enough.

todd yard

After studying theatre in London, then working for several years as an actor in the US, Todd was introduced to Flash in 2000 and was quickly taken by how it allowed for both stunning creativity and programmatic logic application — a truly left-brain, right brain approach to production — and has not looked back. He now works as Creative Director for Daedalus Media in New York City, which specializes in the creation of Flash-based corporate presentations primarily for clients in the investment banking industry. His more frivolous work and experimentation can be found at his personal website, www.27Bobs.com.

Layout
The code in this book is written as it appears in the final files, with one exception: the Continuation symbol (➡) denotes where a line of code is too wide to fit on our page. If you're typing it in, you should just continue on the same line.

A word about source files and technical support
You can download the source files for this book from:

http://www.friendsofed.com/books/flash_mx_titles/inspiring_interfaces/index.html

As with all friends of ED titles, this book is backed up with free, fast and friendly technical support from our editors. If you have a query or problem, mail support@friendsofed.com, and we will get back to you as soon as possible.

If you have any comments about this book, good, bad, or ugly, we're keen to hear from you. Mail feedback@friendsofed.com and have your say!

There's a host of other features at friendsofed.com that may interest you – interviews with top designers, samples from our other books, and a message board where you can post your questions, discussions and answers.

Share the wealth!

Flash as the Ideal Medium

The days of Flash as a creative luxury are long gone. After months of downsizing, Flash creativity has been on a huge rationalization program. It is no longer enough to present animation in millions of colors and a hundred transparencies. It is no longer sufficient to provide interactivity and dynamism for their own sake.

The purpose of this collection is to show how designers have taken Flash and made it work for its supper. What we discover is a series of creations that place Flash at the hub of cutting edge web content.

The end result is a snapshot of Flash as the Ideal Medium.

In these amazing examples we see the software pushed to its limits to create unbeatable applications – a collapsible family tree, an interactive video learning system, and a drawing tool, capable of running online!

Beyond this we dip into the back-end capabilities to look at how to improve Flash still further. Some staple XML and PHP routines are brought in to add a bit of spice, while Flash's mysterious sharedObject command is hunted down and tamed to create a hybrid Tamagotchi-style houseplant – perfectly suited to lure surfers back to your website!

DESIGNING PRELOADERS

Let's begin this chapter with a little honesty – I am an impatient person. I have never been one to wait patiently, as I always feel there is something more productive I could be doing with my time. Traffic jams, delayed flights, shoppers in front of me digging for change at the check-out counter of a grocery store – all anathema to me. I'd speak more on this subject, but you probably get the idea and I'm sorry, I don't really have the time...

Of course my point is that, for most of us, when we have places to go, anything that stands in our way can become an annoyance. With traffic jams, delayed flights and inconsiderate shoppers, we don't have many options other than to wait. On the Web, however, if waiting gets irritating there are an infinite amount of destinations to explore, all just a click away. So if we want to keep our audience's attention, we have to make sure that there is no opportunity for them to get bored. If our site takes too long to load, the chances are that most users will never see our painstakingly designed content. So we need to avoid this risk, by providing a preloader.

This is a 3D preloader used at 27Bobs.com. As the site loads, the sketchy wireframe is replaced by a solid 3D block, representing the "chalk" used to draw the main site.

We'll be seeing more from 27Bobs a little bit later.

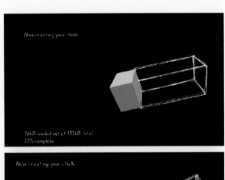

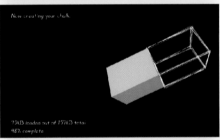

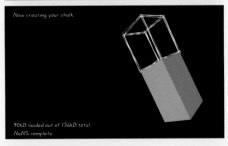

What is a preloader?

Look up "preloader" in Webster's Dictionary and you'll find...nothing. No doubt it will make its way into the reference manuals shortly, but for the time being let's form our own definition. Obviously, the word itself implies that a preloader appears before whatever main content may be loading. Since anything on the Web needs to be loaded to be seen, including a preloader, I would go further and say that a preloader would have a significantly smaller file size than whatever is the main content that is to be loaded. In order to fulfill its function, it must load pretty much instantly.

So we have a small piece of content that loads before, and is the fraction of the size of, the main content. What is the purpose of this smaller content? Well, in its basest form, a preloader simply gives the user feedback that something is occurring. Without a preloader, a user seeing a blank screen with no content might feel that the browser or computer has frozen. A simple "loading..." appearing on the screen would serve this purpose, although if it just sits there for too long we are running the same risk again.

Of course, a preloader could, and should, go further and give the user constant information on what is occurring and what is actually being loaded. Text information displaying what data is being transferred or a loading bar that shows what percentage has been loaded would accomplish this. By keeping the user in the know about what is going on, they will be less frustrated at the delay. A traffic jam would be more bearable with traffic information that kept you updated as to the reason for the delay and when the wait might be over.

Finally, to help pass the time while stuck in that car, what could be better than the radio playing tunes while you wait? Entertainment during delays can make the time pass much more quickly. As the cliché goes, time flies when you're having fun. Why not apply that to your preload time?

Let's amend our preloader definition to express these ideas. We have:

> a preloader is a small piece of content a fraction of the size of the main content, which is quickly loaded before the rest of your movie and offers a combination of feedback, information and entertainment for the user during the time it takes to load the main content.

The preloader at DaedalusMedia.com uses the number of bytes loaded to advance a frame-based animation. This animation, which consists of cracks slowly covering a statue, culminates in the statue exploding into fragments as the site is fully loaded.

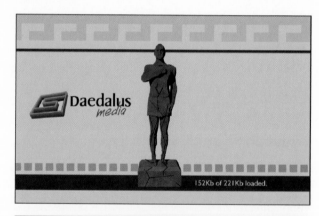

It is important to understand that a preloader is not the same as an intro animation. The former provides information and distraction during the load of the important material, hopefully at a small overhead. An intro animation, however, is usually produced as a sort of advertisement or "Flashy" display of skill and is often placed, as the name implies, as an introduction to the main content of the site. When Flash was first being used to enhance sites, it was all too common for the intro animation to have a large file size and require a preloader itself. At first, the wow factor justified the extra time, but it quickly grew tiresome for many Web users, which is when the "skip intro" button came into prominence. Unless you have good reason to provide an intro animation, or unless you can produce an animation with a small file size, it is usually best to get users directly to the main content of your site. Still, if you insist on a large intro animation, be sure to include a preloader before it so the user knows that something worthwhile is coming.

OK! Now with an idea of what we are trying to accomplish by building preloaders, let's look at some of the common pitfalls we will face.

Stumbling blocks with preloaders

On streaming

One of the terrific features of Flash is its ability to stream information to the user's computer. This allows the user to view content as soon as it becomes available, without having to wait for the content to load in its entirety. By planning the layout of your site or animation to take advantage of this feature, a preloader can become unnecessary since the user isn't made to wait more than a second or two before things begin happening. With long animations, or sites that are broken up into many frames on the main timeline (a practice used less and less frequently now with the powerful new scripting features of Flash MX), this is accomplished by keeping the initial frames' content small so that they can be seen immediately, allowing more time for the "heavier" frames to be loaded later in the timeline.

It is common now, however, to have much, if not all, of your content in a single frame. Animations may be created inside movie clips or through code, and content may be loaded and unloaded onto the stage from your movie's library or externally. When a movie is structured in this way with all of its content in the first frame, the user will see nothing until the content has loaded in its entirety. Because of this, a preloader becomes a necessity, if solely to inform the user that something is indeed coming, despite the lack of activity on the screen.

Since this chapter is on preloaders themselves and not ways of avoiding them, we won't discuss streaming to a large extent. In the examples I present in this chapter, we will work under the assumption that we have a large amount of content contained in a few frames that we need to provide a preloader for.

This doesn't mean that we will ignore the issue of streaming altogether. In actuality, the streaming feature of Flash is what allows us to create a preloader in the first place. By placing a small preloader in the first frame of your movie, it can stream into the user's player almost immediately and give the user feedback as the rest of the site is loading.

You can easily apply the same principles of a preloader to a streaming document if the need arises by simply providing a preloader that looks to load a set amount before the movie begins to play (similar to the buffering that occurs with other streaming media).

After a preloader for a large section at DaedalusMedia.com has loaded a set amount of bytes, the section is presented in part, with additional subsections becoming available as they load. This provides the user with the opportunity to see some content before the section is fully loaded.

Frames versus bytes

In Flash 4, preloaders were accomplished by using the `_framesLoaded` and `_totalFrames` properties of movie clips. By testing the amount of frames that were loaded into the player against the total amount of frames in the movie, you could determine how much was left to be loaded. The problem with this method occurred when the file size was not evenly distributed across frames, so if you had an exorbitant amount of data in the tenth frame of a ten frame movie, the preloader might say 90% loaded (since 90% of the *frames* had been loaded) when in fact only a small percentage of the total bytes for the entire site had been loaded, giving the user slightly misleading information.

A much more accurate way to determine the amount loaded into the player is by using the `getBytesLoaded()` and `getBytesTotal()` methods of a movie clip, which were introduced in Flash 5. These methods will, respectively, return the amount of information in bytes that has loaded into the player and the total bytes of the movie. To then convert these numbers into kilobytes, a unit much more comprehensible to our audience, you must divide the results by 1024, which is the number of bytes in a kilobyte.

We will exclusively use the bytes method over the frames method in our examples, as it gives the user much more accurate feedback and will allow us greater control.

Compression

A minor stumbling block for preloaders has now been introduced in Flash MX with the introduction of the new compression applied during publishing. This wonderful addition to the program further compresses the already small SWFs, making them even tinier. Movies that contain a lot of text and code will benefit greatly from this extra compression (I've seen movies reduced 25-50% in file size, which is nothing to shrug at).

So what could possibly be the problem? Well, the `getBytesLoaded()` and `getBytesTotal()` methods actually return the **uncompressed** file size of the movie. This does not become an issue if you merely use these methods to return a percentage since the relationship between the two remains the same. However, if you wish to display the actual amount of bytes that are loading, or the total bytes that will be loaded, the uncompressed value will be inaccurate since it is the compressed amount that is being loaded into the player.

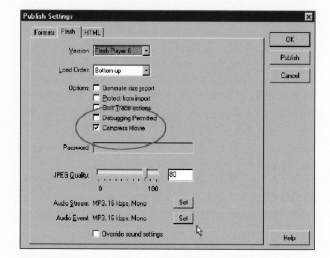

The fix for this is simple, taking little extra time, and really only becomes a nuisance upon updates to the movie. At the end of the first exercise I will demonstrate this fix for you so you may apply it to your own preloaders. Whether you see a need to use the compressed number will depend on your situation. If the difference between the compressed and uncompressed file sizes is merely a few kilobytes, then using the uncompressed value and saving the hassle would probably be preferable. My personal site, 27Bobs.com, which was 200kb when uncompressed, became 150kb after the compression. This tremendous difference was not something I could ignore and so I incorporated the fix.

File size and exported symbols

One last thing to keep in mind is the file size of the preloader itself. Remember that its entire purpose is negated if it does not appear to the user almost immediately. This means that it is imperative to keep your preloader at a tiny size. Simple vectors, small bitmaps, limited sounds, and minimal code will all help ensure the file size remains what it needs to be (and, of course, *not* using sounds and bitmaps will help even more). The last thing you want to find yourself doing is providing a preloader for your preloader.

Sometimes, however, additional data is loaded before the preloader that can delay the appearance of your movie's first frame. If you have exported any symbols from your library, including movie clips, sounds or fonts, these will load by default before the first frame of your movie. It will only be after these symbols are fully loaded that your first frame, and your preloader, will be drawn. Obviously, if you have a lot of symbols exported, which you need to do if you intend to add these items to the stage using code, then this will have an adverse effect on your preloader.

There are several ways around this problem. One common solution is to have your main content load into a separate level after your preloader has loaded. By keeping all of your exported symbols in this separate movie, you can load your preloader almost immediately into a base layer and give the user feedback as the main content loads. A related solution is to load all of your content into movie clips in your main movie. This gets to be a bit more cumbersome, and I usually opt for the former solution of loading into levels.

Another solution, which has been introduced in Flash MX, is to deselect the "Export in first frame" default when creating a new symbol. What this means is that your symbol will not be automatically loaded before the first frame is drawn and will instead be loaded at the frame that you manually place it on the stage. If you do not actually place an instance of the symbol on the stage in the authoring environment before you publish the movie, then you will not be able to access it through code. Using this feature, you can still export the symbols, but you don't have to wait for them to load before the preloader appears.

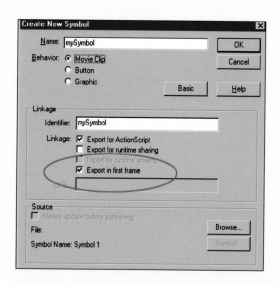

There appears to be a bug with exported fonts in Flash MX, version 6.0. Deselecting "Export in first frame" in the font linkage dialog box does not in fact keep the font from being loaded in the first frame. As long as you have "Export for Actionscript" selected, the font will automatically be exported in the first frame no matter what.

In addition to that, if you have exported fonts for use with `TextFormat` objects in movies that you are intending to load into levels or movie clips, then these fonts will not appear unless you have exported them from your `_level0` movie as well. This of course means that if your preloader is on `_level0`, as it commonly is, any exported fonts will need to load before the preloader appears.

Some possible solutions to this problem include:

- keeping your exported fonts to a minimum

- not exporting fonts containing an excessive amount of vector information

- not using `TextFormat` objects with exported fonts in loaded movies

Although the first two options are good to consider no matter what, the last limits you severely. Macromedia is aware of the problem and hopefully a solution will soon be found.

Creating killer preloaders

For me, preloaders come in three flavors. First, we have textual information on the status of the load. This could be anything from displaying "loading..." to a constant feedback of numbers reporting loading statistics. Building on this idea, you can represent the progress of the load graphically to keep the user informed of the status. The most common example of this, and the most common preloader, is the loading bar. Finally, we can ignore loading status altogether and simply keep the user entertained during the load time. Two effective methods for doing this are providing the user with an animation to watch or a game to play.

Again, most preloaders will be a combination of these types, and the distinction for most is rather blurry. For instance, the very act of a loading bar animating across the screen to show the percentage loaded can be considered a base form of entertainment (that's not to say that this is how you should spend your Saturday nights, but it is a kind of entertainment). Add some relevant numbers to give some textual feedback, and you have all three types rolled into one preloader. Of course, there's nothing that says you have to create a loading bar like everyone else...

Laser Logo

This first exercise is a variation on the classic loading bar and takes advantage of Flash MX's new ability to draw dynamic masks. The idea is to have a logo slowly revealed through the course of the load. The amount that is seen will be the percentage of the total bytes that have been loaded.

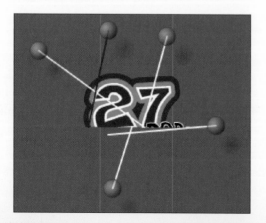

A simple mask wiping across a logo does the trick, but to make it more interesting we will code lasers to actually appear as if they are drawing the logo onto the screen. Open up the file `laserLogo.swf` to see the end result. The accompanying FLA is fully commented.

Let's go over how this effect was accomplished.

Masking the logo

The first thing we will do is create and animate a rectangular dynamic mask for our logo. This is a new option for us in Flash MX thanks to the `setMask` method and the drawing API. Let's see how it works!

Open up the file `laserLogo_start.fla` from the download files. This file has the main timeline already structured for you. You will see that it is a single frame movie with only a few layers. The base layer is simply a vertical rectangle outline. The second layer contains our logo set at center stage. The third layer has two dynamic text fields, both with _sans selected as the font. The two text fields have the instance names loaded and total, respectively. The final layer named code contains a blank keyframe. This is where we will be doing all of our work.

Save the movie with your own filename.

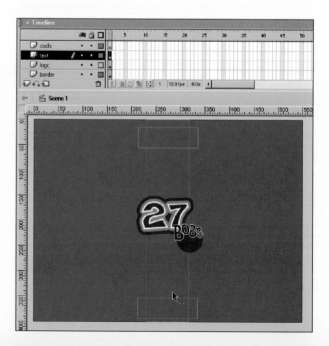

Select the blank keyframe in the first frame of your code layer and open up your ActionScript editor. The first thing we will do in our code is set up a few variables for our movie. Go ahead and type:

```
stageWidth = 550;
stageHeight = 400;

moveWidth = stageWidth*.5;
moveHeight = stageHeight*.5;

totalY = logo._height;
totalX = logo._width;

totalLasers = 5;
```

stageWidth and stageHeight are the dimensions of our movie. Instead of hard coding these, you might want to use the width and height properties of the new Stage object. I have found, however, that at times during testing, the values are erroneous. If you're using _root._width and _root._height, you'll get the width of a bounding box around all the objects on the stage instead of the values you set in Movie Properties, (though it works fine when embedded in an HTML page), and so I prefer to hard code the dimensions in the first few lines of my code.

moveWidth and moveHeight are the maximum distance our lasers (the spheres that fire the beams) will travel as they move about the stage. We will actually center the lasers' movement around the logo, so these two variables will keep the lasers near the center of the screen.

totalX and totalY will be used for the mask that we will draw over our logo. It will be a rectangular mask, and these two variables hold the final size of that rectangle. If you select the logo movie clip on the stage, you will find that I have already given it the instance name logo.

Finally, totalLasers is a variable that holds the amount of lasers we will add to the stage. I found that five was a nice, processor-friendly number for me, but feel free to adjust this number as you test.

The next step is to create the empty movie clip that we will use to draw our logo's mask. Type this code after the preceding lines:

```
this.createEmptyMovieClip("mask", 100);
mask._x = logo._x;
mask._y = logo._y;
logo.setMask(mask);
```

In these lines we create a movie clip named mask and place it at the registration point of our logo (which you will notice is set at the top left of the symbol). We then use the new setMask method to enable it as a mask for our logo movie clip.

With these basic variables and the mask set up, let's write the function that we will call each frame to keep an eye on the loading status:

```
assessLoad = function(clip) {
// var kbLoaded = Math.floor
//➡ (clip.getBytesLoaded()/1024);
// var kbTotal = Math.floor
//➡ (clip.getBytesTotal()/1024);

   // delete these two lines and uncomment
   // the above lines upon publishing
   var kbLoaded = Math.floor
➡ (getTimer()/200) + 2;
   var kbTotal = 150;
```

This is the heart and soul of our preloader. We are creating a function called assessLoad and sending it a reference to a movie clip (clip in the parameters). This will be the clip that we are checking the load status of. This can be the main movie, a movie clip or a level, depending on what we send the function. The first two lines that are commented out are what we would use if we were using this file online. For testing purposes, I've faked some variables in the following lines, which you would delete when you published the final version of this file. Let's take a look at what the commented out lines actually do for us.

The first line following our function declaration creates a local variable named `kbLoaded` and stores in this variable the current number of kilobytes loaded in the clip (`getBytesLoaded` returns bytes, so dividing by 1024 converts this to kilobytes). The next line stores the total number of kilobytes in the clip in a variable named `kbTotal`. These are the numbers this function will need to look at when this movie is online.

For this to work properly during our testing, I've created fake values for these variables in the next two lines. `kbLoaded` gets its value from the current millisecond of the movie. `kbTotal` is simply a hard coded number. You would delete these lines upon the final publishing.

Finish off this function by typing in the following lines:

```
var percentOfLogo =
➡Math.floor(kbLoaded/kbTotal * totalY);
   loaded.text = kbLoaded + "KB";
   total.text = kbTotal + "KB";
   drawLogo(percentOfLogo);
   if ((kbLoaded >= kbTotal) && kbTotal > 1) {
     endPreload(clip);
   }
}
```

Here we calculate the percentage of the bytes that we currently have loaded by dividing the bytes loaded by the total bytes. Since this number will be between 0 and 1, we multiply this by the `totalY` variable (the height of the logo) to determine how far down the logo we should draw our mask (a percentage of the logo's `totalY`). The `Math.floor` rounding method is called to drop the number down to its nearest integer.

The next two lines place our two kilobytes values into their respective text fields on stage, adding the string `"KB"` to the number. We then call a function called `drawLogo` and send it the current percentage of the logo to draw. This function will actually draw the mask and activate our lasers. The final lines are what end our preloading action once the load is complete. The `if` statement checks to see if the amount of kilobytes loaded is greater than or equal to the total amount of kilobytes, which means all of the content has loaded. The second condition of the `if` statement is just a safeguard that I use to ensure that some content has loaded before this check is made (occasionally, the first condition can be `undefined == undefined`, which would evaluate to true). If all of the content has loaded, we call our `endPreload` function, which we will write in a bit.

The next function we will address is the `drawLogo` function we called in the last section of code. Place these lines immediately following the `assessLoad` function:

```
drawLogo = function(percent) {
  mask.clear();
  mask.beginFill(0, 100);
  mask.lineTo(totalX, 0);
  mask.lineTo(totalX, percent);
  mask.lineTo(0, percent);
  mask.endFill();
  for (var i in lasers) {
    lasers[i].drawLaser(percent)
  }
}
```

If you have yet to use the new drawing API (Application Program Interface), it's extremely easy to pick up. In the above code, we first clear out any previous drawing we made in the mask movie clip. This needs to be done each time we intend to draw something new. With the `beginFill` method, we set the color and alpha of our mask. Since the mask won't be visible (just like a mask you create in the authoring environment), neither value is important, so I just set it to black (which has a value of 0x000000, or 0) with an alpha of 100.

The next three lines in this function use the `lineTo` method to draw three sides of our mask's rectangle. It's important to note that each time the `clear` method is called for a clip, the clip's "pen" is moved to the registration point (0, 0). The first `lineTo` then draws a line to the right side of the logo, represented by `totalX`. The second `lineTo` draws vertically down to the amount of the `totalY` that our current percentage of load has determined. The third `lineTo` next draws a line back to the left side of the logo. Calling the `endFill` method automatically closes our rectangle by drawing the final line back up to the registration point.

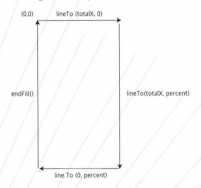

The final `for in` loop runs through each of the lasers we will have placed on the stage. The `lasers` array will actually hold references to each laser movie clip. Each of these clips will hold a method called `drawLaser`. We will look at this method in a moment.

Our last general function is called when our load is complete. Place these lines after the `drawLogo` function:

```
endPreload = function(clip) {
    clearInterval(preload);
    mask.removeMovieClip();
    for (var i in lasers) {
        lasers[i].leaveStage();
    }
    loaded.text = "";
    total.text = "";
}
```

Remember in our `assessLoad` function that `clip` was the movie clip we were assessing. Once the load is complete, this function is called. What we would add here is anything that needs to be cleaned up before we jump to our main content, or our home page, or whatever it was we were loading.

`preload` will be the identifier for the interval that constantly calls our `assessLoad` function above. We will create this using the new `setInterval` function later in the code. Here we get rid of the interval by calling the `clearInterval` function. Next, we remove the mask movie clip that we dynamically added to the stage at the top of our code. The `for in` loop that follows runs through our lasers array and calls each laser's `leaveStage` method which sends the lasers scurrying off stage right. Finally, we clear the text from both text fields by setting their text values to empty strings. If you actually wanted to send the playhead to another frame, this is where you would do it (or perhaps you would wait for all of the lasers to exit the stage).

This next bit of code sets everything in motion:

```
preload = setInterval(assessLoad, 40, this);
```

The new `setInterval` command is simply wonderful. In this form (there are others – we will use another later in this tutorial), it requires at least two parameters, but will take more. The first is the name of the function to be called, `assessLoad` in our case. The second parameter is the amount of time in milliseconds between each call of the function. We are calling our `assessLoad` function every 40 milliseconds. The final parameter we are sending is an argument for `assessLoad`, which you will remember was the clip to watch. We send it `this`, or the `_root` movie. If you were loading into another level or movie clip, you could simply substitute `_level1` or `myMC`, or whatever level or instance name you are dealing with, and the code would work.

We have given our interval the identifier `preload`. This allows us to clear the interval once the preload is complete (we did this in the `endPreload` function above).

Go ahead and test the movie now to see how the mask slowly reveals the logo, and to admire the nice new functionality Flash MX gives us! (If you'd like to see the mask itself being drawn, comment out the `logo.setMask(mask);` line earlier in the code.)

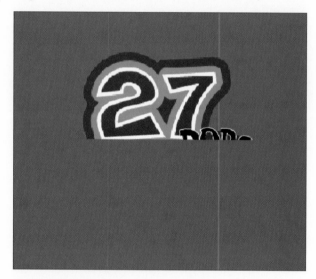

Animating lasers

Now that we have written the functions that reveal the logo, we will add our lasers and make them look as if they are drawing the logo onto the stage. We will accomplish this by creating a custom object for our lasers that will hold all of the methods for each laser movie clip. It's Flash's form of class creation, and it enables us to easily contain the code for our lasers in one tidy chunk.

Type this line after the `endPreload` function (before the `setInterval`):

```
LaserClass = function() {
    this.init()
}

LaserClass.prototype = new MovieClip();
```

`LaserClass` will be the name of our new Class of movie clips. What we will be doing is extending the basic functionality of the movie clip to do what we require of it to perform the laser actions. The line in which we set the prototype of the `LaserClass` to equal a new `MovieClip` is what allows us to do this. The prototype property holds all of the methods and properties of a Class of objects. By setting the prototype of `LaserClass` to be a new `MovieClip`, we are saying that any instance of `LaserClass` (each of our lasers that we place on the stage) will have all the functionality of the `MovieClip` Class plus the functionality of the `LaserClass`. Pretty handy.

The only thing that occurs when a new laser is created is a call to its `init` method (the second line in the code above), so let's write that next.

Place this code immediately following the above lines:

```
LaserClass.prototype.init = function() {
    if (this._parent.lasers == undefined) {
    this._parent.lasers = []
};
    this._parent.lasers.push(this);
    this.direction = Math.random() > .5 ? 1 : -1;
    this.laserPace = Math.floor(Math.random() * 25) + 5;
    this.contactPointX =
➡ Math.floor(Math.random()*totalX);
```

Notice that we are attaching this method to the prototype property of `LaserClass`. This will enable any instance of `LaserClass` access to it. And what does this method do? Well, the first line is a safety check to ensure that we have created the lasers array on the parent timeline (in this case, the main timeline). If we haven't, then we create it as a new instance of the `Array` object (setting a variable equal to square brackets does this). The next line pushes a reference to the current instance (whatever laser was just created) into the lasers array. You will recall that in our above functions we ran through this array to find references to all of our lasers.

The next three lines set properties for each instance. `direction` is set to be either -1 or 1. The way this line works is that it tests to see if a random number between 0 and 1 (the value returned by `Math.random`) is greater than 0.5. If it is, then 1 is assigned to `direction`. If not, then -1 is assigned to the `direction` property. `direction` will be the initial direction on the x axis that a laser will be moving. On the next line, `laserPace`, which is the rate of movement of each laser, is set to be a number between 5 and 30. Again, `Math.random` returns a number between 0 and 1. Multiplying this by 25 gives us a number between 0 and 25, which we round down to the nearest integer using the `Math.floor` method. To ensure that we don't have any lasers moving at a rate of less than 5, we add 5 to this value. Finally, on the last line of the above snippet, we set `contactPointX` to be a random number within the width of the logo. `contactPointX` will be the point of contact on the x axis of the laser beam on the logo.

Finishing off the `init` method, type this code under the preceding lines:

```
    this._x = Math.floor(Math.random()
    ➡ *moveWidth + stageWidth*.25);
    this._y = Math.floor(Math.random()
    ➡ *moveHeight + stageHeight*.25);
    this.setMoveWait();
    this.onPress = this.dragMe;
    this.onRelease = this.onReleaseOutside
    ➡ = this.releaseMe;
    this.useHandCursor = 0;
}
```

The first two lines here set the `_x` and `_y` position of our laser to somewhere within the `moveWidth` and `moveHeight` that we set up earlier. Remember that these variables limited the range of movement of our lasers. To offset these values to center the range on the logo, we multiply these positions by a quarter of the width and height of the stage (the `moveWidth` and `moveHeight` limit the range to 0.5 of the stage, so adding 0.25 to the `_x` and `_y` centers the range on the stage and the logo).

`setMoveWait` is a method we will create in a moment, which sets an amount of time for the laser to wait before moving to a new location. The next two lines then set the `onPress` event handler to equal the `dragMe` method, and the `onRelease` and `onReleaseOutside` event handlers to equal the `releaseMe` method. These two methods of the `LaserClass` will allow the lasers to be dragged around the stage by the user, and we will write them in a little bit. Because enabling these handlers causes our lasers to act as buttons, we disable the default hand cursor in the last line.

This next method, which we called in the previous `init` method, is short and sweet.

```
LaserClass.prototype.setMoveWait =
➡ function() {
    var wait = Math.floor(Math.random()
    ➡ *5000) + 2000;
    this.waitInterval = setInterval(this,
    ➡ "setDestination", wait);
}
```

`setMoveWait` sets the amount of time for the laser to wait before moving to a new destination. We first find a random number of milliseconds between 2000 and 7000 (2 to 7 seconds). Then using the new `setInterval` command, we tell the laser (`this`) to call its method `setDestination` in the amount of milliseconds we placed in the variable `wait`. `setInterval` is often used to create a looping action (indeed, we will do just that to call our `assessLoad` function that runs this entire movie), but it is also a great way to delay an action now in a Flash movie. `waitInterval` is the identifier we have assigned to the interval. We will need that to clear it later on.

That one was pretty simple. Here's the method we just called in our `setInterval`:

```
LaserClass.prototype.setDestination =
function() {
  clearInterval(this.waitInterval);
  this.endX = Math.floor(Math.random()
  *moveWidth + stageWidth*.25);
  this.endY = Math.floor(Math.random()
  *moveHeight + stageHeight*.25);
```

`setDestination` does exactly that – it picks a random destination to move the laser to. First, though, we clear the interval that we created to call this function after a delay. Then we assign an `endX` and an `endY` property to hold the destination coordinates for our laser. These lines are almost exactly the same as the original coordinate assignments in our `init()` method above.

Finishing the function:

```
    this.moveCount = 0;
    this.onEnterFrame = function() {
      this._x -= (this._x - this.endX)/5;
      this._y -= (this._y - this.endY)/5;
      this.moveCount++;
      if (this.moveCount > 20) {
        delete this.onEnterFrame;
        this.setMoveWait();
      }
    }
}
```

First, we initialize a variable. We will use this to limit the amount of time a laser will move. Next, we create a new function for the laser to run on each `enterFrame`. This code should be familiar to anyone who has scripted movement in a Flash movie. We simply move our `_x` and `_y` position a little bit closer to our destination each frame. Once our `moveCount` has exceeded 20 (we add one each frame), we remove the function on the `enterFrame` and call the `setMoveWait` method once again to get ready for the next move. The reason I use `moveCount` instead of

testing when the destination has been reached, as is often the practice, is because in this instance it is unimportant whether the laser gets to its exact destination or not. I would rather limit the amount of times the function loops to a set number as opposed to calling the `Math.abs` method constantly to check the laser position.

This next one's straightforward as well, so I'll give it all to you in one go. I know you can handle it!

```
LaserClass.prototype.leaveStage = function() {
  this.clear();
  clearinterval(this.waitInterval);
  delete this.onPress;
  delete this.onRelease;
  delete this.onReleaseOutside;
  this.xRate = 10;
  this.onEnterFrame = function() {
    this._x += this.xRate;
    this.xRate += 10;
    if (this._x > stageWidth*1.5) {
      this.removeMovieClip();
    }
  }
}
```

What are we doing? Well, when this method is called, we clear it of any beam graphics, we remove any lingering interval calls, we delete all of our button event handler functions, and we send the clip scurrying off the right of the stage. Once it is far enough off, we remove the clip.

Here are the two `LaserClass` methods which allow the user to drag the lasers about the stage:

```
LaserClass.prototype.dragMe = function() {
  delete this.onEnterFrame;
  clearinterval(this.waitInterval);
  this.startDrag();
}

LaserClass.prototype.releaseMe = function() {
  stopDrag();
  this.setMoveWait();
}
```

Once a user clicks on a laser with the mouse it becomes draggable. We remove any interval calls as well as its `enterFrame` handler (in case it is currently moving). Once the laser is released, we stop the dragging and call its `setMoveWait` method to determine when it moves next. This next line of code is what ties this Class definition with a symbol in our library. Place this after the `releaseMe` method:

```
Object.registerClass("laser", LaserClass);

for (i = 0; i < totalLasers; i++) {
    this.attachMovie("laser", "l" + i, i);
}
```

If you right-click on the laser symbol in the library and select Linkage, you will notice that I have exported it as laser. By then registering this symbol with the Class definition `LaserClass` through the `Object` object's `registerClass` method, I have ensured that any instance of laser that I place on the stage will in fact be an instance of `LaserClass`. In the `for` loop that follows, I place all the lasers on the stage.

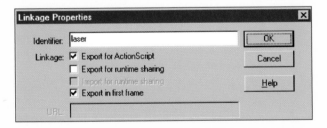

Go ahead and test your movie to see the lasers moving about the logo, each in its own random way, until the preloading is done and they scoot off the right hand side of the stage and disappear.

Drawing the laser beams

Now it's time to complete the effect by drawing beams from the lasers onto the logo. This gets a little tougher, but creates a fantastic effect, so stick with me!

Our next method is called during our `drawLogo` function above and draws the actual laser beam on to the stage.

Place these lines after the `init` method:

```
LaserClass.prototype.drawLaser =
➡function(percent) {
    this.recursiveCount = 0;
    this.beamY = logo._y - this._y + percent;
    this.beamX = this.getContactX();
```

(Really, you can place it anywhere within the `LaserClass` definition as long as it is *after* the `LaserClass.prototype = new MovieClip()` and *before* the `Object.registerClass` line. This goes for all subsequent methods of `LaserClass` as well.)

Remember that `percent` is the percentage of the kilobytes loaded multiplied by the height of the logo. We sent it to this function so that the lasers know at what y position to aim their beams. The first line initializes a variable called `recursiveCount`. We will use this as a safety check in a bit, and I will explain it more fully then. The next two lines find an x and y position for the end of the laser beam (the origin of the beam is always on the laser movie clip itself). `beamY` is found by taking the logo's `_y` position and subtracting the laser's `_y` position. This offset is necessary since we will be drawing the laser inside the laser movie clip. We then add in the current percentage of the logo's total height. Finding the x position of the laser is a bit more complicated, so I placed it inside another method called `getContactX`. We will address that method in a moment.

14

Continue with the `drawLaser` method by adding the following lines of code:

```
for (var i in logo) {
    if (typeof logo[i] == "movieclip") {
        if (logo[i].hitTest(this.contactPoint.x,
        ➥this.contactPoint.y, 1)) {
            var logoColor = new Color(logo[i]);
            var laserColor = logoColor.getRGB();
            break;
        }
    }
}
```

To understand this code, you will need to understand how I have set up the logo. Enter symbol editing mode. You will find that the logo is separated into layers, and each layer contains an element of a different color. If you select any of the elements, you will find that each layer contains its own movie clip, and that the movie clip has been colored in the Properties panel. It is set up in this way so that we can use the Color object's built-in `getRGB` method to determine each clip's color when a laser is over it. For this reason we not only need to separate each color into its own movie clip, but we need to then tint that movie clip 100% of its base color (look down to the Properties panel again to see evidence of this). Currently, there is no way for Flash to determine a clip or pixel's color, so we must create this workaround to accomplish our task.

As to the code, the `for in` loop above runs through each property inside of logo. If a property (which can be an object) is a movie clip, then it tests to see if the point of contact for the laser (stored in `this.contactPoint`, which is set in the `getContactX` function that we will write next) hits that logo movie clip. If it does, then it creates a temporary Color object and uses it to find the color of that element using the `getRGB` method. It stores that color in the variable `laserColor`. Having found one color, we need no longer search and so we break out of the loop.

If you are wondering about the difference between the x and y values stored in `this.contactPoint` and the values stored in `beamX` and `beamY`, you will see when we set up the values for `contactPoint` that they are relative to the main timeline, whereas `beamX` and `beamY` are relative to the laser movie clip. We need the `contactPoint` values in order to call `hitTest`, but we will need the `beamX` and `beamY` values to draw the laser graphic correctly inside of the laser movie clip.

The last bit of this function is a piece of cake. Finish it off by adding these lines:

```
this.clear();
    this.lineStyle(2, laserColor, 100);
    this.lineTo(this.beamX, this.beamY);
}
```

Pretty easy. We clear the previously drawn beam graphic and reset the `lineStyle` (thickness, color and alpha for the laser), which is cleared every time the `clear` method is called. We then draw our line from the laser's origin (0,0) to whatever values we assigned to `beamX` and `beamY`.

The next, and final, method is a bit of a bear, and the most complicated of this project. Let's walk through it slowly.

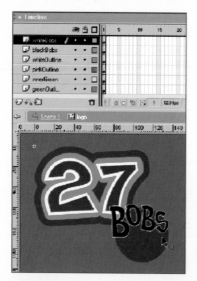

Place it after the `drawLaser` method:

```
LaserClass.prototype.getContactX = function() {
   this.recursiveCount++;
   if (this.recursiveCount > 100) {
     return totalX/2
   }
   this.contactPointX +=
➥this.laserPace*this.direction;
```

`getContactX` is called to determine the beam's point of contact on the logo on the x axis. You will see in a moment that due to the odd shape of the logo, running a simple back and forth sweep isn't possible, so we have to do a little searching for a place to shoot the beam. Because of this, `getContactX` is a recursive function, which means that it's a function that can call itself. This is fine as long as you can ensure that the number of times the function is called isn't infinite, which can sometimes happen in recursive loops. To take care of this, we set the laser's `recursiveCount` property to 0 each time the laser is told to draw itself (in the `drawLaser` method). Each time we enter this method, we add one to `recursiveCount`. If it turns out that this method needs to call itself more than 100 times, we "give up" and simply set the x position to be dead center of the logo.

The final line of code in the above section increments our `contactPointX` property, which is in fact the beam's x point of contact on the logo, by the rate of the laser multiplied by the direction (positive or negative).

Now we need to make some checks to make sure our beam is falling on to our logo. Type these lines after the previous code:

```
if (this.direction > 0) {
   if (this.contactPointX > totalX) {
     this.direction *= -1;
     this.contactPointX = totalX;
   }
} else {
   if (this.contactPointX < 0) {
     this.direction *= -1;
     this.contactPointX = 0;
   }
}
```

The first `if` statement simply checks to see if we are moving in a positive direction. If we are, we then check to see if we have moved off of the right side of the logo. If this occurs, we change direction. The `else` statement simply checks the left side of the logo.

And for the final bit of code for our `getContactX` method (and the final bit in this tutorial!):

```
var beamX = this.contactPointX - (this._x -
➥logo._x);
this.contactPoint = {x:beamX, y:this.beamY};
this.localToGlobal(this.contactPoint);
while (!logo.hitTest(this.contactPoint.x,
➥this.contactPoint.y, 1)) {
   beamX = this.getContactX();
}
return beamX;
}
```

Here we create a local variable named `beamX` and adjust it for the distance between our laser source and the logo. We need to do this since the value for `contactPointX` is simply a number between 0 and the width of the logo. If our laser's `_x` position was equal to the logo's `_x` position, then this value would be fine. Because the laser's position is dynamic, however, we need to make this adjustment.

`contactPoint` is a new object in which we place the `beamX` and `beamY` variables. This object is necessary for the next line in which we call the `localToGlobal` method. `localToGlobal` is an extremely handy method, which converts coordinates from one coordinate space to another. In this instance, it is taking x and y coordinate values inside the laser and converting them to coordinates on the main stage. If we are to perform `hitTests` using coordinate points as we did in the above `drawLaser` function, and as we will in the next line inside this function, then we need to ensure the coordinates are all in the same coordinate space. Since a `hitTest` with the logo will need coordinate positions on the main timeline, we have to convert our laser contact point to suit.

The `while` statement that follows checks to see if the x and y contact points are falling inside the logo. The third argument in the `hitTest` call is a Boolean value which determines if we are using the true shape of the object or simply its bounding box. For our odd shaped logo, it's essential that we use the true shape, and so we set this value to `true`.

If we are hitting the logo with our point of contact, the `while` loop is skipped and we return the `beamX` value to wherever we called it. However, if the point of contact has fallen outside of the logo, we call this function again until we have a value that falls inside the logo. This is what makes this a recursive function. Remember that we will run through this function up to 100 times, adjusting `contactPointX` a little each time and checking to see when it's hitting our logo.

Now test your movie and watch the laser show! How's that for a loading bar? All that at 5KB.

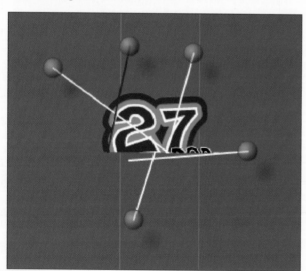

Experiment by dropping your own logo into the movie (remembering to set up the symbol in a similar layered fashion). Play with the number of lasers and their variables, and perhaps alter its graphic. I created a variant where the laser spheres actually appear to refract the logo as they pass over it, as if made of glass, by using additional masking tricks. I have included the file in the download files as `laserLogo_refract.fla`. The possibilities of exploration with this technique are wide and varied.

Accurate kilobytes

Because of the new compression feature in Flash MX, sometimes the amount of uncompressed kilobytes returned in the `getBytesLoaded` and `getBytesTotal` method calls will differ greatly from the compressed amount, as discussed earlier. If you wish to have an accurate display of the kilobytes that are loading, you can do so with just a few steps and a few lines of code. Keep in mind that one of the downsides of having to do this is you must wait until a movie is finished and published before you can incorporate the fix.

1. Publish your movie and write down its file size. In our above example, let's pretend that the compressed file size is 125KB.

2. In the `assessLoad` function after you declare `kbTotal`, create a new variable called `offset` and hard code the compressed file size divided by the uncompressed file size.

    ```
    var offset = 125/kbTotal;
    ```

3. Now in any text field where you display actual readouts of the kilobytes (not percentages, since these are unaffected), multiply the kilobytes by the offset.

    ```
    loaded.text = Math.floor
    ➡ (kbLoaded*offset) + "KB";
    total.text = Math.floor(kbTotal*offset)
    ➡ + "KB";
    ```

It's a fairly simple solution. Of course if you ever update the file, and the compressed file size changes, you will need to repeat the process.

Punchline

This preloader consists of an animation that the user can enjoy as the main content loads. It uses the same principle as the last preloader of testing the bytes loaded against the total bytes to determine when the load is complete. During that process, the user is treated to a series of knock knock jokes and an accompanying animation to keep them from becoming impatient. Open up the file `punchline.swf` from the download files to see the final effect. The FLA of the same name contains fully commented code for you to peruse.

When I was first thinking about creating this animated preloader, the initial challenge was to come up with something that could appear animated and entertaining, but not actually contain an excessive amount of animation (and thus increase the file size). Right away I remembered 'Simpsons' creator Matt Groening's *Life in Hell* comic and two of his characters, Akbar and Jeff, who many times filled a grid of panels without changing position or expression. A lot of the time, the humor actually arose from this fact. So I initially played with creating a two person comic strip with no expressions or movement. It turned to knock knock jokes as I considered the fact that it was obvious back and forth banter and would be easy to extend if necessary (just add more jokes!). The punch just came from the need to add a button to these (admittedly) horrible jokes. That and the fact that I found it funny, and it's all about making me laugh! Let's look at how it was done.

Open the file `punchline_start.fla` and save it as `punchline.fla`. The graphics and layout have already been set up for you so that we may begin looking at the code necessary to achieve this effect. On the main timeline we have two code layers, one named jokes and the other code. Beneath that we have our graphics layers, beginning with continue to hold our continue button and text to hold our two text fields, loaded and total, just as in our Laser Logo example. startLines holds two movie clip instances of the startLine symbol (it's an empty movie clip). These clips, named jokerLine and hitterLine, give us an easy way to define the coordinate position of where we want each character's dialog line to be drawn from. Beneath that layer we have our jokePeople animation movie clip, and on the bottom layer we have our background oval shape.

Now let's take a closer look at the animation so that you can better understand how we use it in the code. Open your library and enter symbol editing mode for jokePeople. You will see that we have several layers of animation divided into four frame sets. The first, which has the label **joke**, is the joker character on the left with his mouth open. **response** has the hitter character on the right opening his mouth while the joker has closed his. The third label, **noTalk**, has both characters with their mouths closed, and the fourth and final label, **punch**, has the hitting animation. The only actions contained in this movie clip, and the only actions outside of the first frame of our main timeline, are a `stop()` action in the first frame to keep the clip from playing at the start of the movie, and a `gotoAndStop("noTalk")` call in the final frame after the hitting animation has played in its entirety. Each time the hitting occurs, the movie clip will automatically return to its `"noTalk"` state and wait for the next joke.

The final thing to look at before we start in on the code is on the main timeline, so return there now and select the first frame of the jokes layer. Open up your ActionScript editor and take a look at how the jokes are set up in the movie. It begins as follows:

```
jokes = [];

joke = [];
joke.push("Knock knock.");
joke.push("Who's there?");
joke.push("Atch.");
joke.push("Atch who?");
joke.push("Gesundheit!");

jokes.push(joke);
```

The first line creates a new array in which we will store all of the jokes. We then create the jokes one by one. We do this by creating another array called `joke`. Each of the subsequent lines pushes a dialog line into the new `joke` array. Once the joke is complete, we push the `joke` array into our larger `jokes` array. This creates a nice clean two dimensional array for us to access as we tell the jokes. Every one added follows the same structure (without, of course, reinitializing the `jokes` array from the top).

After the final joke has been added, we end with the lines:

```
delete joke;

randomSort = function () {
   return Math.round(Math.random());
}
jokes.sort(randomSort);
```

Here, we delete the last `joke` array that we have been using for the individual jokes. The last few lines take advantage of the built-in sorting method of the array object to randomize our array. We send with the `sort` call a compare function that returns either a 0 or 1, which the `sort` method uses to randomly shuffle the array. Usually when you use a compare function, the `sort` method will use it to compare two adjacent indices at a time and place them in an order determined by whatever the compare function returns, -1, 0, or 1. In our example, we simply send a 0 or 1 without a consideration as to the values of the indices themselves. Based on whether the number is 0 or 1 for a particular pair of indices, the `sort` method will swap the two or leave them in place. As it does this throughout the length of the array, the effect is a random shuffle.

With the set-up explained, let's get into the code that creates our joke dialog. Select the first frame of the code layer and type the following into the ActionScript editor:

```
jokeX = 200;
jokeY = 100;
currentJoke = 0;

jokeTF = new TextFormat();
jokeTF.font = "_sans";
jokeTF.size = 18;

this.createTextField("bubble", 0, jokeX, jokeY, 0, 0);
bubble.autoSize = "center";
bubble.setNewTextFormat(jokeTF);
bubble.selectable = 0;
```

The first three lines are variables we will be using in our code. `jokeX` and `jokeY` are the center coordinates position of our joke text field. `currentJoke` is the index number our current position in the `jokes` array.
Next we create a new `TextFormat` object so that we can format our joke text field. We give it a system font choice of `"_sans"` and a point size of 18.

The last block creates a new text field called bubble (I was thinking of little comic dialog bubbles). The create line sets the text field's depth at 0, its `_x` and `_y` to equal the variables we set above, and its width and height to 0 pixels. We can do this because on the next line we set its `autoSize` property to be `center`, which means that the text field will automatically expand from center to contain whatever text we place inside it. On the final lines we set bubble's text format to be our `jokeTF` format and we disable its selectable property so that the user won't get an I bar when they place the mouse over the text field.

Let's continue. Place these lines after the previous code:

```
this.createEmptyMovieClip("speechLine", 1);
jokePeople.gotoAndStop("noTalk");
continue_btn._visible = 0;
```

Three straightforward lines for you. The first creates a new movie clip in which we will draw each character's speech line (the line that leads from the character to text field bubble). Next we send our `jokePeople` movie clip, which is the instance name of the `jokePeople` symbol on our stage, to its `"noTalk"` frame. Finally, we turn our `continue_btn` instance invisible, since it shouldn't be seen until the content has been fully loaded.

The next two functions should look extremely familiar to you if you completed the previous exercise – in fact, with a little tweaking, you could easily add these functions to an ActionScript library that you could pull in to run any preloader you design. For the time being, let's simply type them into our movie.

```
assessLoad = function(clip) {
// var kbLoaded = Math.floor(clip.getBytesLoaded()/1024);
// var kbTotal = Math.floor(clip.getBytesTotal()/1024);

   // delete these two lines and uncomment
   // the above lines upon publishing
   var kbLoaded = Math.floor(getTimer()/200) + 2;
   var kbTotal = 150;

   loaded.text = kbLoaded + "KB";
   total.text = kbTotal + "KB";
   if ((kbLoaded >= kbTotal) && kbTotal > 1) {
     endPreload(clip);
   };
};

endPreload = function(clip) {
   clearInterval(preload);
   loaded.text = "";
   total.text = "";
   continue_btn._visible = 1;
   continue_btn.onPress = function() {
     //clip.gotoAndStop("main")
   };
};
```

Since the `assessLoad` function is exactly the same as in Laser Logo, you can look there for a longer explanation. Suffice it to say that it records the amount of bytes loaded and the total bytes of the movie, places these values in text fields, and checks to see when the movie is fully loaded. The `endPreload` function contains a few different lines for you to consider. You can see that we clear our preload interval as before, wipe our text fields clean and make our button visible. That's it. The jokes will continue until the user has grown tired of them and clicks on the `continue_btn`, at which point the playhead is sent to another frame, or whatever you need to have happen to get to your main content.

Now we have four functions that control the telling of the jokes. The first initiates the entire process. Type these lines after the `endPreload` function:

```
startJoke = function() {
   currentLine = 0;
   clearInterval(nextJokeInterval);
   startLine();
}
```

`startJoke` first sets the current line of the current joke to 0. Remember that each index in the `jokes` array contains another array. The variable `currentJoke` that we set above represents the index position in `jokes`. `currentLine` then represents the index in the sub-array, and since each joke will begin on its first line, the index is set to 0. The next line in this function clears the interval we will set that will create a pause before the joker begins his next joke. Finally, we call the `startLine` function, which will do just that: start the display of the line on the screen. Let's write that function now.

Type this to follow the previous code:

```
startLine = function() {
   currentLetter = 0;
   clearInterval(nextLine);
   bubble.text = "";
   speechLine.clear();
```

At the start of this function call, we set the current letter to 0 (the first letter in the line), we clear the interval used to delay the display of the next line, we erase the current text in bubble and clear the speech line drawing from the `speechLine` movie clip.

Add this to finish the `startLine` function:

```
if (currentLine >=
➡jokes[currentJoke].length) {
     jokePeople.gotoAndStop("noTalk");
     hitInterval = setInterval(hitJoker, 1000);
   } else {
     speechLine.lineStyle(1, 0, 100);
     if (currentLine%2 > 0) {
       speechLine.moveTo(hitterLine._x,
       ➡ hitterLine._y);
       jokePeople.gotoAndStop("response");
     } else {
       speechLine.moveTo(jokerLine._x,
       ➡ jokerLine._y);
       jokePeople.gotoAndStop("joke");
     }
     speechLine.lineTo(jokeX, jokeY + 30);
     letterInterval =
     ➡ setInterval(revealLetters, 50);
   }
}
```

Before we display any text, we first check to see if we have reached the last line of the joke. `jokes[currentJoke]` contains an array holding each line of our joke, so if the `currentLine` is equal to or greater than the length of this array, we know we have reached the end. If this is the case, we send our jokers to `"noTalk"`, and set up a one second delay before we call our `hitJoker` function, which we will create next. We give this the identifier `hitInterval`.

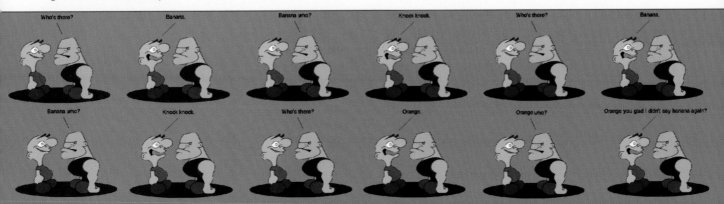

If we have not reached the last line of our joke, we go ahead and start displaying the line. First, we set the lineStyle for our speechLine movie clip to be 1 pixel black at 100% opacity. We then look to see if the currentLine is odd or even. Since the jokes are a set back-and-forth banter and the first line always goes to the joker, we know that any odd index numbers mean that the hitter is speaking. The modulo operator (%) is an easy way to determine odd or even since it returns the remainder of the two operands. Any odd number divided by two will have a remainder of 1, so we check to see if this occurs with our current line index. If indeed we do have an odd number, we move our speechLine's starting draw position to the hitterLine movie clip coordinates and send our animation to the "response" frame. If instead the index is even, we know that the joker is speaking and so move the speechLine to draw from jokerLine and send the animation to the "joke" frame.

Finally, we draw the speechLine from whatever starting position it is at to the bubble text field (plus a 30 pixel offset) and use setInterval to call the revealLetters function every 50 milliseconds. revealLetters will add letters one by one to the bubbles text field.

That was the longest of the lot. Here's a function that's short and sweet, to be placed after the startLine function:

```
hitJoker = function() {
  if (Math.random() > .33) {
    clearInterval(hitInterval);
    jokePeople.gotoAndPlay("punch");
    nextJokeInterval =
➥ setInterval(startJoke, 3000);
    currentJoke++;
    if (currentJoke >= jokes.length) {
      currentJoke = 0;
    }
  }
}
```

You will recall that hitJoker was called after the last line of the joke was given (right above in the startLine function). There was a one second delay before this function was called. After one second has passed, we test a random number between 0 and 1 to see if it is greater than 0.33. If it's not, nothing happens and we wait another second before this function is called again. This keeps occurring until a random number crops up that is greater than 0.33. I have set it up in this way so that the punch does not happen at a regular interval for each joke, which provides just a little more fun (well, it makes *me* laugh!).

Once a random number meets the if conditional's requirements, we clear the interval that is calling this function every second. We then send our animation to play the punching sequence and set up another interval to delay the start of our next joke. The three seconds we wait (3000 milliseconds) is just enough for the punch to occur and a brief pause at the "noTalk" frame (remember we have an action inside the animation that sends the playhead to "noTalk" upon the punch sequence's conclusion).

The final lines increment our current joke index. If we have reached the end of our jokes array, we loop back to the top. By adding enough jokes, you should be able to ensure that the user won't reach the end of the sequence before the content has loaded.

One last function for our movie. Type these lines after the hitJoker function:

```
revealLetters = function() {
  var line = jokes[currentJoke]
➥ [currentLine];
  bubble.text += line.charAt
➥ (currentLetter);
  currentLetter++;
  if (currentLetter > line.length) {
    clearInterval(letterInterval);
    currentLine++;
    nextLine = setInterval(startLine, 2000);
  }
}
```

revealLetters takes care of the actual animation of our text. This is called every 50 milliseconds (set up in our startLine function). We first place the current line into a variable for easy access. Next we add the current letter to our bubble text field and increment the currentLetter variable. If we have reached the last letter of the current line, we clear the interval that is calling this function, increment our line variable and finally create a new interval to call the startLine function after 2 seconds have passed (can you tell how much I love the new setInterval command?). The 2 second delay should be enough for the user to read the entire line.

And now for the final two lines:

```
startJoke();

preload = setInterval(assessLoad, 20, this);
```

startJoke calls the first joke and starts the entire ball rolling. The last line should look familiar to you from the last exercise. It sets up an interval to call assessLoad every 20 milliseconds, sending the additional argument of "this" to let the function know that we are loading the main movie.

Test your movie and see how it works. Try adding some jokes, or perhaps changing the structure into a dialog instead. Consider a professor offering instructions on site navigation, or a newsreader updating the user on recent events at your company. Keep in mind that if you add longer lines, you will have to account for multiline and wordwrap in the bubble text field.

The load time will pass in no time, and all for a measly 7KB!

And even more preloaders!

I've prepared a few additional preloaders for you to play with and build upon. You can find them all fully commented in the download files for you to open up and look under the hood.

Falling tiles – 3KB

This preloader, `fallingTiles.fla` allows you to place an image on the screen that will appear to be made up of many tiles. The tiles will slowly fall away into space depending on the amount of the site that has been loaded. The beauty of this is that you can easily drop in your own images for both the tiled image and the background to use it for your own projects.

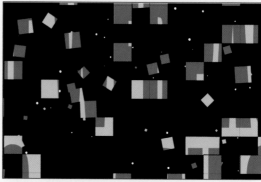

Text scroller – 18KB

This preloader, `textScroll.fla`, is a bit larger in file size since it requires an embedded font for the animation. Still, it provides a simple, entertaining and familiar effect that will cause the time to pass quickly as the users read whatever it is you have prepared. Taken from the opening sequences of the Star Wars films, the textScroll effect provides a way to communicate some useful information as well as a diversion.

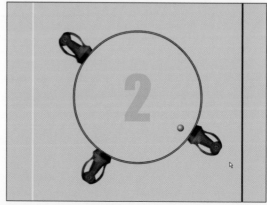

Perimeter Sweep – 7KB

The final preloader, `perimeterSweep.fla`, is a fully functioning game that a user can be challenged by as the site loads in the background. A circular variation on Pong, Perimeter Sweep gives the player three paddles to use to keep multiple balls within the perimeter of the circle. With a few additional tweaks, this could be turned into site content itself, but as it stands at 7KB, it makes a great diversionary preloader.

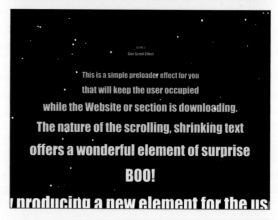

Conclusion

As long as our eyes are bigger than our stomachs (or our imaginations are bigger than our phonelines), we will demand and produce more than our bandwidth will easily accommodate. This isn't a problem as long as you provide the user with something either entertaining or productive (or both!) as your main content loads in the background. Don't ever leave the user with any idle time during which they can click to somewhere that doesn't make them wait. And of course, if you can do it in style, that's all the better.

CREATING INTERFACES WITH THE DRAWING API

The interface – aesthetics, interaction & usability

Humans have always used graphics to represent the world around them. From cave paintings to technical diagrams, we have constantly sought new ways of depicting information in pictographic form. The use of computers in the last few decades brought to us the GUI – Graphical User Interface. Prior to the forward-looking work done at Xerox, most interfaces required their users to remember and type esoteric text commands to get things done. But with the GUI, computers were made accessible to the masses, and the technical revolution began to take hold. Our culture is now so saturated with information and communication technologies that the design of interfaces has increasingly become a challenging key issue of culture. I think it's probably to our benefit that we should consider what we are trying to say about our information in the way that we present it.

We are at the early evolutionary stages regarding interface design. In many cases computer interfaces still reference the real physical world. They mimic mechanical devices, dashboards and control systems. As a result we find our computer interfaces with bevel-edged buttons in rows and grids, just as they appear in aircraft cockpits for example. The downside of trying to make an interface like something in the real world however is that it misses the point when it comes to representations of human experience and subjectivity – it says nothing about the information it represents.

Another problem is the fact that after some years of experience with interactive interfaces there seems to be a standard school of thought about guidelines for producing interfaces. Quite often these functionality-centric models favor a productivity context, designing to get work done, rather than taking any account of the notion of playfulness for the designer or the user. As a result the magic of innovation gets lost, as designer-developers get obsessed with the usability of their e-commerce sites. While usability and functionality are important, there are occasions where it's valuable to experiment at the fringes, in order to make breakthroughs and find new aesthetically interesting ways of representing information.

Designing for interactivity means asking the question 'how can we give a user an experience?' and 'what kind of experience do we want our users to have?' I think quite often that usability can create a gulf between user and experience – I'd like to produce an interface that could almost be seen as a work of art itself, responding creatively to user input.

Spirals in nature

As anyone with an eye for patterns will know, nature seems to be attracted to repetition, symmetry and geometrical exactness, and this has been an ongoing interest for me, from both an artistic and philosophical point of view, for quite some time. From the recursive branching seen in trees to the delicate mirrored patterns on moths' wings, in the six-fold symmetry of snowflakes and in chaotic fractal geometry of clouds, we are immersed in repetitive forms.

One particular universal form that nature seems content in showing off whenever it gets the chance is the humble spiral – we find it almost everywhere. At the microscopic end of the scale we find the smallest of all living creatures is spiral shaped, the spirillum bacteria. The building blocks of life, DNA, are well known to exhibit a double helical spiral formation. Moving up the ladder we find an amazing amount of spiral shaped shells. The shell of the nautilus, the only surviving cephlapod, is a fine example of a growth or logarithmic spiral – its ancestor is the well known ammonite. The sunflower head reveals two sets of opposing spirals formed by individual florets – the number of arms in each opposing spiral are two adjacent numbers in the Fibonacci sequence, 34 and 55. The Fibonacci sequence of numbers runs 1,1,2,3,5,8,13,21,34,55 and so on. The series is generated by adding the two previous numbers in the sequence to produce the third. This sequence of numbers is the blueprint to the spiral growth formation of petals and leaves in nearly all plants. Continuing upwards in scale we find whirlpools, hurricanes and tornados, and finally as we look into space we see that galaxies have radial arms that spiral out into the universe.

Man has also been inspired by the spiral – a great deal of artifacts, both ancient and modern, employ the spiral as a decorative motif. Architecture has repeatedly used the constructional properties of spirals from both a utilitarian and an aesthetic point of view. In 1919 the great philosopher and psychologist Carl Jung posited the notion of symbol sharing in the collective unconscious. The spiral, he believed, was one of these genetically shared archetypes linking all societies and all cultures, ancient and modern.

Spirals as interface – concepts

I've used the spiral as inspiration to produce an interface using Flash MX's native drawing API. There are a couple of reasons why I chose the spiral archetype. Firstly I wanted to produce an interface with some aesthetic beauty of its own. What better way than to borrow one of nature's prototypes? Most of the interfaces on the web are often nothing more than rows of buttons in grid formation, a bit like a few rows of a spreadsheet!

My second reason for using the spiral as a prototype has to do with the utilization of space. Using the spiral as a model, Nature expertly makes the most out of its spatial confines. DNA is a great example of the economical use of space for storing information, as it coils information into a dense double helical formation – any other way and these chains would take up much greater volume. Since Web design is continually concerned with real estate it's probably to our advantage to take on some of nature's answers to the constraints of space, and so the spiral is a good structural model to base an interface upon.

To give wholeness to this interface I decided that the site's content would also be spirals. When each item of the interface is rolled over or clicked it will allow us to view a picture of a particular spiral form and provide us with information about the spiral, such as its natural size and its type in terms of mathematical terminology. I've kept the structure of data to one level since this chapter is more interested in the utilization of the drawing API to produce interfaces than the subtle intricacies of information hierarchy.

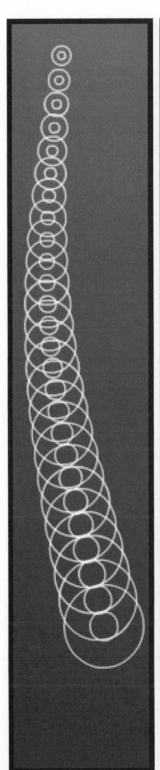
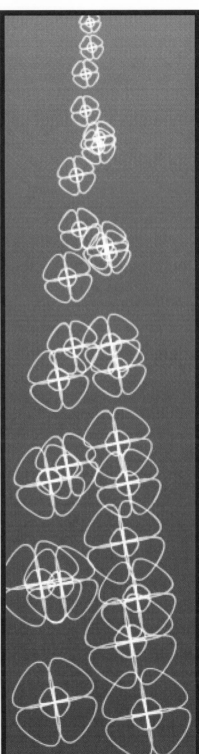

The Flash MX drawing API and its uses for interface design

The drawing API (Application Programming Interface) is a new addition to Flash with the release of Flash MX, and for many it is the high point of the upgrade. It encompasses an excellent little set of movie clip methods that allow us to draw lines and curves to make shapes and then fill those shapes with color. The important thing here is that these lines and shapes are drawn at runtime, thereby minimizing the need for symbols in the library. This has the obvious advantage of keeping file sizes small and performance fast – something that is highly desirable for an interface.

Another great new feature of Flash MX is the ability to create empty movie clips as holders for our drawing API shapes. This, in affect, allows us to control shapes made using the drawing API methods in much same way as we would do ordinary movie clips from the library.

Interface interactivity using the drawing API is given its final boost with the arrival of an enhanced Event methods model in Flash MX. Basically it allows any shape drawn using the drawing API to be given button interactivity. So, as you can see, we have all the tools we need to produce an interactive interface using only the drawing API. Shapes produced at runtime that can be manipulated and animated on screen, and what's more these shapes can behave just like buttons? That sounds like an interface to me.

The interface

Perhaps it's time to open the file in Flash MX and have a play. Open `API_spiral01redg6.swf` from the download files. Above a deep red gradient we find two sets of buttons. Towards the right-hand side of the stage we have a vertical column of downward spiraling buttons, increasing in size the nearer each button is to the bottom of the stage. The column can be twisted in either direction by the relative positioning of the mouse pointer. On rolling over these buttons a floating label appears with the name of a spiral in it. On clicking one of these buttons a pseudo-ornamental frame appears to the left-hand side of the screen, and in it an illustration of the corresponding type of spiral with its name above it (note that the shape of this frame changes shape with a degree of randomness).

We can also see that two other groups of concentrically positioned shapes appear. The one to the left of the spiral column contains a label describing the type of spiral we are looking at, logarithmic or archimedian for example. The group to the right contains a label describing a unit of measurement and a simple dial-system indicating a value of that particular unit measurement for our chosen spiral. Notice how the dial-system works as a button is clicked – the dial (a simple line) rotates around a center point to a final position like a clock-hand, and a label indicating the value appears at the end of the line. I don't want to worry too much about information regarding spiral type and scale, suffice to say they are not based on any accurate model and are used for the purpose of displaying related information within the confines of this interface demonstration.

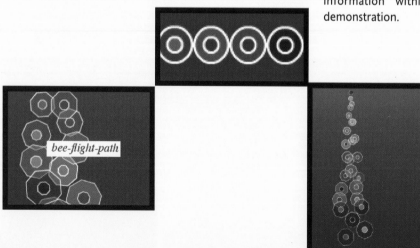

The second set of circular buttons located near the bottom left of the stage controls the configuration layout of the spiral-buttons. It's an interface inside an interface! When one of these 12 buttons is pressed the spiral-buttons are re-plotted into a new configuration, re-shaped and re-colored. I like the idea of having this recursive functionality, whereby the interface itself can be reconfigured according to user preference.

The interface resides on a stage with the dimensions of 660 x 400 and runs at a rate of 50 frames per second. The JPGs called-up by clicking on any one of the buttons are located in the same root directory as the Flash file.

A quick glance at the code shows you that this is an entire interface generated at runtime using the drawing API, and `CreateTextfield` methods coupled with the `TextFormat` object. Information used by, and to build the interface, as well as reconfiguring it, is provided by a couple of dimensional arrays. Since the file size is less than 3k the interface would load virtually instantly, even on a 56k dial-up modem.

Now let's scrutinize the 3 frames of code in detail – a chunk of code at a time starting at the beginning.

Frame one

We get things underway by setting the quality of the movie to medium.

```
_quality = "medium";
```

On my machine, a fairly outdated P3 500, this facilitates speed and smoothness of animation. An important consideration in the design of interactive navigation systems in Flash is the average target spec of the user's computer. The speed and smoothness of movement of graphical elements in Flash is very much dependent on processor speed. Performance becomes impaired and movement starts getting jerky as soon as processor limitations are exceeded. By reducing the quality level, the time used by Flash to render animations is reduced – so we can see there is a pay-off between quality and speed. When testing navigation systems its always a good idea to test on a range of computers. It's very nice to have the latest speed-machine but I prefer working on an older machine happily knowing I'm coding for the common ground, and that my files will more-than-likely perform as good, if not better, on other people's machines.

Next we initialize some important configuration variables:

```
cshape = 0.4786;
dshape = 0.4571;
rota = 45;
kolor = 5;
pha = 80;
```

`cshape` and `dshape` are important factorial variables that are used to describe the shape of the buttons – they are used in a prototype function called `drawshape` that we will define later in the code. `rota` defines a rotational constant that is used in the plotting positions of the buttons and this variable affects the final configuration of the buttons on screen. The `kolor` and `pha` variables affect the coloration and alpha values of each individual button.

Next up we declare the contents of a dimensional, or nested, array (an array stored inside an array):

```
var link = [ [ "dna", "helical", 10, "nanometers" ],    [ "dna02", "helical", 15, "nanometers" ],
    ➡[ "particle-path", "root", 20, "nanometers" ],    [ "spirillum", "helical", 30, "nanometers"],
    ➡[ "rhodospirillum", "helical", 35, "micrometers" ], [ "rhodospirillum02", "bernoulli", 40, "nanometers" ],
    ➡[ "liquid-crystal", "growth", 45, "nanometers" ], [ "cochlea", "equiangular", 45, "millimeters" ],
    ➡[ "shell", "logarithmic", 50, "millimeters" ],    [ "shells", "growth", 60, "millimeters" ],
    ➡[ "zebra-shell", "growth", 70, "millimeters" ],    [ "nautilus", "logarithmic", 80, "millimeters" ],
    ➡[ "sunflower", "fibonacci", 100, "millimeters" ], [ "horn", "logarithmic", 110, "millimeters" ],
    ➡[ "pine-cones", "growth", 130, "millimeters" ],    [ "ammonite", "logarithmic", 150, "millimeters" ],
    ➡[ "bee-flight-path", "irregular", 160, "meters" ], [ "whirlpool", "vortex", 170, "meters" ],
    ➡[ "artifact", "archimedian", 180, "centimeters" ], [ "fort", "equiangular", 210, "meters" ],
    ➡[ "mosque", "archimedian", 230, "meters" ],    [ "cyclone", "vortex", 240, "meters" ],
    [ "star", "unknown", 250, "kilometers" ],    [ "galaxy02", "unknown", 270, "100lightyears" ],
    ➡[ "galaxy03", "unknown", 290, "100lightyears" ], [ "galaxy04", "unknown", 300, "100lightyears" ] ];
```

This 2 dimensional array stores all the data regarding our spiral classification. Although far from being the most robust or versatile method for holding data, it's a quick and simple way of organizing data to be used/or called up by an interface. In this case our link array contains 26 nested arrays, each containing 4 elements. The 4 elements in each array represent the spiral's name, its terminology (spiral type), a quantity of scale and its unit of measurement of scale, in that order. The data in these arrays will be used for a number of purposes – to locate a specific JPG to load into the player, to give screen elements labels, and to effect the positioning of parts of the interface during interaction. As you will see this is a useful way of identifying a particular spiral in the list along with any associated information.

Following this we declare the contents of a similarly defined 2 dimensional array, this time containing data used in the configuration options of the interface:

```
var conf = [ [ 0.4786, 0.4571 , "reset", 45, 5, 80 ],
        ➡[ 0.0086, 0.7071 , "config 01", 250, 4.1, 70 ],
        ➡[ 0.4086, 0.9071 , "config 02", 120, 5.2, 40 ],
        ➡[ 0.786, 0.6571 , "config 03", 15, 9.8, 130 ],
        ➡[ -0.9086, 0.8071 , "config 04", 45, 12, 50 ],
        ➡[ 0.0086, -0.7071 , "config 05", 210, 160, 90 ],
        ➡[ 0.4086, 0.7071 , "config 06", 5, 260, 0 ],
        ➡[ 0.1086, 0.7071 , "config 07", 30, 5, 80 ],
        ➡[ 0.4086, 0.7071 , "config 08", 20, 4.4, 50 ],
        ➡[ 0.2086, 0.9071 , "config 09", 45, 10.91, 100 ],
        ➡[ -1.2086, -1.0071 , "config 10", 200, 5.4, 100 ],
        ➡[ -1.2086, -0.0071 , "config 11", 270, 10.95, 0 ] ];
```

Remember the row of buttons to the bottom left of the stage? Here the nested arrays contain information regarding the shape, color and alpha values of the buttons as well as the overall structure of the spiral shape. There is also an element that provides a string containing a label name for each of the buttons.

We will return to these arrays later in the chapter as we look at pulling data from them through button interaction.

The next block of code defines a prototype for drawing a shape, and in essence provides us with a new movie clip method called drawShape. This prototype is basically an extension of one I used in an earlier set of interface experiments that appeared in another friends of ED book called **Fresh Flash – New design ideas with Flash MX**. 10 arguments are passed to the function once it is called and these are used to produce an eight-sided shape – where each of the sides can vary between a straight line to an oblique or obtuse curve. Originally the prototype function was used to draw perfect circles made of 8 curves, something that Flash is not too accurate at doing with the standard 4.

```
MovieClip.prototype.drawShape =
➡function(xpos,ypos,radius,lWidth,lColor,
➡fColor,fAlpha,distorta,distortb,kolor) {
x = xpos;
y = ypos;
r = radius;
u = r*distorta;
v = r*distortb;
    this.lineStyle(lwidth,lColor,100);
    this.beginFill(fColor, fAlpha);
    this.moveTo(x-r, y);
    this.curveTo(x-r, y-u, x-v, y-v);
    this.curveTo(x-u, y-r, x, y-r);
    this.curveTo(x+u, y-r, x+v, y-v);
    this.curveTo(x+r, y-u, x+r, y);
    this.curveTo(x+r, y+u, x+v, y+v);
    this.curveTo(x+u, y+r, x, y+r);
    this.curveTo(x-u, y+r, x-v, y+v);
    this.curveTo(x-r, y+u, x-r, y);
    this.endFill();
    }
```

Taking a look at the 10 parameters in order we have xpos and ypos, which define the x and y co-ordinates of the drawn shape relative to the _root or the movie clip it is in. lWidth describes the thickness of the shape's perimeter line, and lColor its color as a hexadecimal value. fColor and fAlpha describe the respective colour and alpha values of the shape's fill. The parameters distorta and distortb are ratio values that affect the curve angles – for a perfect circle to be produced these need to be 0.4086 and 0.7071 respectively. The final parameter, kolor, is used to affect the final output color of the shape when the drawShape method is invoked. Note the use of this to define the scope within which the shape is drawn – it will be drawn inside the movie clip from which the drawShape method is invoked (or if called upon in the main timeline the shape will be drawn at the _root level). We will see how the newly defined drawShape method works in detail when we come to invoke it later in the second frame.

The actual drawing of the shape is performed by the curveTo drawing method, which has four parameters. The curve is drawn from the current pen position (in this case defined by the moveTo drawing method) to the first two parameters representing the x and y position of the end of the curve. The second two parameters in the curveTo method represent a control point to which the line curves out. The additive and subtractive maths used to define these points in this prototype produce an eight-sided symmetrical curved shape.

The rest of the code in frame 1 is concerned with textual elements that appear within the interface – the static and floating labels, and the dial-system describing a value of scale. Flash MX introduced a great new set of ActionScript objects and methods for dealing with our every textual need. We can create text fields on the fly and control them as we would any other movie clip, and we can give these text fields a range of properties and apply formatting in much the same way as you might do with style sheets in HTML. I could have added these text fields to the stage using the authoring environment but that would mean another library of symbols and we've avoided them so far so for the sake of purity why not carry on that way!

First off I created two `TextFormat` objects called `Tformat` and `Uformat`:

```
        Tformat = new TextFormat();
        Tformat.color = 0x660000;
        Tformat.align = "center";
        Tformat.italic = true

        Uformat = new TextFormat();
        Uformat.color = 0x993300;
        Uformat.align = "center";
        Uformat.italic = true
```

We will apply our `TextFormat` objects to our text fields in much the same way as we would use a CSS style sheet to control the style formatting of text elements in an HTML document. This has the obvious advantage of being the most efficient way of allowing changes to be made to groups of text with the minimum of fuss. In both we define the particular color of our text, and set the text to center within its text field. We then set the text to be italicized.

The next six lines of code instruct Flash to create three new text fields for our disposal and set the selectable property for each to be `false`:

```
 _root.createTextField("titletext",
 ➥ 700, 77, 83, 100, 20);
 _root.titletext.selectable = false;
 _root.createTextField("spiraltype",
 ➥ 701, 237, 181, 100, 20);
 _root.spiraltype.selectable = false;
 _root.createTextField("measurement",
 ➥ 702, 437, 81, 100, 20);
 _root.measurement.selectable = false;
```

The parameters for the `createTextField` method are as follows:

- a string identifier
- the depth at which the text field is placed
- the x and y positions of the text field
- the width and height of the text field

What this amounts to on screen is three invisible text fields waiting to be populated with text.

The following block of ActionScript is also used to create a text label, but this one is responsible for the floating title label that we see whenever we roll over a button.

```
 _root.createEmptyMovieClip('label', 1002);
 _root.label.createTextField("insidelabel",
 ➥1003, -20, -30, 85, 18);
 _root.label.insidelabel.background = true;
 _root.label.insidelabel.selectable = false;
 _root.label.insidelabel.autosize = true;
 _root.label.onEnterFrame = function() {
    yslide = (_root._ymouse-this._y)*.2;
    this._y += yslide;
    xslide = (_root._xmouse-this._x)*.2;
    this._x += xslide;
 _root.label.insidelabel.text = _root.select;
 _root.label.insidelabel.setTextFormat(Uformat);
 };
```

The first line of this block of code creates an empty movie clip instance named `label` at a depth of 1002. There is no magical reason why it's at a depth of 1002, I just like to space my movie clips over a range of depths just in case I need to place a new one at an intermediate depth between two others.

The next line of code nests a text field called `insidelabel` inside our freshly created empty movie clip.

The subsequent three lines set some properties of the text field to be switched on or off. The `background` is switched on, giving us a default white rectangle in which to contain our text. The `selectable` property is set to `false` and this prevents the cursor from changing from pointer to text-selectable if it inadvertently rolls over the floating label. (Try commenting this line out and you will see that it causes all sorts of problems if we leave the default setting as on.) Next up is the `autosize` property, and we've set this to be on by giving it the Boolean value of `true`. This essentially fits the text field snugly around the text it contains – it resizes our white rectangular text container depending on the number of characters the text field displays.

Following on, we see that the next line defines an `onEnterFrame` function that is used to animate the floating label and update its contents as buttons are rolled over. The first four lines of code in our callback function provide the sliding inertia movement to the label so that the label floats towards the pointer in the both the x and y axis. The line `_root.label.insidelabel.text = _root.select;` populates the text field with the value `_root.select`, which as we will see later is updated every time we roll over a button. The last line of code in this block sets the text field to our previously defined `Uformat` text format.

The last block of code in frame 1 is partly similar to the previous block, dealing specifically with the 'size label' – this time the label is animated around a circular path when a button is clicked, its final position on the path being dependent upon the value it is displaying, `_root.sise`:

```
_root.createEmptyMovieClip('sizelabel', 993);
_root.sizelabel.createTextField("insidesize", 0, 0, 40, 30, 18);
_root.sizelabel.insidesize.selectable = false;
_root.sizelabel.onEnterFrame = function() {
    this._x = 470 + Math.cos(degrees / 180 * Math.PI) * 75;
    this._y = 140 + Math.sin(degrees / 180 * Math.PI) * 75;
    if (count*10 < _root.sise) degrees+=7;
    count++;
    _root.dial.createEmptyMovieClip('indial', -387);
    with (_root.dial.indial) {
    lineStyle(1, 0xFFFFFF, 60);
    moveTo(486, 191);
    lineto(this._x+20, this._y+50);
    }
    _root.sizelabel.insidesize.text = _root.sise;
    _root.sizelabel.insidesize.setTextFormat(Tformat);
    }
```

The `onEnterFrame` callback function plots the size label in positions on the stage using a formula to describe points on a circle. The formula is:

```
X position = Xposition of center point + Math.cos(degrees / 180 * Math.PI) * radius;
Y position = Yposition of center point + Math.sin(degrees / 180 * Math.PI) * radius;
```

The next conditional checks to see if a variable called `count` has reached 10 times the value of `_root.sise`. If it has, the animation of the size label around the circular path stops – so the final distance it moves around is dependent on the value of `_root.sise`. For every frame that passes, the label moves 7 degrees around the circular path and a value of 1 is added to the variable `count`.

The next few lines of code in this block are responsible for the rendering of the 'hand' of the dial that points to the size label. Inside a freshly created movie clip called `indial` a 1 pixel thick line is drawn from a center point and outwards towards a position relative to the size label – the end result is an animated hand that points to the size label.

The line `_root.sizelabel.insidesize.text = _root.sise;` populates the text field with the value `_root.sise` – this value is derived from our dimensional array, as we will see later. The last line of code in this block sets the text field to our previously defined `Tformat` text format.

Frame 2

If frame 1 was used primarily for setting things up ready to generate the interface, frame 2 is the part where the actual generation is accomplished. There is nothing to be seen on the screen until the commands in frame 2 have been carried out.

The first block of code tells Flash to draw a rectangle the size of the stage and fill it with a deep red gradient – this will provide a backdrop for our interface. Again we put the drawing API to good use:

```
_root.createEmptyMovieClip("background", -2000);
with (_root.background) {
    colors = [0xD83D3D, 0x990000];
    alphas = [100, 100];
    ratios = [0, 0xFF];
    matrix = {matrixType:"box", x:100, y:100, w:200, h:200, r:(90/180)*Math.PI};
    beginGradientFill("linear", colors, alphas, ratios, matrix);
    moveto(0, 0);
    lineto(660, 0);
    lineto(660, 400);
    lineto(0, 400);
    lineto(0, 0);
    endFill();
}
```

First we create an empty movie clip called `background` at a depth of -2000 to ensure nothing we generate later on appears below it, then we define four arrays which are default parameters for the `beginGradientFill` method applied to our `background` movie clip. These are, in order:

- the `colors` array – our two colors through which our gradient will move

- the `alphas` array – defining the alpha values of the two colors

- the `ratios` array – containing color distributions

- the `matrix` array – containing a string identifier, x and y positions, width and height and the relative rotation of the gradient.

Note that the last element of the matrix array, the rotation, is measured in radians, so we must divide by 180 and multiply by PI in order to convert from the more universally understood measurement of degrees.

The `beginGradientFill` method instructs Flash to proceed filling the area enclosed by any shape that occurs after the method has been invoked. In all the method uses 5 parameters, a string representing the type of gradient (either `linear` or `radial`) and the other four arrays we just discussed. A rectangle is then drawn using the `moveTo` and `lineTo` methods and the size of the stage. The gradient fill is terminated using `endFill`.

Ok, so this deep red gradient could have been made using the drawing tools in the authoring environment and converted to a symbol and placed on the stage. Easier and quicker perhaps, yes, but the beauty of using the API version is that we can dynamically change the gradient in many ways as the user interacts with the interface. Perhaps we may want to change the gradient colors as the user makes a new selection? We can simply introduce a dynamic variable to the color array, which has got to be better than producing, say, ten gradient symbols, one for each selection. In fact this is one of the great reasons for producing an entire interface dynamically using the API. It makes it very easy to add dynamic elements that are governed by a few variables, that are in turn affected by choices the user makes. There is no conceivable reason why the whole interface couldn't be built in this manner, where all the elements' properties are affected by user interaction. We then have something of a chameleon interface that morphs as it is being navigated, hopefully engaging the user as he is directly participating in the interface's structure and restructure.

The following lines of code in frame 2 create an empty movie clip called dial ready to house the dial-system:

```
_root.createEmptyMovieClip('dial', -88);
  _root.dial._visible = false;
  _root.sise = "";
```

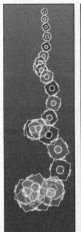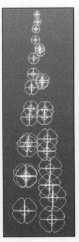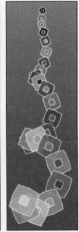

The visibility of the newly created clip is set to `false`. The last line in the block sets the variable `_root.sise` to equal an empty string.

The next block of code in the sequence gets down to the nitty gritty of actually generating the buttons in a spiral formation:

```
for (i=0; i<link.length; i++) {
    _root.createEmptyMovieClip('mc'+i, i);
    with (_root['mc'+i]) {
        drawShape(i*1.4, 0, 5+i/1.5, 1,
        ➥ 0xffffff, 0x666699*i/kolor, pha,
        ➥ cshape, dshape);
        drawShape(i*1.4, 0, 2+i/4.5, 1,
        ➥ 0xffffff, 0x999900*i/5, pha,
        ➥cshape, dshape);
        _x = 375;
        _y = 20+i*13;
        _rotation = i*rota;
        _alpha = 80;
    }
```

First up we've set a for loop to loop as many times as there are first level arrays in the link array. `length` is a property of an array returning the number of elements in the array, in this case 26. So we will have 26 buttons, each corresponding to a second level array, containing all of our spiral data.

The next line creates an empty movie clip as a container for our generated buttons. Using the `with` statement to prevent us from having to rewrite the object's full path for each of our applied methods, we instruct Flash to invoke the `drawShape` method twice, drawing two concentric shapes (in this case the outcome is flower-shaped) inside the freshly created empty movie clip. The arguments passed to the prototype function have been discussed earlier – in this case the size, the fill color, and relative position of the circles are dependent upon the position of `mc`'s generated sequence, a factor of the variable `i`. The alpha values of the buttons are dependent upon the value of `pha`. The final shape of these buttons is also dependent on the variables `cshape` and `dshape`. To make a perfect circle these variables need to have the values of 0.4086 and 0.7071 respectively. It is also worth noting that as well as being dependent on a factor of `i`, the fill color of the first shape or circle is dependent on the variable `kolor`. The four variables `cshape`, `dshape`, `pha` and `kolor` are the variables used by the bottom left row of buttons to reconfigure the look of the interface – but more on that as we get to it.

The last four lines of code in this block position `mc` in the x and y axis and rotate it by a factor of `i*rota`. As we shall see, the variable `rota` is also used in the reconfiguration of the interface using the bottom left row of buttons. Finally we've set the `alpha` of `mc+i` to 80.

Still within the `for` loop the next thing to do is define our rollover callback function:

```
_root['mc'+i].onRollOver = function() {
    this._alpha = 100;
    ref = Number((this._name).substring(2));
    _root.select = _root.link[ref][0];
    _root.label._visible = true;
}
```

First up we have set the alpha of our rolled-over mc to 100. Previously when we generated the button mc in the block of code we set the alpha to 80, so doing this gives the button a rollover effect of becoming subtly highlighted. As you'll see later, when we roll-out of our specific button mc the alpha will be set back to 80.

Following on we have set the value of a new variable ref to the value of Number((this._name).substring(2));. This equates to the third character in the string identifier for that particular instance name, converted to the number data type. So this gives us a variable representing which button has been rolled-over in the button sequence, basically a number between 0 and 25, which will be very handy indeed.

Moving to the next line we can see that the variable _root.select has been set to the value of _root.link[ref][0]; So we are using ref to reference the nested link array, in this case the first element. For example if we rolled over button 9 in the sequence we will be referencing the first element of the ninth nested array in the link array, in this case returning the string shell.

This method is used extensively throughout this example as a way of referencing data from our arrays corresponding to the button that is being interacted with.

The next line sets label to visible, and so our button label appears on the screen and floats around following the pointer wherever it goes, as long as it is over a button. The onEnterFrame call-back function for label defined in frame 1 keeps updating its contained text with the value of _root.select for every frame that passes, thereby showing the correct label at all times.

Moving on – the subsequent onRollOut function simply sets the alpha of our button movie clip back to 80 and sets label's visibility back to false.

```
_root['mc'+i].onRollOut = function() {
  this._alpha = 80;
  _root.label._visible = false;
};
```

The onRelease function in the next block of code tells Flash to do a number of things – first it draws shapes:

```
_root['mc'+i].onRelease = function() {
count = 0;
degrees = -90;
_root.dial._visible = true;
_root.createEmptyMovieClip('shapes', -1000);
  with (_root.shapes) {
  drawShape(486, 191, 57, 1, 0xFFCCCC,
➥0xFFCCCC, 40, cshape, dshape);
  drawShape(286, 191, 57, 1, 0xFFCCCC,
➥0xFFCCCC, 40, cshape, dshape);
  drawShape(486, 191, 134, 1, 0xFFCCCC,
➥0xFFCCCC, 40, cshape, dshape);
  drawShape(286, 191, 100, 1, 0xFFCCCC,
➥0xFFCCCC, 40, cshape, dshape);
  }
```

The variables count and degrees are set to 0 and -90 respectively, and this essentially sets the hand of the dial and position of the size label back to 12 o'clock as soon as a button is clicked. The dial is made visible by setting the dial's visibility property to true.

Two sets of concentric shapes are then drawn using our prototype function, and these are used to house the spiral-type label and our dial-system.

The next step is concerned with setting our empty labels, which we defined in frame 1, with textual data regarding the correspondingly clicked buttons:

```
_root.sise = " "+_root.link[ref][2];
_root.titletext.text = select;
titletext.setTextFormat(Tformat);
_root.spiraltype.text = _root.link[ref][1];
spiraltype.setTextFormat(Tformat);
_root.measurement.text = _root.link[ref][3];
measurement.setTextFormat(Tformat);
```

As we already have a clicked-button reference number, ref, we can use it to retrieve corresponding elements from our dimensional link array just as we did before. For example _root.sise = " "+_root.link[ref][2]; sets _root.sise to the value of the third element in the corresponding array in the dimensional link array, and adds a character space to the start. This value is then used by the sizelabel movie clip to produce the floating label on the far left of the stage indicating the size of the spiral. The titletext, spiraltype and measurement text fields are similarly given values using our ref variable to reference our link array.

Going onwards, we now create a new empty movie clip called jpgframe, and in it we use our drawShape method to produce a frame holder, again consisting of concentric shapes, for our JPGs:

```
_root.createEmptyMovieClip('jpgframe', 300);
with (_root.jpgframe) {
    drawShape(130, 193, 82, 1, 0xFFCACA, 0xFFCCCC, 40,
    ➥ Math.random(1)*1.3, 0.7071);
    drawShape(130, 193, 52, 1, 0xFFCACA, 0xEF9790, 100,
    ➥ 0.4086, 0.7071);
}
```

Notice that this time we have passed Math.random(1)*1.3 as an argument to the distorta parameter, and this has the effect of producing a random but somewhat ornate pink frame with a light border. Inside of this frame we've drawn a simple circle in which to house the relevant JPG.

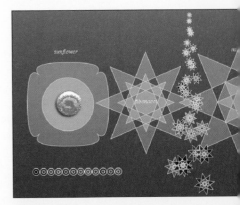
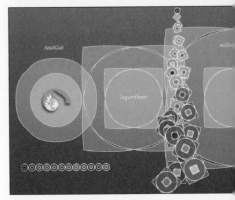
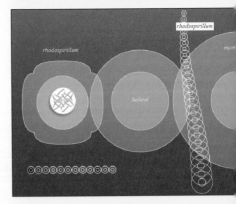
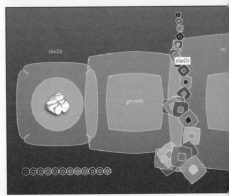

Next up is the block of code that loads our particular JPG into its frame:

```
toload = select+".jpg";
_root.createEmptyMovieClip("jpgholder", 301);
with (_root.jpgholder) {
    _x = 91;
    _y = 163;
    loadMovie(toload);
}
};
```

First we set the variable `toload` to add together the value of `select` (which will be set to the string name of one of our spirals) and `.jpg`. Then inside a freshly created movie clip called `jpgholder`, placed in the correct position on the stage, we load our JPG represented by `toload`.

Moving onwards, we come to the `onEnterFrame` function:

```
_root['mc'+i].onEnterFrame = function() {
    this._rotation -= 6*(2-(_root._xmouse/200));
}
}
```

This simple line of code is responsible for the directional rotation of our spiral interface, dependent on the x position of the mouse pointer. Because of the specific spatial distribution of our buttons a rotation of the clips brings about a pleasing 3 dimensional depth to our interface. It allows us to twist our spiral around and reach buttons that are on the far side – the buttons are partially transparent so we can see what's on the other side as the spiral moves around.

The final curly bracket closes our `for` loop and within a small fraction of a second all of the buttons generated have been given full functionality by the attachment of the `callback` functions we have just described.

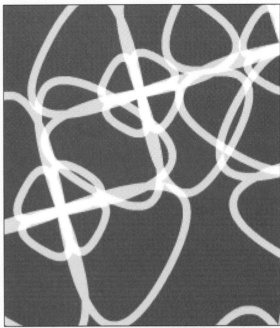

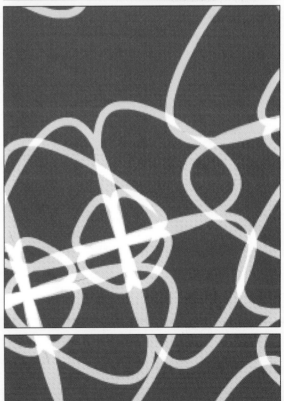

The configurations interface

I was going to leave it there, but then I had the idea of adding an interface inside the interface – one that utilized constructional variables (remember cshape, dshape, pha, kolor and rota?) to affect the shape and colors of the buttons as well as the spiral configuration of the main interface:

```
for (j=0; j<conf.length; j++) {
   _root.createEmptyMovieClip('nc'+j, 100+j);
   with (_root['nc'+j]) {
        drawShape(0, 0, 7, 1, 0xffffff, 0x666699*j/3.5, 40, 0.4086, 0.7071);
        drawShape(0, 0, 3, 1, 0xffffff, 0x999900*j/kolor, 30, 0.4086, 0.7071);
        _x = 30+j*15;
        _y = 375;
   }

   _root['nc'+j].onRollOver = function() {
        ref = Number((this._name).substring(2));
        _root.select = " "+_root.conf[ref][2];
        _root.label._visible = true;
      this._xscale = this._yscale=110;
   }

   _root['nc'+j].onRollOut = function() {
        _root.label._visible = false;
      this._xscale = this._yscale=100;
   }

   _root['nc'+j].onrelease = function() {
        cshape = _root.conf[ref][0];
        dshape = _root.conf[ref][1];
        rota = _root.conf[ref][3];
        kolor = _root.conf[ref][4];
        pha = _root.conf[ref][5];
        _root.jpgholder.unloadMovie(toload);
        jpgframe.clear();
        _root.titletext.text = ""; _root.spiraltype.text = "";
        _root.measurement.text = ""; _root.dial.visible = true;
        gotoAndPlay(2);
   }
}
```

The configurations interface is very similar in nature to the spiral interface – it relies on a two dimensional array called conf to hold data that is passed to those constructional variables and uses the same method for referencing them. This time the buttons are arranged in a row at the bottom left of the stage – again the buttons are generated using the drawShape prototype. A new label name is given to each button as it is rolled-over, and this time the scaling of each button is increased by 10 percent, and reduced back to its original size on roll-out. When one of these buttons is clicked, the five constructional variables are set to values that I have found to produce interesting effects in terms of shape, color and formation. Try experimenting with different values in the conf array to see the vast range of geometrically exact and interesting shapes that arise.

Within our onRelease function and after the setting of our configuration variables, we've asked Flash to unload the JPG using the unloadMovie method and clear the jpgframe movie clip using the clear method. We've set the visibility of _root.dial to true ready for the next instance of redrawing the 'hand' and we've also set our label's contents to equal empty strings, thereby removing all our content from the stage ready for the interface to be re-built to its newly selected configuration – and this we've done by simply instructing Flash to gotoAndPlay(2). So frame 2 goes about generating the interface once again, this time using a new set of constructional variables to affect the final color, shape and configuration of the spiral.

Frame 3

Frame 3 contains a humble stop, and so this is where our story ends.

Onwards and tangents

In this example I've used the Flash drawing API to generate all of the onscreen interface elements at runtime. I've shown how the basic API methods can be extended through the use of prototyping to provide us with methods for drawing more complex shapes. I've then utilized these shapes as buttons by attaching to them a sequence of event callback functions to provide user interactivity. Our data has been referenced from a couple of simple two-dimensional arrays – in fact the generated structure of the interface itself is also derived from these arrays. Textual information pulled from our arrays has been utilized by dynamically created and updated text fields. In all we have fairly tight piece of code weighing in at around 2.68 kilobytes and without a single symbol in sight.

Aesthetically I think we have an interesting interface that is perhaps only a few steps away from acting as an animated database front-end. I hope there will be some degree of enjoyment in the twisting and turning of the interface, coupled with the ability to reconfigure the shape, color and structure of the final interface column. In the presentation of information I do think it's to our advantage to provide experiential navigation – an interface that has an element of playfulness about it. I would encourage you to add more constructional variables to this system and play with the values of the existing ones, adding randomized variables and even pushing it to a point beyond functionality – for this kind of experimentation is the only way to break through into new ideas about user interaction and navigation.

Technically, this simple system has some great advantages too, for updating a site would be made easy as all we would need to do is update our `link` array with new array elements containing the names of the new spirals and all their associated data. We then drop the new JPGs into the root folder and there we have it – the number of buttons in the spiral will always be the same as the number of elements in our array.

In terms of further development to this interface model I think there are many routes we might take. We might for example derive our structure and data from a more versatile system such as XML schema, or link it to a living database. We could perhaps extend the use of our constructional variables to allow online users to reconfigure the interface and leave a new configuration for subsequent users. Perhaps we could store information regarding the online use of the interface and evolve its structure related to that use – for example color coding according to the most frequently visited links. I think there are many ways we could link live dynamic data to the evolving interface structure – anything to avoid looking at the same formation of buttons again and again on repeated visits would be a good thing. All in all, as always, the amount of directions this interface could be taken in is endless. Experimentation is an end in itself.

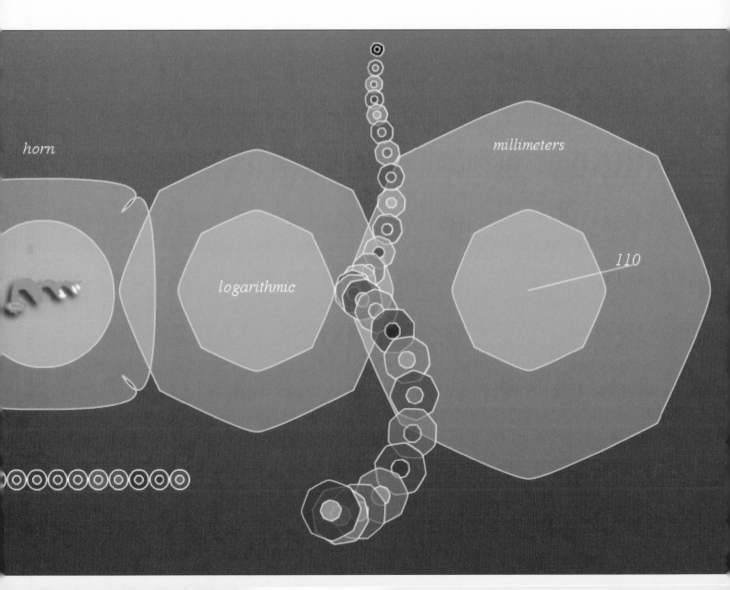

millimeters

sunflower

REAL FEEL INTERFACES

Every popular piece of software has a bit of the 'real feel' about it. Windows is called Windows because it pretends to open a bunch of windows. These windows pretend to have buttons on them, and those buttons pretend to depress when they are clicked on.

It all feels pretty real, and it's a good way of understanding all the code executions that are being performed. There is comfort in this familiarity.

The Web represents, to an extent, a whole new unfamiliar world. Information is being presented in another medium, one that many people are not yet familiar or comfortable with. To help ease the transition into this new medium, designers have been taking advantage of what can be referred to as 'real feel', by incorporating real-world metaphors into the design elements of the web site.

When the Web was a purely textual medium, pages (note how already we referred to information on a computer monitor as a "page") contained a similar layout to a magazine or newspaper article. Footnotes and references became hyperlinks in the text, and so a new concept was introduced amidst the familiar. Even when graphics became an option, the periodical-style layout was still the norm, with each site looking more and more like a magazine transferred to your screen. Of course, early web designers using HTML were limited by the language.

And then along came Flash, and with it new possibilities in layout, navigation and design. We must now be careful, however, that we do not overwhelm the audience with all these possibilities and ideas at once. A dynamic new navigation system is useless if a user cannot figure it out. An interface built solely from your imagination and based on a Dali-like dream you had last night might be a wonder to look at, but if a user is too confused (or frightened!) to interact with it, then nothing further can be communicated. A great way to invite users to interact with your site is give them something they are already familiar with. This can range from items as simple as a graphic that looks like a 3D button that depresses when clicked, or something as standard as a control panel resembling VCR controls to manage playback of a movie, to something as quirky as a box of crayons to alter and customize the colors of a product. By offering such real-world items with functionality already familiar to the user, you can then bring in new and fresh ideas that the user can recognize and respond to with without feeling overwhelmed.

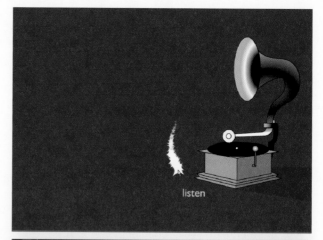

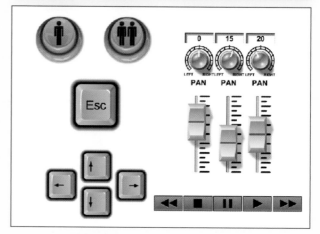

Embracing the metaphor

I will readily admit that I am not an abstract thinker. I gravitate more towards stories that focus on a strong plot, paintings and sculpture with realistic depictions and music with a discernable beat and melody. When I am creating, I am more productive when I have a literal theme to concentrate on and use as a catalyst for perhaps more abstract ideas. In such a way, I created the current version of my personal web site found at www.27Bobs.com, which is what we will be dissecting for the rest of this chapter.

A good example of a metaphor is www.marvel.com, which features a section presenting online comic books using the metaphor of...well, comic books. Metaphors can be used for single elements or as themes for entire sites.

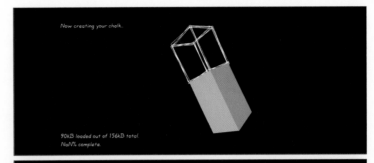

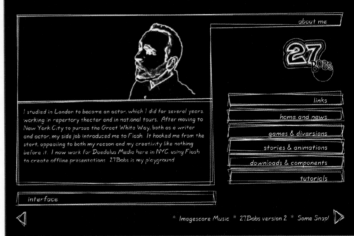

Personally, I like to carry a metaphor throughout the entire site as it allows for more creativity by limiting the range in which to work. For instance, if someone tells me to draw a picture of anything, the complete freedom of subject matter doesn't necessarily challenge me into creative corners, whereas if I am told to draw a picture of a castle, then immediately the mind starts playing with ideas and variations such as who (or what) owns the castle, the real or imaginary land it where might be located, or what elements the castle might have been built from. In the end I might draw a sand castle that a quixotic crab has chosen to inhabit and defend against the coming tide, which would not be an idea I would have come up with if I had not been given limitations.

Creating the metaphor

With 27Bobs.com, my thought was to create an "unfinished" site – one that would display experiments, tutorials, games, images, odds and ends and anything else I wanted to put up, with the idea that I would continue to add more to it as time went on. I wanted the layout and the graphics to evoke this unfinished feeling, and so immediately began seeking a metaphor that I could use as a theme for the site.

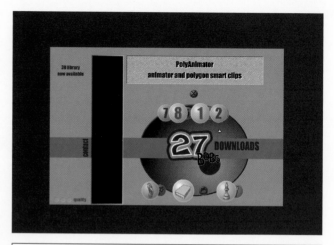

The previous version had been a bit too "crisp" for my current tastes, built from straight rectangles and smooth ellipses. I knew I wanted something more seemingly haphazard and for a time played with the idea of simply sketching all of the elements with pencil and scanning them in, but then Flash MX was released and I found a new toy in the drawing API.

One of my first drawing API experiments was building a 3D engine, and one of its variations was an engine to produce 3D "sketches", where several lines were randomly placed on a polygon's edges. I've included the file `sketch3D.swf` in the download files, so you can have a look at this experiment.

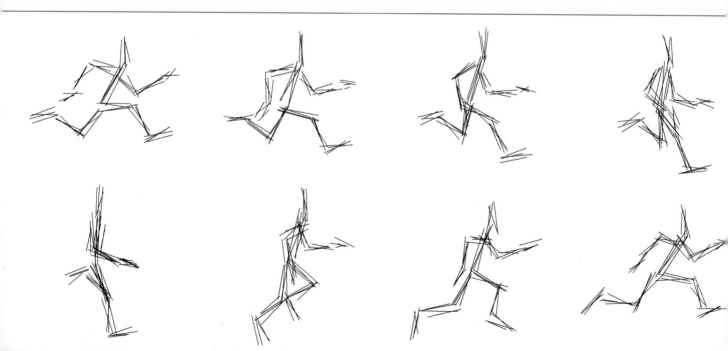

I then adapted another early experiment of mine, a smart clip to animate biped symbols, but replaced body parts with movie clips that would redraw several sketch lines each frame. You can see the result in the file `runner_sketch.swf`.

I liked the sketchy feel and decided that this is what I wanted to do with the site, which would be composed of basic boxes that expanded and contracted based on the section selected. As the boxes transformed, though, I wanted them to redraw using the sketchy animation I had been playing with as opposed to adjusting scale, so that it might appear as if the page was being redrawn each time the user made a selection.

But what was my metaphor? Well, I had a sketchy feel and a site with little purpose other than to serve as my playground. It was a small step to find the metaphor of a sketchpad. The page would be my collection of Flash "sketches" – some complete, some in the process, some abandoned – made up of two colors, as my real-world sketchpad most usually is, though I would offer the user the ability to alter the two colors. The users, although presented with (hopefully) a different kind of site, would feel a bit familiar with the territory since they could apply their real-world knowledge to the metaphorical landscape. This left me free to create a new and exciting interface that I felt users would be comfortable exploring.

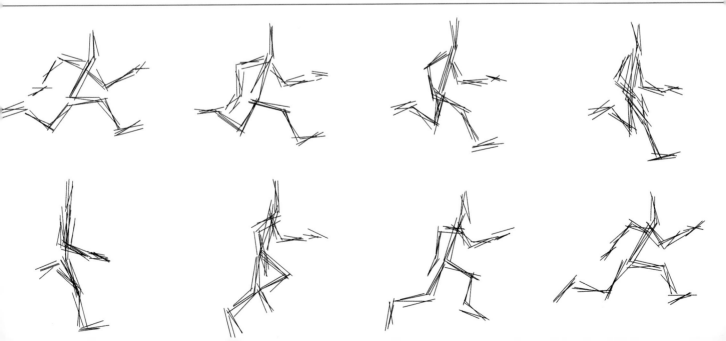

27Bobs.com

In this chapter, I am going to walk you through the majority of the code I used to create my site. If you open up `27Bobs_book_finished.swf` from the download files, you will see the result of this tutorial, and the accompanying FLA has all of the code commented as well. There are certain things that I built into the finished version of the site that would be too difficult to fit into one chapter, such as the history list and the interface window that allows the user to adjust interface colors, although I included these additions in the file `27Bobs_further.swf` so you can take a look, and hopefully gain some inspiration in how to move such a project forward. As it stands, we have plenty of code to examine, so let's get going!

Movie preparations

I have left the majority of work to be covered in this section, but there are a few items I prepared for us so that we may hit the ground running. If you open the file `27Bobs_start.fla` from the download files you will see what I have set up in preparation for this exercise.

First, you will notice that the stage is empty. The entire web site will be built from code, plus a few graphics that we will attach to the stage at run-time. Open the library to see how these graphics have been prepared.

The logo movie clip (exported as logo) and its associated PNG are in their own folder. All of the other images that will be placed for each section as it opens are located in the section images folder, the exported symbols in the section images exported subfolder and the associated PNGs in the section images png subfolder. These images, including the logo, were prepared in Photoshop to appear as if roughly sketched with the same line width that we would be using for our boxed sections, then exported as PNGs with transparency so that we could alter the foreground color of the image in Flash without having to worry about a background.

The final two items in the library are our exported font, called scriptFont, and an empty movie clip named subButtonSymbol, which we will use to extend the movie clip object. The font I have chosen to use as `scriptFont` in my finished version is QuillScript, though if you do not have the font or would like to use another, simply double-click on the font symbol in the library and pick another font in the drop-down list. Note that the file actually has Arial currently selected as the exported font so that readers without QuillScript installed won't get a warning message. As we work through the tutorial, keep in mind that using a different font might mean some adjusting of a few variables to account for the different font size.

The only other prepared feature in this movie is a layer of code on the main timeline (in fact, all of the code will be located on the first frame of the main timeline). Select the top layer, sections set up, and open your ActionScript editor to see the code included with the file. Basically, I have populated an array with objects containing information on all of the sections.

```
sections = [];
```

This line is where the array is created, then each individual section is an object pushed into this array:

```
sections.push({name:"home and news",
➥info:"", image:"home"});
```

Here we have created an anonymous object with three properties, `name`, `info` and `image`, and pushed it into the `sections` array. `name` is obviously the name of the section, `info` is any text we wish to have placed in the textbox at the top left of the stage, and `image` is the name of the linkage identifier of the image symbol in the library to be used with this section. We then give one or two new properties to our anonymous object. For the first two sections, we fill a new property called `textBlock`, which will be a text field at the bottom left of the stage, with text:

```
sections[0].textBlock = "Welcome to the
➥ new version of 27Bobs, updated to
➥utilize some of the new features of Flash MX. ";
sections[0].textBlock += "I thought the
➥ theme of a sketchbook or a drawing
➥board for the new interface was appropriate ";
sections[0].textBlock += "given the
➥purpose of this site." + newline + newline;
sections[0].textBlock += "Keep an eye out
➥ for Flash MX Studio, out in July from
➥ friends of ED. I contributed three
➥ chapters to this book in which I
➥ discuss the drawing API and using it to
➥ code 3D in Flash.";
```

For later sections, I added a new property called links and filled it with information on hyperlinks for that section. First, a temporary array is created to hold a number of objects:

```
links = [];
links.push({title:"Cassie", url:"",
info:"My first Flash experiment and a
tribute to my favorite canine, who just
happens to be the cutest dog... ever."});
links.push({title:"Fluppets", url:"",
info:"I've always been a big Jim Henson
fan, so I was excited to attempt this
interactivity experiment."});
links.push({title:"MazeMaker", url:"",
info:"I don't recall what prompted this
experiment, but I used a variation as a
navigation tool in the first version of
my site."});
```

You can see that each index in the new links array contains another anonymous object with three properties, title (the name of the link), url (which would contain the URL itself) and info (the information about the link that will be displayed on rollover). Once links has been filled with all of the link objects for that section, it is assigned to the links property for that section:

```
sections[3].links = links;
```

This is done for all of the sections of the site and can easily be updated when changes need to be made. I wanted to provide a file for you where all of the work was done in Flash to show how it's possible. There are, of course, other ways to accomplish the same set-up. Included with the download files is 27Bobs_further.fla, which loads an XML file, sections_27Bobs.XML, containing all of the section information. If you are interested in seeing how to use XML to achieve the same state, I would encourage you to look at the files.

That's it for the preparation. I tried to do as little as possible beforehand so that I could really take you through the process of creating this site. So let's get to it!

Movie variables

The remaining time in this tutorial will be spent in the ActionScript editor, so stretch those typing fingers and then open up the editor if it is not already opened. Select the first frame of the variables layer to begin.

We need to establish some values that we will use throughout our movie. Type the following into your ActionScript editor:

```
stageWidth = Stage.width; //800
stageHeight = Stage.height; //400
sectionXPos = stageWidth*.8;
halfButtonWidth = (stageWidth*.8)/5;
buttonHeight = 25;
subButtonWidth = halfButtonWidth*1.2;
subButtonHeight = buttonHeight*1.2;
```

The first two variables are the current dimensions of the stage, which we access through the Stage object. The sectionXPos variable holds the _x position of our section buttons at the right of the stage. The next four variables hold dimensions for our section buttons and subsection (or link) buttons. I've tried to make these all relative so that I could come back and quickly change a single value if I wished to alter dimensions for the site.

Continue by adding these variables to our code:

```
topSectionY = buttonHeight*1.5;
branchDown = halfButtonWidth*1.3;
extendedButton = halfButtonWidth*4.75;
windowHeight = 400;
windowWidth = extendedButton - branchDown;
sectionButtons = [];
```

topSectionY is the _y position that a section will move to when selected. branchDown is a bit less obvious, being the _x distance from the center of the section button where the main section window will open and drop down from. extendedButton is the distance across the stage a section button will extend to when selected. windowHeight and windowWidth are the dimensions for our opened section's window. Finally, sectionButtons is an array that will hold references to all of our section buttons so that we may quickly loop through every button. The next piece of code holds all the information we will need to try different color schemes. Place this after the previous code:

```
colorSchemes = {};
colorSchemes.blackboard =
{foreground:0xFFFFFF, background:0x000000};
colorSchemes.chalkboard =
{foreground:0xFFFFFF, background:0x003300};
colorSchemes.blueprint =
{foreground:0xFFFFFF, background:0x000033};
colorSchemes.sketchpad =
{foreground:0x000000, background:0xDDDDDD};
colorSchemes.custom =
{foreground:0x000055, background:0xDDDDAA};
currentColorScheme = colorSchemes.blackboard;
```

I initially tried the site with white as a background color and black as the foreground, as you might find in a traditional sketchpad. As I developed the site further, I found it might resemble more of a chalkboard and so inverted the colors. This gave me the idea to provide a number of color schemes for the user, plus the ability to choose custom colors as well. As you can see, each scheme is a property of the colorSchemes object (blackboard, chalkboard, blueprint, sketchpad and custom). Each of these properties contains an object consisting of a foreground and background property. By changing the scheme then stored in the variable currentColorScheme, you can experiment with your own colors and schemes.

Now we have established our variables and color schemes, it's time to place a few movie clips on our stage to hold the actual graphics. This code is still located on the variables layer:

```
this.createEmptyMovieClip("sectionHolder", 1);
```

`sectionHolder` is the clip that will hold all of the section buttons themselves. I often like to place attached graphics into holders, rather than to adding them directly to the stage, because it gives more freedom for placing, rotating and scaling the entire group if need arises.

The next movie clip will serve as the background of our stage. Since we will be changing colors dynamically, we can't rely on the stage color itself. Instead we draw a box around the stage, using the drawing API, and color it as needed:

```
this.createEmptyMovieClip("bg", 0);
bg.beginFill(currentColorScheme.background
➡ , 100);
drawBox(bg, 0, 0, stageWidth,
➡ stageHeight);
bg.endFill();
```

OK, the `beginFill` (where we send a color and alpha value) and `endFill` lines might be familiar to you if you have used the drawing API at all, but where does `drawBox` come from? Well, since we will be drawing plenty of boxes in this movie, it's best that we place this in another function that we can easily call up over and over. What we are sending to this new function are the clip in which to draw, and the left, top, right and bottom boundaries for the box. Let's take care of this function now so you can see how we accomplish this.

Go to the functions layer of code (which should be empty) and type the following:

```
drawBox = function(clip, l, t, r, b) {
  with (clip) {
    moveTo(l, b);
    lineTo(r, b);
    lineTo(r, t);
    lineTo(l, t);
    lineTo(l, b);
  }
}
```

As simple as this function might seem, it will help us out tremendously. Using the four boundaries sent, the function draws a box in the given clip. Notice how we have kept the fill methods (as well as `clear` and `lineStyle`) outside of the function so that we can handle these for differing clips. With that taken care of, jump back to the variables layer so we can finish up there.

Back on the variables layer, we need to add the lines that will format all of our text fields. Add these lines to follow the creation of the background graphic (bg):

```
headingTF = new TextFormat();
headingTF.align = "right";
headingTF.font = "scriptFont";
headingTF.size = 18;
headingTF.color = currentColorScheme.foreground;

infoTF = new TextFormat();
infoTF.align = "left";
infoTF.font = "scriptFont";
infoTF.size = 15;
infoTF.color = currentColorScheme.foreground;

buttonTF = new TextFormat();
buttonTF.align = "center";
buttonTF.font = "scriptFont";
buttonTF.size = 16;
buttonTF.color = currentColorScheme.foreground;
```

Here we are using the new `TextFormat` object to provide formatting for our text fields. Each formatting object has the same font, since we only exported one from our library, though each has a different size and alignment. Notice too how each establishes its color (which is the same for each) by looking in the foreground property of the `currentColorScheme`. Since we set the `currentColorScheme` to be `blackboard`, then that color will be `white`.

If you are using a font other than QuillScript as your exported font, this is the area where you might need to come back to adjust the font size. Simply alter each text format's size property if my values are not working for your choice of font.

That takes care of all of our variables. Now it's time to add the code that will actually draw our buttons on our stage.

54

Drawing the buttons

It's frustrating typing a lot of code without seeing any results, so let's write some code that will quickly show us a result and reward us for our efforts so far. This will add new movie clips on the stage to represent the section buttons at the right of the interface.

Go to the set up stage layer (which should be empty at this time) and type in the following:

```
for (i = 0; i < sections.length; i++) {
   clip = sections[i].clip =
   ➥ sectionHolder.createEmptyMovieClip
   ➥ ("sectionButton" + i, i);
   sectionButtons.push(clip);
   clip._y = ((i*2) * buttonHeight) +
   ➥ buttonHeight*2;
   clip._x = sectionXPos;
```

We start with a `for` loop to run through the amount of sections we have already established in the section set-up layer. For each of these sections we create a new movie clip and place a reference to this movie clip in the new `clip` property of that section. We also place a reference into a variable to make it easier to use in the rest of our code here. The line following the clip's creation pushes a reference to the clip into the `sectionButtons` array that we created earlier. The final two lines place the clip on the stage. Although the `_x` position is the same for each clip, the `_y` position changes based on the current iteration of the loop. It's not terribly important how I arrived at this value, as it is simply a starting position from which the clip will fall (and never be assigned again).

The next piece of code, to be placed immediately after the previous section, adds and formats a text field in the `sectionButton` movie clip:

```
clip.createTextField("label", 0,
➥ halfButtonWidth*.75, -buttonHeight/2,
➥ 0, 0);
label = clip.label;
label.setNewTextFormat(headingTF);
label.embedFonts = 1;
label.autoSize = "right";
label.selectable = 0;
label.text = sections[i].name;
label._y -= label.textHeight/2;
```

To understand how `label` is placed, we first need to look at how the `sectionButton` graphic will be drawn. Basically, a border will be drawn from the center of the `sectionButton` clip to the left and right (positive and negative `_x`) by `halfButtonWidth`, and from 0 to `-buttonHeight` on the `_y` axis. So placing the `label` text field at `halfButtonWidth*.75` and `-buttonHeight/2` puts it off on the far right on the x axis and in the middle on the y axis. We give it a height and width of 0 since in a few lines we set its `autoSize` property to `right`, meaning it will automatically resize from the right depending on the text we place inside it. We also apply the `headingTF` text format and embed the exported font so that it can be seen. After disabling the text field's selectable property, which would allow the user to select the text, we place the corresponding section's name in the text property and adjust the y position based on the `textHeight` to keep the text in the middle of our clip.

The next bit of code adds a new movie clip inside of our `sectionButton` to hold any drawings we do with the drawing API. Place it after the previous code:

```
drawing = clip.createEmptyMovieClip
➥ ("drawing", 2);
drawing.leftSide = halfButtonWidth;
drawBorders(drawing);
```

After creating a new clip named drawing, we give it a variable to hold the current left side of the drawing (right now, simply half of the sectionButton's width from sectionButton center). This will change as we extend the left side of the button to the left as the section opens. The next line is another function I've added to encapsulate code that we will use throughout. drawBorders will add randomized borders to a movie clip. Let's jump back to our functions code layer and add this new function now.

In the functions layer, immediately following our drawBox function, write the following:

```
drawBorders = function(clip) {
    clip.clear();
    clip.lineStyle(1,
    ➥ currentColorScheme.foreground, 100);
    drawRandomBox(clip, -clip.leftSide, -
    ➥ buttonHeight, halfButtonWidth, 0);
}
```

In this function, we accept a movie clip as a parameter and clear it of any previous drawings, reset the lineStyle based on the current color scheme's foreground color, and call a new function, drawRandomBox, sending it the clip and its four boundaries. This function is similar to our earlier drawBox function, but instead will draw a box with randomized borders. Let's write the necessary code now.

Below the drawBox function, add the following new function:

```
drawRandomBox = function(clip, l, t, r, b) {
    with (clip) {
        for (var i = 0; i < 3; i++) {
            moveTo(getRandom(10) + l,
            ➥ getRandom(10) + b);
            lineTo(getRandom(10) + r,
            ➥ getRandom(10) + b);
            lineTo(getRandom(10) + r,
            ➥ getRandom(10) + t);
            lineTo(getRandom(10) + l,
            ➥ getRandom(10) + t);
            lineTo(getRandom(10) + l,
            ➥ getRandom(10) + b);
        }
    }
}
```

In this function, we run through a for loop three times and draw from and to randomized positions about the box's boundaries. What's getRandom? Why, another function we're just about to write.

Add this above the drawBox function, still on the functions layer:

```
getRandom = function(range) {
    return Math.random()*range - range/2
}
```

Pretty simple. We call this function and send a range in which to find a randomized number. The function uses Math.random to find a number between 0 and 1, multiplies this by our range so we have a number between 0 and our range maximum, then we subtract half of our range so the final number returned falls within the specified range but on either side of 0 (so a range of 10 will return a number between –5 and 5). Now we have our drawBorders function call complete and we can return to the set up stage layer to finish our script there.

After returning to the set up stage layer, add these lines to finish up the for loop:

```
        btn = clip.createEmptyMovieClp("btn", 1);
        btn.beginFill(0, 0);
        drawBox(btn, -halfButtonWidth,
        ➥ -buttonHeight, halfButtonWidth, 0);
        btn.endFill();
        btn.onRollOver = sectionOver;
        btn.onRollOut = btn.onReleaseOutside =
        ➥ btn.onDragOut = sectionOut;
        btn.onRelease = function() {
        ➥ selectMe.apply(this._parent) };
    }
    delete clip;
    delete btn;
    delete drawing;
    delete labelHolder;
    delete label;
    delete i;
```

56

btn will be the final movie clip inside of our sectionButton. We need this clip for all of the actual button functionality, since at this time we only have a text field and clip of line drawings. btn will serve as our solid hit area for the user's mouse to click. To accomplish this, we call the drawBox function, but only after setting the clip's fill alpha to 0. This will give us a solid, rectangular hit area that's invisible to the user. The final lines in the for loop assign the button actions, sectionOver, sectionOut and selectMe, the third of which we will write in the next section (where we will discuss the use of apply). After we close the for loop, we delete all of the unnecessary variables we no longer need.

Finally in this section, we will write the functions that will control our rollover effects. Go to the sections code layer (which should be empty at this time) and type the following:

```
sectionOver = function() {
   this.onEnterFrame = function() {
      drawBorders(this._parent.drawing) };
}

sectionOut = function() {
   delete this.onEnterFrame
}
```

These are two simple functions that are called when our section buttons are rolled over and off. sectionOver has the clip call the drawBorders function on each enterFrame event (sending the appropriate drawing clip, located on the parent's timeline since the onEnterFrame lies on the btn timeline). sectionOut simply deletes that handler.

All right! Test your movie now to see the section buttons placed on the stage and their borders drawn and redrawn. A pretty nice beginning, and it only gets more fun from here!

Making the buttons bounce

The next section of code will deal with the bouncing effect that occurs when one of the `sectionButtons` is selected. Here you'll notice we've got a whole bunch of real-feeling going on. We've got the interface pretending to be a chalkboard, we've got areas that pretend to be buttons, and now those buttons are going to pretend to be bouncy – all in the name of making our user feel comfortable!

This is probably the toughest code in this entire tutorial, so stick with me and we'll make it through. It's all downhill from there!

The concept for this code is that each button will have a ground and ceiling (usually another button), and it will look to these as it's falling or rising to determine when it needs to rebound. As a new section is selected, the button selected will be moved from the stack of buttons bouncing, and so a new order, with new ground and ceiling clips, will need to be determined. The first thing we will need to do is add a few variables to the variables layer to take care of the values driving the fall.

Go to the variables layer and add the following lines of code before our `colorSchemes` declaration:

```
gravity = .6;
bounceFactor = .1;
buttonEnergy = .5
```

Although it is all fake physics that I employ (I practice a lot of "that looks good to me" physics), I tried to name the variables to match their real-world functions. Therefore `gravity` will control how quickly a section will fall. `bounceFactor` is how high a button will rebound once it hits the ground (or another button). `buttonEnergy` controls how quickly the buttons will come to rest after falling and bouncing.

Now add the following lines after the creation of the `sectionHolder` movie clip (still on the variables layer):

```
windowBottom = sectionHolder.
➥ createEmptyMovieClip("ground", 500);
windowBottom._y = windowHeight*.95;
windowTop = sectionHolder.
➥ createEmptyMovieClip("ceiling", 501);
windowTop._y = 0;
```

Inside `sectionHolder`, I create two empty movie clips to serve as position holders at the top and bottom of the window. When the `sectionButtons` are finding the other buttons above and below them, these two new clips will act as book ends so that each `sectionButton` has clips on either side, including the `sectionButtons` at the top or bottom of the stack.

Now go to the sections code layer and place the following lines of code after the `sectionOut` function:

```
selectMe = function() {
  delete this.btn.onEnterFrame;
  this.btn.enabled = 0;
  this.onEnterFrame = moveUp;
  for (var i in sections) {
    if (sections[i].clip == this) {
      currentSection = i;
      break;
    }
  }
}
```

`selectMe` will be called when a `sectionButton` is clicked. The first thing it needs to do is to delete the `drawBorders` call that is occurring on its `btn`'s `onEnterFrame`. It then disables the button so that it can no longer be clicked. The `moveUp` function assigned to the `sectionHolder`'s `onEnterFrame` will do exactly that – move the button up to the top of the screen. We will write this function in a moment. Finally, the `for in` loop goes through the `sections` array and finds the reference to the clip that was clicked so that we can know what section has been selected. We store this index number in the `currentSection` variable.

If you look back to the code located in the set up stage layer where we called this function in btn's onRelease handler, you will see that we incorporated a rather odd way of calling the function:

```
    btn.onRelease = function() {
  selectMe.apply(this._parent) };
```

apply is an interesting new addition in Flash MX that allows you to specify what clip is represented by this inside a function. In the above example, I apply the selectMe function to the _parent of btn, which is the sectionButton itself. Therefore in the code for selectMe, any time this appears, it now refers to the sectionButton sent. In addition, you can send parameters inside of an array, a process I will demonstrate shortly.

Next we need to find a reference to the sectionButton in the sectionButtons array, which we will use to determine the ground and ceiling for each sectionButton. Type this code after the previous lines:

```
    for (var i in sectionButtons) {
  if (sectionButtons[i].selected) {
    sectionButtons[i].btn.enabled = 1;
    delete sectionButtons[i].selected;
  }
  if (sectionButtons[i] == this) {
    sectionButtons.splice(i, 1);
    sectionButtons.unshift(this);
    this.selected = 1;
  }
}
```

Before we search for this sectionButton's reference, we first find the previously selected sectionButton so that we can re-enable it. After this is accomplished, we find reference to this sectionButton in the sectionButtons array and remove it from its position and place it at the beginning instead using the built-in unshift method. We also give it a new property, named selected, which will serve as a flag to find it when another button is clicked (as you can see in the previous if statement).

With the selected sectionButton placed safely in the first index of our sectionButtons array, we can look at all of the other buttons and determine each one's ground and ceiling clip. Write this code after the previous lines:

```
for (var i = 1; i < sectionButtons.length;
i++) {
  if (i == sectionButtons.length-1) {
    var params = [windowBottom,
    ➥ sectionButtons[i-1], i]
  } else if (i == 1) {
    var params = [sectionButtons[i+1],
    ➥ windowTop, i]
  } else {
    var params = [sectionButtons[i+1],
    ➥ sectionButtons[i-1], i]
  }
  initFall.apply(sectionButtons[i], params);
}
```

Looping through our sectionButtons array, skipping the first index which contains the selected section, we call the function initFall for each sectionButton. First, however, we need to determine the two clips above and below each sectionButton so that it will know its ground and ceiling. If you read the note above dealing with the apply function, you will recall I mentioned that you can send parameters as well inside an array. You can see that for each sectionButton, I create a local array named params, which contains three indices.

The first is the sectionButton's ground clip, the second is its ceiling, while the third is simply its index position in the array. For the bottom sectionButton, which will be located at the end of the sectionButtons array, the ground clip will be the windowBottom clip that we created previously, located at the bottom of the interface. For the top sectionButton (excluding the selected button), we send windowTop as its ceiling so that it cannot bounce above the screen. For the remaining sectionButtons, the sectionButton on either side of it in the array serves as the top or bottom. Once params has been set for each, we can apply the initFall function, sending the params on as a second argument.

We will write initFall in a moment, but let's first finish up the selectMe function.

Here are the final lines:

```
    buttonFallers = sectionButtons.slice(1);
    clearInterval(buttonFall);
    buttonFall = setInterval
➥ (this._parent._parent, "fall", 20);
}
```

By slicing from index 1 of sectionButtons to its end, we effectively place all of the buttons that need to fall and bounce inside a new array named buttonFallers. With that set, we create a new interval call (after first clearing any previous calls that might still be being made) that will call the fall function (yet to be written) on the _parent._parent's timeline, which works out to be the main timeline. We will call this function every 20 milliseconds and give this call the identifier buttonFall, which we can then use to clear the interval call (as we do in the previous line). Though you might think that 20 milliseconds is a bit too often to call this function, I found it gave the best results even after altering the gravity variable and the frame rate.

OK, with this function we have named three other functions that we will need to take care of: moveUp, initFall and fall. Let's take care of moveUp first, since it is the simplest.

Still in the sections code layer, directly beneath the selectMe function, add this new function:

```
moveUp = function() {
    this._y -= (this._y - topSectionY)/2;
    if (Math.abs(this._y - topSectionY) < 1)
{
        delete this.onEnterFrame;
    }
}
```

That's pretty easy to deal with, isn't it? Each frame, the sectionButton is moved half of the remaining distance to the top of the stage. When it is close enough, the onEnterFrame is deleted. Now let's take care of the initFall function, which we will place in the bouncing code layer.

Go to the bouncing code layer, which should be empty at this time, and type the following code:

```
initFall = function(ground, ceiling, place) {
    var finalVicinity = windowBottom._y -
➥ (((sectionButtons.length-1)-place)
➥ *(buttonHeight*1.5));
    if (this._y >= finalVicinity) { return false };
    this.moving = 1;
    this.velocity = 0;
    this.energy = buttonEnergy;
    this.ground = ground;
    this.ceiling = ceiling;
}
```

Even though the arguments sent to `initFall` were placed in an array, we do not need to access them in such a way thanks to the nature of the `apply` function. Instead, we simply have them separated into separate arguments. We place `ground` and `ceiling`, which are references to other clips, in this `sectionButtons`'s `ground` and `ceiling` properties, and we initialize a few variables, `moving` (a Boolean flag to determine whether the button is moving), `velocity` (its current rate) and `energy` (which equals the `buttonEnergy` variable we set earlier).

Before we set these properties, however, we make sure the button should be falling at all. Basically, any `sectionButtons` that are already in their final resting position needn't (and shouldn't) fall at all, so we quickly determine the general whereabouts of that final position. By finding the button's place from the bottom of the `sectionButton`'s stack and multiplying this value by 1.5 the height of the button (the height can vary thanks to the sketchy border) and then subtracting this from the bottom of the interface represented by `windowBottom`, we can see if the button is in the area where it will come to rest. If it is, then we exit the function without initializing anything, which will leave its `energy` as undefined.

`fall` should be added directly after the `initFall` function, still on the bouncing code layer:

```
fall = function() {
  for (var i in sectionButtons) {
    var which = sectionButtons[i];
    if (which._yscale < 100) { which.
    ➥ _yscale++ } else { which._yscale = 100 };
    if (which._xscale > 100) { which.
    ➥ _xscale— } else { which._xscale = 100 };
  }
```

This is the start of our `fall` function, which you will recall we set up to be called at a set interval after a button had been clicked. These first few lines simply run through all of the buttons and make sure they are at 100% scale, and if they're not, adjust them a little each interval call.

Continuing with the `fall` function:

```
for (var i in buttonFallers) {
  var which = buttonFallers[i];
  which._y += which.velocity;
  which.velocity += gravity;
```

Now we run through all of the buttons that are falling. We place a reference to the current button in the variable `which` and adjust its `_y` position by its current `velocity`, which could be positive or negative. We then adjust its `velocity` by the `gravity` constant.

Here is the biggest chunk of code from this function, which deals with a button hitting its ground clip:

```
if (which._y > which.ground._y -
➥ which.ground._height) {
  squish(which, which.ground);
  which._y = which.ground._y -
  ➥ which.ground._height;
  which.velocity *= -which.energy;
  if (which.energy < .1) {
    delete which.moving;
    delete which.energy;
    delete which.velocity;
    which._xscale = which._yscale = 100;
    buttonFallers.splice(i, 1);
  } else {
    if (!which.ground.moving) {
      which.energy -= bounceFactor
    }
  }
}
```

If the `sectionButton` is hitting its ground clip, it squishes the two (a function we will write in a moment), absolutely places its `_y` position so the two don't overlap, and reverses the button's direction. We then make a check to see if all of the `sectionButton`'s energy is depleted, which means it should come to a rest. If it has lost all of its energy, it removes all of the added properties, resets itself to 100% scale, and removes itself from the `buttonFallers` array since it no longer is falling. However, if energy does remain in the `sectionButton`, it checks to see if the ground clip was actually moving up when they hit. If this is the case, nothing happens (no loss of energy), but if not, then some energy is removed.

Now that we have taken care of the ground clips, we need to do the same for the ceiling clips. Place this code next:

```
if (which._y + which.height < which.ceiling._y) {
    which._y = which.ceiling._y + which._height;
    which.ceiling.energy += bounceFactor;
      }
    }
```

This is much simpler than the previous section. Basically, if a button is hitting the clip above it, it readjusts its position and adds some energy to the ceiling clip.

This last piece of code finishes up our `fall` function:

```
    if (buttonFallers.length < 1) {
      clearInterval(buttonFall);
    }
  }
```

Each time a `sectionButton` comes to rest, it removes itself from the `buttonFallers` array. Once all of the clips have been removed, the interval call is cleared.

To complete the bouncing code, we need to code in one last function, `squish`, an easy addition.

Add these lines directly after the fall function, still on the bouncing code layer:

```
squish = function(one, two) {
    var totalEnergy = one.energy + two.energy;
    one._yscale = two._yscale = 100 -
  ➡ (30*totalEnergy);
    one._xscale = two._xscale = 100 +
  ➡ (10*totalEnergy);
  }
```

With `squish`, the total energy of the two colliding clips is used to determine how much to scale those clips. The clips are actually squished on the y axis and stretched on the x axis. The code at the top of our `fall` function is what slowly returns the clips back to normal.

If you can believe it, only one line remains to get our bouncing sections working. Go to the set up stage layer and add this line at the very end. Basically, it will be the final line of code before the stage is drawn the first time.

```
selectMe.apply(sections[0].clip);
```

This will select the first section (home) automatically when the movie starts. If you look back at the `selectMe` code, you will see that this is where we called the `initFall` and `fall` functions, so selecting this clip sets the falling in motion as the movie begins.

Test your movie now to see the squishy, animated chalk sections.

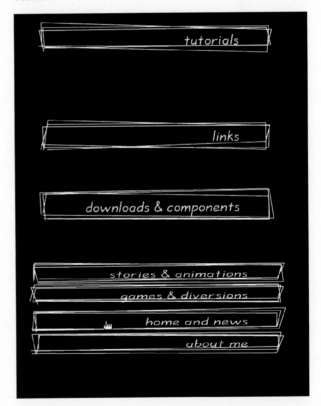

Adding the content

Well, we now have a nice effect to enhance the otherwise familiar menu on the right. Of course, now we need the menus to actually load the content that they are advertising. We will take care of this with four functions that will not only attach the content links, but also animate each section after it has been clicked and moved to the top of the interface so that the content can be revealed in a more engaging way.

The first item we need to address is when to actually begin the animation and loading of content. I chose to initiate these actions once a section had reached the top of the interface after being clicked. In the sections code layer, alter the `moveUp` function to read (changes in bold):

```
moveUp = function() {
   this._y -= (this._y - topSectionY)/2;
   if (Math.abs(this._y - topSectionY) < 1) {
      this.onEnterFrame = extendLeftSide;
   }
}
```

Now instead of merely deleting the `onEnterFrame`, we assign another function to it named `extendLeftSide`. Let's write that function now.

Still on the sections code layer, add the following function directly after `moveUp`:

```
extendLeftSide = function() {
   this.drawing.leftSide += (extendedButton
   ➡ - this.drawing.leftSide)/1.2;
   drawBorders(this.drawing);
   if (extendedButton -
   ➡ this.drawing.leftSide < 1) {
      addContent.apply(this);
   }
}
```

There's really nothing here that you've not seen before, though you might be more familiar with such easing animation code being used to adjust stage coordinates (just as we used in `moveUp`). What we are easing here instead is the `leftSide` property of our `sectionButton`. By calling the `drawBorders` function immediately after, we have accomplished the animation of our extending button across the stage. Once the left side of the stage has been reached (represented by `extendedButton`), we call another function named `addContent`, which we will write in a moment. First, go ahead and test your movie to see how these additions work.

Obviously, one thing we have to deal with is retracting our extended sections, so let's write that code next. Place this new function directly after `extendLeftSide`:

```
retractLeftSide = function() {
   this.drawing.leftSide -= (this.drawing.
   ➡ leftSide - halfButtonWidth)/2;
   if (this.drawing.leftSide -
   ➡ halfButtonWidth < 1) {
      this.drawing.leftSide = halfButtonWidth;
      delete this.onEnterFrame;
   }
   drawBorders(this.drawing);
}
```

This does the exact opposite of our `extendLeftSide` function. Now we just need to call it when a new section has been clicked, so the obvious place is in the `selectMe` function.

Amend the `selectMe` function as shown:

```
for (var i in sectionButtons) {
   if (sectionButtons[i].selected) {
sectionButtons[i].onEnterFrame =
➡ retractLeftSide;
      sectionButtons[i].btn.enabled = 1;
      delete sectionButtons[i].selected;
   }
```

So now when a new section is pressed, the previously selected section will retract its left side. Test your movie to see how this works.

After the `retractLeftSide` function, begin the `addContent` function that we called earlier:

```
addContent = function() {
    this.drawing.bottom = 0;
    this.onEnterFrame = extendBottomSide;
}
```

Obviously this doesn't yet add any content at all, but we will take care of that in a moment. In the meantime, let's focus on the `extendBottomSide` function we just set to be called on the `onEnterFrame` handler. This is what will take care of extending the window down once the section button has extended to the left of the interface. Notice how first we have set the bottom property, which represents the current position of the bottom side, to 0. Let's take care of `extendBottomSide` to see how it works.

Place this code immediately above the `addContent` function:

```
extendBottomSide = function() {
    var mc = this.drawing;
    mc.bottom += ((windowBottom._y -
    ➥ topSectionY) - mc.bottom)/1.2;
```

It starts off simple enough, using the same easing code we used in our previous functions to adjust the bottom side a little each call. The next bit of code will take care of the drawing itself.

Place this code after the previous lines:

```
with (mc) {
    clear();
    lineStyle(1, currentColorScheme.foreground, 100);
    for (var j = 0; j < 3; j++) {
        moveTo(getRandom(10) - leftSide, getRandom(10) - buttonHeight);
        lineTo(getRandom(10) + halfButtonWidth, getRandom(10) - buttonHeight);
        lineTo(getRandom(10) + halfButtonWidth, getRandom(10));
        lineTo(getRandom(10) - branchDown, getRandom(10));
        lineTo(getRandom(10) - branchDown, getRandom(10) + bottom);
        lineTo(getRandom(10) - leftSide, getRandom(10) + bottom);
        lineTo(getRandom(10) - leftSide, getRandom(10) - buttonHeight);
    }
}
```

We cannot call the `drawBorders` function in this case since now we are dealing with a polygon of six sides instead of four. The concept is still the same, however, despite the extra sides. We loop three times and draw randomized lines for each side as the bottom side of the window extends down. Now of course, we need to check when we reach the bottom.

Type these lines to finish the `extendBottomSide` function:

```
    if ((windowBottom._y - topSectionY) - mc.bottom < 1) {
        delete this.onEnterFrame
    }
}
```

Just as before, we check each function call to see when we are close enough to our destination to stop, at which point the `onEnterFrame` handler is removed. Test your movie now to see the result.

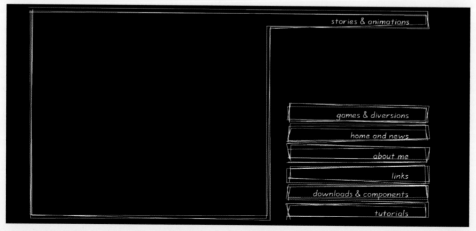

Well, now we can see where the content needs to be added, so let's take care of that by adding the following lines to our `addContent` function as shown:

```
addContent = function() {
    this.drawing.bottom = 0;
    this.onEnterFrame = extendBottomSide;
    var content = this._parent.createEmptyMovieClip("content", 50);
    var margin = sectionXPos - extendedButton;
    content.createTextField("info", 0, margin*1.6, windowHeight*.25,
    ➥ windowWidth*.45, windowHeight*.45);
    var info = content.info;
    info.setNewTextFormat(infoTF);
    info.embedFonts = 1;
    info.selectable = 0;
    info.wordWrap = 1;
    info.text = sections[currentSection].info;
    info._y -= info.textHeight/2;
```

`content` is a movie clip we add to the main timeline (`this._parent`) that will hold all of the content. `margin` holds the amount of space to the left of the open window, which will help us when we start placing items. The text field we add is at the upper left of the window, a quarter of the way down and about half the width and height of the window itself. We give it all the necessary formatting, including the ability to wordwrap, and place whatever `info` text we included with the section.

Next, we're going to attach and color the appropriate image for the section. Place this code immediately following the last line above, but before `addContent`'s closing bracket (this code is all a part of `addContent`):

```
    var image = content.attachMovie(sections[currentSection].image,
    ➥ "image", 500);
    imageColor = new Color(image);
    imageColor.setRGB(currentColorScheme.foreground);
    image.onRollOver = function() { info.text = sections[currentSection].info };
    image.useHandCursor = 0;
    image._x = windowWidth*.65;
    image._y = windowHeight*.1;
```

This code is all fairly straightforward. We attach an image, color it based on the foreground color, give it a button action to place the section info back into the `info` text field upon `rollOver`, disable the hand cursor and finally place the image at the upper right of the window.

Continuing with addContent, place this code after the previous image code (again, before addContent's closing bracket):

```
var midLine = content.createEmptyMovieClip("midLine", 250);
midLine.lineStyle(1, currentColorScheme.foreground, 100);
for (var i = 0; i < 4; i++) {
  midLine.moveTo(getRandom(10) + margin, getRandom(10) +
  ➥ windowHeight/2);
  midLine.lineTo(getRandom(10) + windowWidth + margin, getRandom(10)
  ➥ + windowHeight/2);
}
```

midLine is the line that is drawn between the two halves of the window. Here we simply create a new movie clip and draw a line randomly across the general vicinity of mid-window a total of four times in a similar way that we have drawn our box borders in previous code.

This final piece of code should be placed directly after the midLine code above and immediately before addContent's closing bracket:

```
content.createTextField("textBlock", 777, margin*1.4,
➥ windowHeight*.53, windowWidth*.95, windowHeight*.4);
var tb = content.textBlock;
tb.setNewTextFormat(infoTF);
tb.embedFonts = 1;
tb.wordWrap = 1;
tb.selectable = 0;
tb.text = sections[currentSection].textBlock;
```

To end addContent, we add and format another text field to hold the text at the bottom of the interface. This is where text stored in a section's textBlock property will be displayed. Go ahead and test your movie now to see the result.

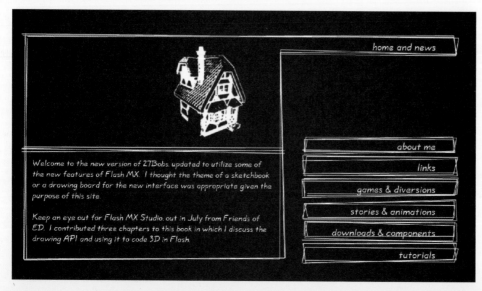

We're almost there, but you can see we have a few problems that have cropped up. First, the content is seen before the window is fully open, and second, the content is not removed immediately when a new section is selected. Let's take care of the first problem by adding a mask to reveal the content. We will do this in our `addContent` code.

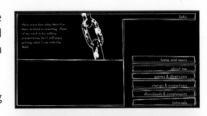

Place these lines at the end of the `addContent` function, immediately after the formatting of `tb`:

```
this.createEmptyMovieClip("contentMask", 50);
content.setMask(this.contentMask);
```

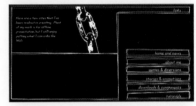

That's easy enough, but all we actually have is an empty clip. We need to draw something inside it to serve as our masked region. We will take care of this in the `extendBottomSide` function, which is appropriate since this is where we want the mask to slowly reveal the content.

Place these lines before the final `if` statement in the `extendBottomSide` function:

```
this.contentMask.clear();
this.contentMask.beginFill(0,0);
drawBox(this.contentMask, -mc.leftSide, -buttonHeight, -branchDown,
➥ mc.bottom);
this.contentMask.endFill();
```

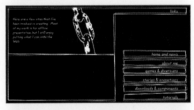

Now we have something! The box inside `contentMask` can be drawn with the `drawBox` function since we want a rectangular mask for our content. As `mc.bottom` is adjusted a little each function call, the mask will extend with the drawn borders to reveal more content.

One last thing to take care of, and that's the removal of previous content. This can be accomplished with just a few extra lines within the `selectMe` function, which is the point where we need previous content removed.

Add the following line to the beginning of `selectMe` (still on the sections code layer). It can be added anywhere before the first `for` loop.

```
this._parent.content.removeMovieClip();
```

So the content is removed. To take care of the mask as well, add the following new line to the second `for` loop:

```
for (var i in sectionButtons) {
    if (sectionButtons[i].selected) {
        sectionButtons[i].onEnterFrame = retractLeftSide;
        sectionButtons[i].contentMask.removeMovieClip();
        sectionButtons[i].btn.enabled = 1;
        delete sectionButtons[i].selected;
    }
```

With these additions, test your movie and see what we've accomplished!

Providing links

There is only one final step before we are finished, and that is to add the link buttons to our content. We are going to take a slightly different route in creating these buttons than we have used for the rest of the site. With these buttons, we are going to extend movie clips to hold all of the functionality of the subsection buttons as additional methods. This is fairly easy to do and can be wonderfully modular for future projects. Before we code this, however, let's quickly write the code that will place these new clips on the stage. Of course, this is done in the addContent function as well.

OK, brace yourself, because I'm giving it to you all in one blow. Place this code after the formatting of the info text box and before the attaching of the image, all inside the addContent function:

```
var linksNum = sections[currentSection].links.length;
var rows = Math.ceil(linksNum/2);
for (var i = 0; i < rows; i++) {
  var props = {};
  props._x = windowWidth*.25 + margin;
  props._y = windowHeight*.6 + subButtonHeight*i;
  props.num = i;
  content.attachMovie("subButtonSymbol", "b" + i, i+1, props);
}
for (var i = rows; i < linksNum; i++) {
  var props = {};
  props._x = windowWidth*.75 + margin;
  props._y = windowHeight*.6 + subButtonHeight*(i-rows);
  props.num = i;
  content.attachMovie("subButtonSymbol", "b" + i, i+1, props);
}
```

It might seem like a lot, but the two for loops are actually almost identical, so it's really not so bad. The first two lines of code at the top take the number of links in the currentSection and use this to determine the number of rows to place the subButtons in. The two for loops then run through the first column of rows, then the second. For each subButton attached, I first create a new local object called props. I place in props the co-ordinate position at which I want to place the new subButton. I also include a property called num, which holds the links index position for this particular subButton (it will need this number later to access its information). With props all set, I attach the subButton and send props as the initObject, which is an optional fourth parameter for attachMovie that allows you to give and set properties for a newly attached movie clip. By doing it this way, my subButton is automatically placed at the position I need it.

All right, now with that set up, we need to write the code that will control our subButtons.

Go to the subButtons layer (which should still be empty), and type the following code:

```
SubButton = function() {
   this.init();
}

SubButton.prototype = new MovieClip();
```

This is the way to extend a movie clip in Flash MX. You simply create a new class constructor function as I do in the first line. You then set the new class's prototype to be an instance of the MovieClip object. Now any instance of your new class will have all of the MovieClip's properties and methods, plus anything you add to the new class. The only method I have called inside the constructor is the init method for the class, so let's write this now.

Place this code directly after the previous lines of code:

```
SubButton.prototype.init = function() {
   this.createTextField("label", 0, 0, 0, 0, 0);
   this.label.setNewTextFormat(buttonTF);
   this.label.autoSize = "center";
   this.label.embedFonts = 1;
   this.label.selectable = 0;
   this.label.text = sections[currentSection]
   ➥ .links[this.num].title;
   this.label._y -= this.label.textHeight*1.25;
```

By attaching this, and all of the following methods of SubButton, to its prototype object, I have enabled each instance of SubButton to have access to these methods without having to duplicate functions. This is the beginning of the init method, and all these lines do is create and format a text field that will display the link's name. The name itself is found in the sections array, using this.num (passed in the initObject, remember?) to access the proper link information.

Continuing on with the init method, type the following lines of code:

```
this.width = this.label.textWidth/2 + 20;

this.onRollOver = this.rollOverScript;
this.onRollOut = this.onReleaseOutside
   ➥ = this.onDragOut = this.rollOutScript;
this.onRelease = this.releaseScript;

var fill = this.createEmptyMovieClip("fill", 1);
fill._x = buttonWidth/2;
fill.beginFill(0,0);
drawBox(fill, -this.width, - buttonHeight,
   ➥ this.width, 0);
fill.endFill();
```

These lines give our subButton all of its button abilities. First, we establish its width based on the amount of text (plus a 20 pixel buffer). We then assign functions to each of its button handlers – we'll write these in a moment. Finally, as we did with our sectionButtons, we need to draw a hit area for the user's mouse. To do this, we create a new movie clip called fill and place it in the center of the button, using drawBox to draw a 0% opacity box around our button.

The following lines complete our init function:

```
   if (sections[currentSection]
   ➥ .visited[this.num]) {
     this.drawCrossOut()
   }
}
```

This will draw a line through a link that has already been visited when a section is reopened. visited will be the name of an array property of a section that will be created once a link in a section has been clicked on. Once the array is created, it will store a true in the index of a link that has been visited in that section, so the next time the section is opened, the line automatically appears drawn through the previously visited link. We'll look at the drawCrossOut method in a moment, but let's first take care of our rollOver functions.

These next two methods really go together, so I include them both in the next block. Place these after the `init` method:

```
SubButton.prototype.rollOverScript = function() {
   this._parent.info.text
   ➡ sections[currentSection].links[this.num].info;
   this._parent.info._y = ((windowHeight*.5) -
   ➡ this._parent.info.textHeight)/2;
   this.clear();
   this.lineStyle(1, currentColorScheme.foreground, 100);
   drawRandomBox(this, -this.width, -buttonHeight, this.width, 0);
}

SubButton.prototype.rollOutScript = function() {
   this.clear()
}
```

`rollOverScript` first places its link's information in the `info` text field and adjusts that text field's position based on the amount of text. It then draws random borders around itself in the same way that our random borders have been drawn throughout our code. `rollOutScript` simply removes these borders.

Place `releaseScript` immediately after `rollOutScript`:

```
SubButton.prototype.releaseScript = function() {
   if (sections[currentSection].visited == undefined) {
sections[currentSection].visited = [] };
   if (sections[currentSection].visited[this.num] != true) {
     sections[currentSection].visited[this.num] = true;
     this.drawCrossOut();
   }
   if (sections[currentSection].links[this.num].url != undefined) {
//    getURL(sections[currentSection].links[this.num].url, "_blank");
   }
}
```

The first line of code inside `releaseScript` checks to see if the `visited` property of the current section exists yet, and if it doesn't it creates it. It then checks to see if its corresponding index inside this array has a true value, meaning it has already been visited. If it finds it hasn't yet been visited, then a `true` value is placed into this index and the `drawCrossOut` method is called to draw a line through the link name. Finally, if a URL exists for the link, then the page is opened. Notice here that I have commented out this line so you won't be given an error message that the paths are not correct while you test this file.

It's finally time to write the `drawCrossOut` method we have already referred to twice, which also happens to be the last method for `SubButton` (and nearly the last block in our tutorial!). Place this code after `releaseScript`:

```
SubButton.prototype.drawCrossOut = function() {
    var cross = this.createEmptyMovieClip("crossOut", 2);
    cross.lineStyle(1, currentColorScheme.foreground, 100);
    cross.moveTo(getRandom(10) - this.width, getRandom(10) -
➥ buttonHeight/2);
    cross.lineTo(getRandom(10) + this.width, getRandom(10) -
➥ buttonHeight/2);
}
```

This, of course, creates a new empty clip and draws a randomized line through the link name. Easy enough. One final line now to complete our `SubButton` code.

Place this line at the end of the code in the subButtons layer:

```
Object.registerClass("subButtonSymbol", SubButton);
```

`Object.registerClass` associates an exported library symbol with a particular class. In this case, the symbol exported as `subButtonSymbol` (an empty clip in the library) is associated with the `SubButton` class we just created as an extension of the `MovieClip` object. Now any instances of `subButtonSymbol` placed on the stage will automatically be instances of `SubButton`.

That takes care of it! Test the movie to see where we stand.

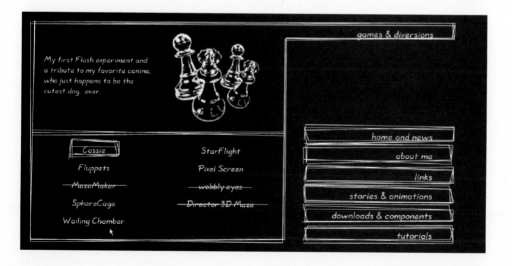

Branding the site

Of course, the last thing I need to add before the page is complete is my logo so people know where they're at (hey, I have to take *some* credit for all my hard work!). I left a nice little space for the logo up right. Go to the variables layer for this final bit of code.

Add the following lines after the creation of the bg movie clip:

```
logo = sectionHolder.attachMovie("logo",
➥ "logo", 12);
logo._x = 630 - sectionHolder._x;
logo._y = 64;
logo.onRelease = function() {
getURL("mailto:toddyard@27Bobs.com") };
logoColor = new Color(logo);
logoColor.setRGB(currentColorScheme.foregr
ound);
```

That's all it takes to place and color the logo, and give it an e-mail contact button functionality. And with that final touch, the page is complete. Congratulations! Test the final version to see how all your hard work paid off.

Conclusion

My hope with this site was to create a unique interface that evoked a sense of a work in progress. The sketchy feel of the scribbles of chalk aided this since we are already used to chalk markings being temporary and utilized in the planning stages of a project. Here, the real world, tactile metaphor applied, and the use of a real feel interface to familiarize the user with the purpose and subject matter, helped me in getting across what I wanted to communicate in a playful way without alienating or overwhelming the user.

When you are experimenting with interfaces and tools for navigation, I would invite you to explore incorporating metaphors to better communicate your ideas. Sometimes, the limitations you place on yourself by attempting to follow a theme will unlock creative ideas you would never have otherwise considered, in addition to giving users something familiar to grasp hold of as they are swept up in your imagination.

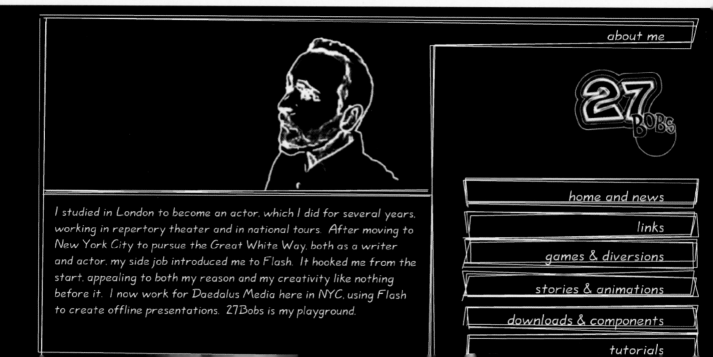

A FLASH FAMILY TREE

It's almost certain you've faced the problem at some point. You want to draw up your family tree, but you can't quite get it right. Then you regret starting the whole thing in permanent pen.

Even with the advent of computer genealogy, things look a bit blocky. Sure it's useful, but where's the love in all that square data storage? What we need is beauty! A tree you can grow! Data you can bring in on a whim. It needs to be intuitive, and this is where Flash presents itself as the ideal medium.

In this chapter we will look at how we can use Flash and a branching structure to help communicate and illustrate a large amount of related information without overwhelming the user. Flash, with an authoring environment that facilitates the combination of code and animated graphics, is a fantastic tool for the dynamic display of information. Let's take a look at one exciting way to take advantage of that.

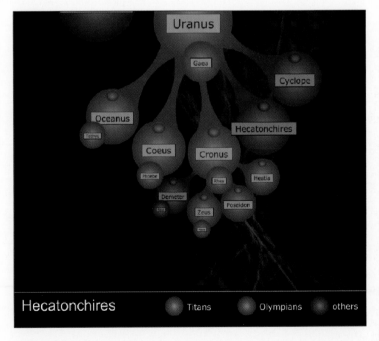

Hierarchy of the gods

I think the best way to begin this tutorial is to actually start at the end and show you the final project that we will be building in this chapter. Open up the file `gods_tree.swf` from the download files to see the end result, a branching hierarchical structure to display the gods and titans of Greek mythology. Have fun exploring the structure, by rotating and expanding the nodes to see how we could use such a system to display a large amount of information. Notice the gloopy connectors that stretch between the nodes, and how a smooth gradient can be drawn to ease color from a parent node to its child. Try opening a node to access more information and then using the combo boxes to navigate to a different node. Once you close the interface, the tree structure has been updated to your new position. Think about how you might go about structuring, drawing, expanding, and navigating such a system – then read on to see how I approached it.

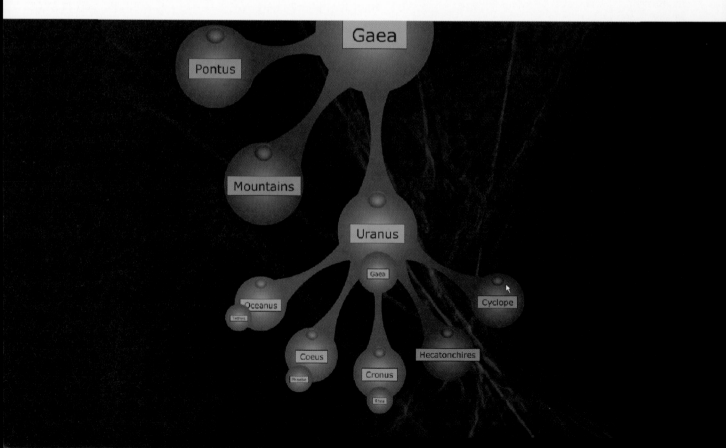

The process

As often happens with projects and experiments, what started out as one idea quickly grew into another, shifting through a myriad of stages to finally arrive at the product that you have just been looking at. The original idea happened to be the construction of an interface that would allow the user to quickly and easily navigate through a family tree structure, like the one shown here of some early generations of the British Royal Family.

The more I worked at it, however, the more I became aware of the anomalies that can occur in such a structure, such as multiple marriages (oh, that Henry VIII), interfamilial marriages and the existence or nonexistence of ancestor information for spouses. There were quite a lot of if...then statements flying about and I realized that such a chapter would have to be a study in conditions and little more. Instead, I wanted to write a chapter about the **display** of such data and different ways of presenting it.

In my job, I spend a lot of time inventing interesting methods to display data graphically. We are a visual society, and there is truth to the adage that a picture is worth a thousand words. Even more so, a picture is worth a thousand numbers – figures are much more easily understood when they are translated into a pictorial form. And so I create charts, graphs, timelines, and maps in order to communicate information more clearly. This is something that I wanted to accomplish with a branching family tree structure.

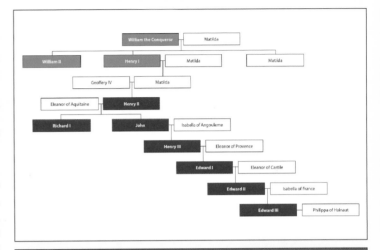

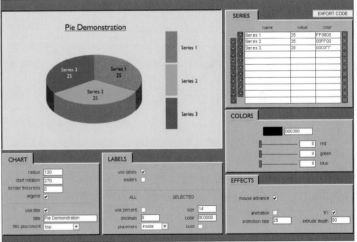

I'll admit that I got a little lucky in that I hit upon my metaphor fairly early in the process. As I explained in the last chapter on real-feel interfaces, my creative process is all about metaphors. If I find one that at least pushes me in the right direction, even if it exists solely in my mind and not the finished project, I'm happy. With the family tree, one of the first things that came to mind was a molecular structure – the ultimate nuclear family! Anyone who has played with 3D in Flash should be familiar with the radial gradient spheres circling about. It was a subject I was well versed in from Flash 5, and one of my first Flash MX experiments with 3D was to build a molecule engine using the drawing API to draw the bonds and give the atoms cell-shading.

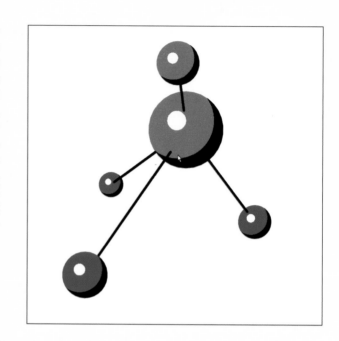

I wasn't certain at first, though, whether there needed to be any 3D involved with my family tree at all. Initially, I chose to "fake" the 3D by simply choosing smaller scales for each generation, similar to what you might find with fractal experiments in Flash.

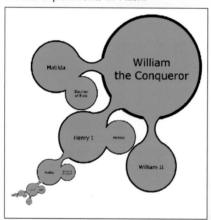

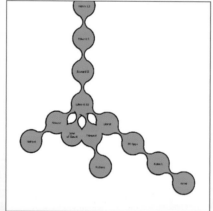

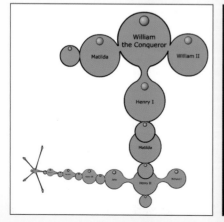

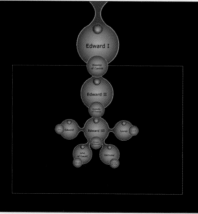

The idea I planned to work with was to house all of the nodes in one movie clip, and each time I attached additional nodes for a new generation at a smaller scale, I'd zoom-in by scaling up the parent movie clip. One thing I hadn't foreseen, however, was that if I kept scaling up, I'd eventually reach a scale that was too small for Flash to place new movie clips accurately. It became apparent that if I wanted to have each generation smaller than the previous (which I did) I'd have to resort to using 3D to get my desired effect.

Along the way, I also decided that I wanted something a little different for the connectors or bonds between each node in the tree. As I worked more with the animation of each child from its parent, the nodes began to look more like cells that were splitting through something akin to mitosis. I thought it might be fun to create something a bit more organic in nature than the straight line bonds of my molecule engine. I've always been enthralled by the work of H.R. Giger and his work on transforming the usually cold, straight lines of sci-fi into his biomechanic vision. I too wanted to make something more fluid and organic, especially as this seemed to suit the nature of the data. And with the drawing API, why settle for straight lines when we can just as easily make curves?

As a final piece of functionality for this system, I wanted to allow the user the ability to access more information from each node. One of the terrific advantages of displaying data on a computer, as opposed to paper, is that you can jump to additional pages of information instantaneously without losing your place within the structure. On paper, if I included extra information on each family member in a tree, in addition to the display of his or her relation to other family members, then anyone reading the chart would quickly become overwhelmed with the amount of information provided. In contrast, I wanted Flash to offer the user the ability to expand each node to display more information if they required it. In this way, I could cram as much data as users might need into one chart – without overloading them with information.

Unfortunately, we don't have the pages to cover the expanded interface in this chapter's tutorial, but the fully commented finished version of the family tree is included in the download files. Once you have completed this chapter, if you are interested in taking the system further, I'd encourage you to open the file `gods_tree.fla` and have a look at what additional code is needed to complete the effect.

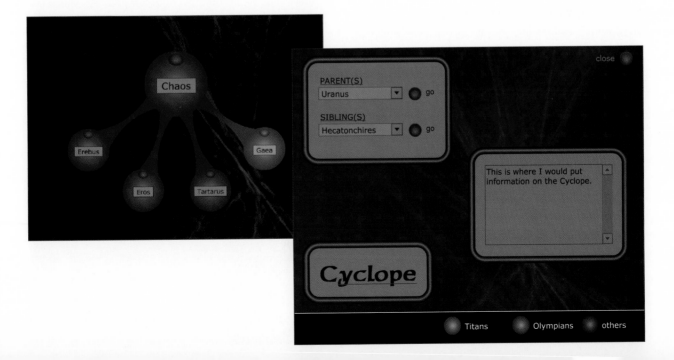

The family tree that wasn't

If you have played around at all with the finished SWF, you might notice that there are certain things that take this system out of the category of true family tree. First and foremost, although I have included spouse nodes, you are unable to access them directly. In addition, the existence of a spouse node isn't necessary to produce children (although, as I think on it, the situation would occur in real life with adoption by a single parent). Finally, I have not accounted for multiple spouses (and Zeus got around...). These weren't oversights, but merely different directions I chose to take. I felt that the creation of a single node branching structure might be more useful for more projects. As it happened, I still (successfully, I believe) displayed a family tree, but you could quickly adapt this system for a menu, game, gallery, index, and so on. It's all about modularity.

The base FLA

As you might imagine, there is a decent amount of code involved in creating this effect ("decent" is a less intimidating way of saying "a lot"), so I have prepared a base file that has all the elements we need to begin, including some of the code already prepared for you (just like on the best cooking shows!). Open up the file `gods_tree_base.fla` from the download files, and let's go over these elements so you can see what we're working with.

The timeline

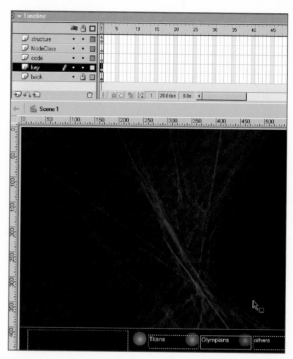

The main timeline of the movie is fairly straightforward, consisting of five layers. The top three layers will hold our code, while the bottom two hold our graphics, which are already drawn and placed. The key layer contains the key information for our chart (which obviously applies specifically to this chart, so it would be the first thing to change if you were charting another family) as well as a dynamic text field at the lower left named rollOver_txt. This text field has titleFont* selected as its font, while the three to its right have sansFont* selected. The asterisk indicates that these are exported fonts, and when we look at the library in a moment you will see how I did this. Finally in our layer structure, the bottom layer, named back, contains the background image (goo.jpg) inside an unnamed movie clip instance.

The library

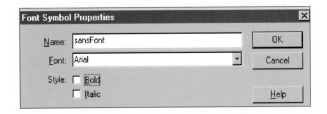

Next in our journey through the base file, let's take a look at our library to see what symbols I've included, as we won't be adding any more during the course of this chapter.

The background folder contains the background symbol and JPG, so there's nothing to see there (move along now!). The Flash UI Components folder came along with the combo box component I used, and if you've worked at all with MX components you should be familiar with its appearance. For this project, I didn't touch any of the contents of these folders, except for adding three lines to the constructor function of the combo box (I've commented these lines rather flamboyantly if you care to take a look).

The first folder we should look more closely at is the fonts folder. If you expand this, you'll notice it contains two fonts, sansFont and titleFont. For my finished project I used Verdana and American Unciale for these, respectively. In the base file, however, I have left them as

standard fonts (Arial and Times New Roman) so you can choose your own fonts for your version of the project. All you need to do to change the fonts is double-click either font name (or right-click and select Properties) and select a different font for your own movie. This is one of the great advantages to using exported fonts. At any time you can change the fonts you've used through the whole movie with just a few clicks, allowing you to try different faces with little extra time spent. I love that versatility.

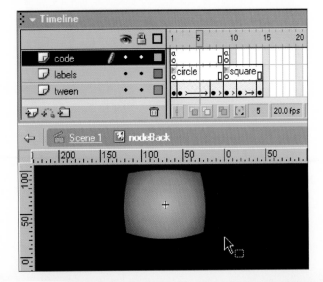

The last three folders to look at all contain something of interest, so we'll spend a little more time examining the items.

The node graphic

First, let's look at the contents of the node assets folder in your library. Most are simple symbols without any code, though you will note that nodeSymbol, nodeGraphic and spouse are all exported so we can dynamically attach them with our code. The symbol of most interest is nodeBack, which you should take a look inside by entering symbol editing mode.

Two `stop` actions make up the sole code in this clip, which is merely a shape tween from a circle to a rectangle and back to a circle. This is the animation that occurs when a node is opened and it transforms and covers the interface. If you select the rectangle on the stage, you will see that it is 110 x 80 pixels, which will scale up nicely to 550 x 400, the size of the viewing window we will be using. How convenient! So when a node is opened, we will need to scale it up to 500% to cover the window in its entirety. At that point, we will attach the nodeInterface to the stage, which is the next symbol we will look at.

The node interface

Have a look inside the interface assets folder. It only contains three symbols, a graphic, interfaceBack, a movie clip, jumpTo, which simply contains a button and a text field, and the movie clip nodeInterface. Enter symbol editing mode for this final movie clip.

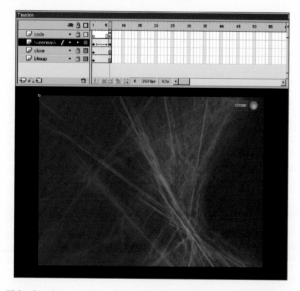

This is the movie clip that is attached to the stage whenever a node is opened in the tree and its interface is accessed (something the finished file allows, but we won't be covering in this tutorial). The movie clip is extremely straightforward, with a single `stop` action at its final frame being the only code. The tween is simply an alpha motion tween of the interfaceBack symbol (which is only a white rectangle). When a node is opened, you saw that its graphic tweens from a circle to a rectangle and scales to fill the stage. It will be at this point that this symbol, nodeInterface, is attached to the stage. The alpha tween produces a brief white flash that fades to slowly reveal the information we attach (in the form of a series of combo boxes). There are actually two things to note if you intend to adapt this project for your own purposes. First, this clip contains graphics that are 550 x 400 pixels in total, which is the size of the window I've chosen to display the tree (not the stage size necessarily). That way, as I said, when a node is opened, this interface will cover the viewing window in its entirety. Second, since this clip is attached to the stage dynamically, it is obviously separate from the node graphic and symbols, so you can easily create a different background and use it for your interface without the need to worry about how it will affect the nodes. It gives you some freedom to play.

The bevelBox

The last folder to examine is the bevelBox assets folder. The bevelBox is a handy little clip that I use in the expanded interface window (so we will not be using it specifically in this tutorial, though it will be handy for you to know if you wish to look at the finished project). The way I have set it up, I can simply attach it and give it a size, using a custom `setSize` method, and it will automatically expand to that size (without scaling the border). I've set it up in a similar fashion to the way Macromedia created their components that expand without distorting the graphics. If you enter symbol editing mode for the symbol bevelBox itself (which you will notice is also exported), you will see how this was done.

The movie clip only contains two layers, one of graphics, the other of code. The code is obviously what does all of the work, but since we have plenty of code to cover for the rest of the project I won't go over the code contained here. Briefly, what I've done is create a custom class by extending the `MovieClip` object. The `BevelBoxClass` really only does two things: expands to a set size, and makes itself draggable. We will create another custom class by extending the `MovieClip` object in the code later in this chapter, so I would encourage you to come back and take a look at this code then and apply your knowledge. It really is no different (and is actually much simpler) than the coding we are about to embark on, except for the existence of the `#initclip` and `#endinitclip` lines as the bookends of the code. All these lines do is allow us to place this code inside a movie clip as opposed to on our main timeline, and the code will still run before the movie begins, initializing our object.

The structure

The last item that has been prepared for this project is the code in the layer named structure on the main timeline. If you select the frame in this layer and open your ActionScript editor, you will see the code I use to populate the tree. Since you will want to alter this for your own projects, it's important that we look at it more closely so you understand how I accomplished it.

First, we have three objects in which I store the color values for the nodes:

```
chaosCol = {params:{ra:50, rb:32, ga:50,
➡gb:-10, ba:50, bb:0}, connector:0x471D27};
titansCol = {params:{ra:50, rb:17, ga:50,
➡gb:34, ba:50, bb:36}, connector:0x38494B};
olympiansCol = {params:{ra:50, rb:32, ga:50,
➡gb:13, ba:50, bb:37}, connector:0x47344C};
```

Each object contains two properties: `params` and `connector`. `params` holds another custom object containing values to send to the `Color` object's `setTransform` method. We will use the `params` object to tint the nodes themselves. `connector`, on the other hand, contains a hexadecimal value that we will send to the `beginGradientFill` method when we draw our connectors with the drawing API.

The rest of the lines of script in the structure layer deal with populating our tree. Let's look at the first two lines of this code:

```
chaos = {name:"Chaos", col:chaosCol};
chaos.info = "This is where I would put
➡information on Chaos."
```

Each node in our tree will be an object holding at least three properties. The first property is the node's name, the second is a reference to our custom coloring objects created above, and the third is any information we wish to have related about that node in its expanded interface.

If you are not familiar with the number of ways to create custom objects, it's important for you to know that all of the following methods accomplish the exact same thing:

```
chaos = new Object();
chaos.name = "Chaos";

chaos = new Object();
chaos["name"] = "Chaos";

chaos = {};
chaos.name = "Chaos";

chaos = {};
chaos["name"] = "Chaos";

chaos = {name:"Chaos"};
```

The way I have chosen is to give the object a name and color property on the first line, and an info property on the second. I felt this method was clear and easy to update, as well as keeping the number of lines at a manageable length.

Now to build on this first object, which will be the patriarch for the entire tree, I added these lines:

```
gaea = {name:"Gaea", col:titansCol};
gaea.info = "This is where I would put
➡information on Gaea."

tartarus = {name:"Tartarus",
col:chaosCol};
tartarus.info = "This is where I would
➡ put information on Tartarus."

eros = {name:"Eros", col:chaosCol};
eros.info = "This is where I would put
➡ information on Eros."

erebus = {name:"Erebus", col:chaosCol};
erebus.info = "This is where I would put
➡ information on Erebus."

chaos.children = [gaea, tartarus, eros,
➡ erebus];

delete tartarus;
delete eros;
delete erebus;
```

Each child is set up in the same way as its parent. Once all of the children of a parent node are created, we add them to the parent's `children` array, which is a new property we create to hold the references. Once the references to the children are stored, we can delete those variables that we won't use again. In this instance, we delete all of the children but the `gaea` object, since it will have children to store in a moment. If you continue on down through the code, you will see that this pattern is followed to the end. It is important that you understand that all of the variables we are using (such as `gaea`, `tartarus`, and `eros`) are just that – **variables** holding references to objects in memory, and not the objects themselves. Once an object has been stored in its parent's `children` array and, if necessary, given its own `children` property full of object references,

we can safely delete the variable. The objects themselves are not deleted, merely the variables referencing them. When we have completed storing the entire family, we will be left with only one variable, `chaos`, which will hold references to all of our objects within its many dimensions. The only other item to note is that if a node has a spouse, I add another property, as I do here with the `cronus` node:

```
cronus.spouse = {name:"Rhea", col:titansCol};
```

The `spouse` property contains an object holding a name and color as well.

If you wished to build your own tree, you'd simply have to alter these properties, since the system to display the tree works independently of the information. You might also consider building the tree in XML and bringing it into and parsing it in Flash, which was a bit too much to cover in this already hefty chapter. Check out Jamie Macdonald's chapter after this one to find out about XML structuring. You might want to have a go at blending the techniques! Included in the download files you will find `gods_tree_XML.fla`, uses XML. The SWF allows you to toggle between two trees, those of the Greek gods and the Norse gods, which are loaded from XML files when a button is clicked. The two files in which the information is stored, `Greek_gods.XML` and `Norse_gods.XML`, show how easy it is to structure and set up your own files to load into the interface. By adding additional elements to the tree, you could create added functionality. For instance, an image element might contain the file name of a JPG to load into the interface.

And now, the code

Now we get to the good stuff! The code to generate and navigate this interface is broken down into two parts – the nodes themselves and everything else. The "everything else" is actually very slight, since most of the functionality is contained in the nodes themselves, so let's do a little typing and take care of that right away.

Everything else

This is where we will set up some global variables for our movie, including objects to control text formatting for our interface, dimensions, rate of animation and a few factors to control the 3D look of our nodes. We will also create the movie clips that will house and mask our tree.

Select the first frame in the code layer on your main timeline and open up your ActionScript editor, typing the following:

```
windowWidth = 550;
windowHeight = 400;
intervalTime = 40;
intervals = 10;
```

`windowWidth` and `windowHeight` hold the dimensions of our viewing window (which is actually smaller than the stage). `intervalTime` is the amount of milliseconds between interval calls in the movie. Nearly all of the animation for the tree is accomplished using `setInterval` as opposed to `enterFrame` events, so it's good to have a variable here that we can quickly alter to change the rate of our animation. The final variable, `intervals`, is used for all of our easing motion tween functions. This interface uses the classic (and easy) Zeno's paradox method of tweening, which means we simply divide the distance a clip is going to move by a certain number each frame. This variable contains that number. Using 10 means that a clip will travel a tenth of its remaining distance each frame.

Next, here are four more variables for you to add directly following the previous four lines:

```
childDistance = 2;
childDepth = 100;
scaleFactor = .4;
pi = Math.PI;
```

`childDistance` is a number we will multiply a parent's diameter by to get a distance at which to place its children. `childDepth` is the distance on the z axis (remember, we're doing 3D here, so z is perpendicular to your computer screen) between a parent and child node. `scaleFactor` is a variable I added to give more control over the appearance of a node. By altering this number you can make a node bigger or smaller on screen without going into all the 3D rendering code. Finally, I've placed the value for pi, which we will access a lot in the code, into a variable, so that we don't have to keep looking into the Math object each time, as this would slow us down a little.

Next comes the font formatting for our movie. Type these lines to follow the previous code:

```
nameTF = new TextFormat();
nameTF.font = "sansFont";
nameTF.align = "center";
nameTF.size = 12;

underlineTF = new TextFormat();
underlineTF.underline = 1;

infoTF = new TextFormat();
infoTF.align = "left";

titleTF = new TextFormat();
titleTF.font = "titleFont";
titleTF.size = 32;
```

I love `TextFormat` objects, I really do. One thing that is rather neat is the fact that you can compound them. So if I add one `TextFormat` object to a text field that already has one applied, it will simply apply the extra formatting without wiping away the previous formatting (unless of course all the property values are different). This is the concept I use here. `nameTF` is my main `TextFormat` for my movie. It uses the `sansFont` I exported from the library, centers it and makes it 12 pts. The next two `TextFormats` merely add to that, one adding an underline and the other left aligning the text (which I use in the info box of the node interface). The final `TextFormat` is used for the titles of the nodes in the node interface.

The final piece of font formatting is necessary for the components I use:

```
globalStyleFormat.textFont = "sansFont";
globalStyleFormat.embedFonts = 1;
```

The `globalStyleFormat` affects any components I use in the movie, in this case the combo box. I want the text to match the text elsewhere, so I change its font to be the font I exported from the library.

The variables are now all set, so it's time to start creating the movie clips we will need to make our interface run. Go ahead and add these lines directly after the text formatting code.

```
this.createEmptyMovieClip("window", 1000);
window.beginFill(0, 0);
window.lineTo(windowWidth, 0);
window.lineTo(windowWidth, windowHeight);
window.lineTo(0, windowHeight);
window.endFill();
```

`window` is a movie clip that we are creating to cover the entirety of the viewing area of our tree. We will use this clip to center our tree, as well as to run `hitTests` on our nodes to make sure they are within the viewing area defined by the window (and if they aren't, we will make them invisible). Using the drawing API, we draw a black box (0x000000 and 0 are equivalent) with a 0% opacity to cover the viewing area. The 0% opacity means that the window won't be seen by the user, but Flash will know its dimensions. It's also interesting to note that we only have to draw three sides of our box, as the `endFill` method will automatically close an open shape by drawing a line back to the starting position of the fill.

The next movie clip to create is the actual tree itself. Place this code after the previous lines:

```
this.createEmptyMovieClip("tree", 0);
tree._x = windowWidth*.5;
tree._y = windowHeight*.5;
tree.depth = 15000;
```

After creating an empty movie clip, we place it in the center of the viewing window. `tree.depth` is the depth level inside of `tree` where we will start placing the nodes. We will count down from this number, so each subsequent node will be placed beneath the previously placed node. Finally, although we will add more functionality to the tree later, let's get the ball rolling with our nodes by placing the first one:

```
tree.attachMovie("nodeSymbol", "rootNode",
➡ tree.depth --, {node:chaos});
delete chaos;
```

We attach a nodeSymbol from the library to our tree, calling the instance `rootNode`, at the tree's current depth, which we then decrement to make way for the next node. You will also see that we send an additional object with our `attachMovie` call as a fourth parameter. This is a new feature of Flash MX, which allows us to include an object containing properties and values that we wish to pass to our newly attached clip. You can use it to set a preexisting property, like `_x` or `_y`, or to create an entirely new property, which I do here by creating the property name `node` and setting it to the value of our `chaos` node from the structure layer. Once I've passed the value of `chaos` to the new node, I can delete the variable on the next line.

For the time being, that's all of the preparation we'll need outside of our `nodeSymbol` code itself. Right now, testing your movie would reveal nothing, as all we have done is place a few empty movie clips on our stage. How about we make those movie clips do something?

  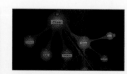 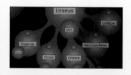 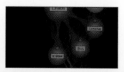

The node code

Nearly all of the work in this project rests on the rounded little shoulders of the nodes themselves. The way we will handle this is by using movie clips for their basic functionality, but then extending them to hold the methods we will need to run this system. Let's get right into it so you can see how this is done.

The first thing we will take care of is the constructor function for our nodes, and the passing of necessary information to each node created so that it displays itself correctly on the stage.

Go to the first frame of the NodeClass layer and type the following into the ActionScript editor:

```
NodeClass = function() {
    this.init();
}

NodeClass.prototype = new MovieClip();

NodeClass.prototype.focalLength = 600;
NodeClass.prototype.hither = -210;
NodeClass.prototype.yon = 210;
```

The first line of code looks like any function declaration you might have used in the past. This is how class constructors work in Flash. All we are doing is creating a function to hold the methods, and the first method we call – the only method involved directly in the constructor – is this.init, which we will write in a moment. The important line to understand is the line of code that follows, in which we set the prototype of the NodeClass to equal a new MovieClip instance. This is Flash's form of inheritance, which allows us to use all of the properties and methods of a movie clip for our NodeClass instances. The prototype property is a special property of an object that holds all of its methods and properties. By storing the methods and properties of NodeClass in its prototype, each instance of NodeClass will have access to these without having to duplicate functions and unnecessary code.

It is purely a personal choice which one of the following lines of code you choose to use to create a function:

```
NodeClass = function() {};

function NodeClass() {};
```

I opt for the former, as I like to have the name of the function at the beginning of the line – it makes it easier for me to spot if I have a lot of functions.

I should note, though, that the latter method is more widely used, and if your background is in another programming language, you will probably not care to change for ActionScript. If you choose to write your functions in the style of the latter method, the code will run exactly the same. Whichever method you choose, however, you should probably remain consistent throughout your code.

The next three lines of code establish three properties for our NodeClass. focalLength will be used in our perspective formula when we render our nodes, and controls the amount of depth distortion, similar to altering lenses on a camera. hither and yon are used as z positions at which we make our nodes invisible. It makes sense when we draw our tree to only show a certain range of nodes, so using these values we determine which nodes are too big or too small. Notice again how we have attached these properties to the prototype of NodeClass so that any instance will have access to these values.

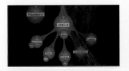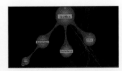

The next method to write is the one we called in our constructor. This will set up all of the graphics and values that our node will need to run initially:

```
NodeClass.prototype.init = function() {
    if (this._parent.nodes == undefined) {
    this._parent.nodes = []
};
    this._parent.nodes.push(this);

    this.attachMovie("nodeGraphic",
    ➡ "nodeGraphic", 10);
    this.diameter = this._width;
    this.radius = this.diameter/2;
    var col = new Color(this.nodeGraphic);
    col.setTransform(this.node.col.params);
```

This is the start of our init method, which will be one of the longest of our NodeClass, as we need to establish a number of things before our node is functional. The first thing we want to do is store a reference to this node (whichever node was just created) in an array located on the parent timeline, in this case tree's timeline, since we are attaching all of the nodes to tree. Before we do that, though, we need to make sure that the array exists, which we take care of in the first line. If the array is undefined, we create a new array instance. We then push a reference to this node into that array.

The following line of code attaches the nodeGraphic on to the clip. I did it this way for two reasons. First, we can easily swap out to another graphic if we so desire, and second, we need to place the graphic at a higher depth than other clips we will add to this node (like the connector). Once the graphic is attached, we can find our diameter and radius based on that graphic. We will need these for later operations.

Finally, we color the graphic based on whatever color parameters are stored in this node's node.col.params property. Remember that when we create a node, as we did with our rootNode above, we will send with it an additional property called node, which will store all of the information that we established in our structure layer. It

follows then, that an instance of NodeClass will have access to name, col, info, and sometimes children and spouse in its node property.

Now that we've placed and colored our node, let's add the text field to display its name:

```
this.nodeGraphic.createTextField
➡ ("name_txt", 0, 0, 0, 0, 0);
    var label = this.nodeGraphic.name_txt;
    label.setNewTextFormat(nameTF);
    label.border = 1;
    label.background = 1;
    label.autoSize = "center";
    label.selectable = 0;
    label.embedFonts = 1;
    label.text = " " + this.node.name + " ";
    label._y -= label.textHeight/2;
```

This text field will hold the name of our node, and we place it in the center of our nodeGraphic movie clip, at 0,0, which are the third and fourth parameters of the createTextField method. Notice that we also give it a width and height of 0 and 0 (the fifth and sixth parameters). We can do this because in a few lines we set the text field's autoSize property to center, which means that the text field will automatically expand from the center to fit whatever text we place inside. In the other lines that follow the text field's creation, we turn on its border and background; we make sure it isn't selectable so the I bar doesn't appear over it, and we embed the fonts so that we get the font we included with our TextFormat (which we applied on the second line directly following the createTextField). Finally, we place the node's name into the text property of the text field (buffering it with spaces on each side) and adjust its _y position based on the size of the text so that the text field will appear centered in the node.

That was a lot of work for a text field! So let's just add a line or two more so that we can see what we have created so far. Finish up the init method with the following code:

```
    this.render();
}
```

render is the next method we will create, which will correctly place and scale our node based on its 3D coordinates. Let's write the function now so we can test our movie.

Place this method directly after the init method:

```
NodeClass.prototype.render = function() {
    var depthFactor = this.focalLength/
    ➥ (this.focalLength - this.z);
    this._x = this.x * depthFactor;
    this._y = this.y * depthFactor;
    this._xscale = this._yscale = this.z *
    ➥ depthFactor *scaleFactor + 100;
}
```

This, you might be happy to know, is the extent of the 3D calculations involved in this project. We don't have time to go into much theory about what's occurring here, and if you've worked with any 3D in Flash you will have already encountered similar methods. Suffice it to say that this is a method which transforms our 3D coordinates (x, y, z) into 2D coordinates on our screen. We simulate depth on the 2D screen by scaling the movie clip and adjusting the _x and _y 2D properties based on the z 3D property and the focalLength. Using this depthFactor, as I called it, we set the _x, _y, _xscale and _yscale properties of our clip to make clips that are nearer on the z axis appear larger and farther away from the 3D vanishing point at (0, 0, 0). The scaling itself is determined by the z value multiplied by the depthFactor. 100 is added to get the scale up into a workable range (since we deal with negative z depths). scaleFactor is something I added to give a little bit more freedom in how we display the nodes (we set this variable right near the top of our code, on the code layer).

This is the final line we will need for our NodeClass to work initially:

```
Object.registerClass("nodeSymbol",
➥NodeClass);
```

registerClass associates a movie clip symbol in our library with a Class definition in our code. If you access the linkage properties of the nodeSymbol in the library, you will see that I have already set it up to export as nodeSymbol. With the registerClass line above, any nodeSymbol we attach to the stage will automatically be an instance of our NodeClass.

OK! Test your movie. You should see our first node appear, all ready to go! Although it might seem like that's a lot of preparation for a single node, the groundwork for the entire tree has been set. It will now be small steps to making our tree do some really cool things!

Displaying children

The next section we will deal with is the display of a node's children whenever it is clicked. We will create a few new methods to take care of this feature. The first thing to consider is what we want to have happen when a node is clicked on. In addition to simply showing a node's children, we need to have the node that was selected move to the center of the stage. Let's write that method first.

Place this method directly after the `render` method (make sure it's above the `Object.registerClass` line, which should always remain the final line in our `NodeClass` code):

```
NodeClass.prototype.center = function() {
    clearInterval(translateInt);
    this.showChildren();
    this._parent.tNodes = [];
    var x = -this.tX;
    var y = -this.tY;
    var z = -this.tZ;
    var i = 0;
    while (i < this._parent.nodes.length) {
      this._parent.nodes[i].setTranslate(x, y, z);
      i++;
    }
    translateInt = setInterval(this._parent,
    ➥ "translate", intervalTime);
}
```

This method introduces a number of new items that we will address in a moment. Skipping the first line of code in the method for a moment, notice we are calling a new method `showChildren`, which will take care of adding the necessary nodes for children. We then create a new array on the `_parent` (tree) timeline called `tNodes`, which will hold references to all the nodes we need to translate. The next three lines create three variables to hold the distance this node will need to travel to reach (0, 0, 0). `tX`, `tY`, and `tZ` will eventually hold translated coordinates, the ending position of a node after movement. If a node is at (100, 100, -100), then it will need to travel negative 100 on the x axis, negative 100 on the y axis and positive 100 on the

z-axis to reach (0, 0, 0). That is what we store in the `x`, `y` and `z` variables. Now, if every node retains its same relation to every other node, it follows that each node will have to travel the same distance on each axis.

So with these values decided, we call another new method for each node called `setTranslate`. Using a `while` loop (which is slightly faster than the `for` loop), we run through the `_parent`'s node array, which stores references to all the nodes (we took care of this in the `init` method) and have each node set up its own translation. On the line that follows, we use `setInterval` to call the `translate` method on the tree timeline (which we've yet to write). `translate` is what will move the nodes at each interval.

Now let's quickly look at the methods we just called in `center` so you can see how they all work together.

The first method to add is the `NodeClass`'s `setTranslate`. Add these lines after the `center` method:

```
NodeClass.prototype.setTranslate =
➥ function(x, y, z) {
    this.tX += x;
    this.tY += y;
    this.tZ += z;
    if (this.tZ > this.yon || this.tZ <
➥ this.hither) {
      this.x = this.tX;
      this.y = this.tY;
      this.z = this.tZ;
      this.render();
    } else {
      this._parent.tNodes.push(this)
    }
}
```

setTranslate, as we saw above in the center method, is called for each node when the tree needs to be translated. We send to this method the x, y and z distance the node needs to travel, which we add on to the node's current translated position. The next statements make sure that we need to animate a move at all. Basically, we test to see if the ending z position for this node is going to be outside our specified rendering range (as determined by hither and yon). If it's not in the range, we set our x, y and z coordinates to equal our translated coordinates and render the node in its final position (later, we'll add a visibility check that will turn this node off since it's outside the range). If the node's z position is inside the rendering range, we simply push a reference to the node into the _parent timeline's tNodes array, which will hold all of the nodes that need to be translated. Let's take care of that method now.

You need to head back to the code layer for these lines, as they are not a part of the NodeClass code. Place this method after the line tree.depth = 15000;:

```
tree.translate = function() {
   var i = 0;
   while (i < this.tNodes.length) {
      this.tNodes[i].translate();
      this.tNodes[i].render();
      i++;
   }
   if (this.tNodes.length < 1) {
      clearInterval(translateInt) };
   }
}
```

This one's pretty self-explanatory. Each time this function is called (which is determined by our setInterval), tree runs through its list of nodes and tells each one to translate and render itself. The nodes, once they have reached their destination, will individually remove themselves from the tNodes array. Once the array is empty, we clear the interval since the function no longer needs to be called.

Alright! One more method to cover to get our translation happening. Go back to the NodeClass layer and place this new method after the setTranslate method:

```
NodeClass.prototype.translate = function() {
   this.x -= (this.x - this.tX)/intervals;
   this.y -= (this.y - this.tY)/intervals;
   this.z -= (this.z - this.tZ)/intervals;
   if (Math.abs(this.x - this.tX) < 1 &&
➥ Math.abs(this.y - this.tY) < 1 &&
➥ Math.abs(this.z - this.tZ) < 1) {
      var i = 0;
      while (i < this._parent.tNodes.length) {
       if (this._parent.tNodes[i] == this) {
        this._parent.tNodes.splice(i, 1);
        break;
      }
      i++;
     }
     this.x = this.tX;
     this.y = this.tY;
     this.z = this.tZ;
   }
}
```

And here's our easing animation code. Each time translate is called, the node is moved a fraction of the distance it needs to travel on each axis. The if conditional is there to determine when the current coordinates are close enough to the ending coordinates. When that point is reached, we use a while loop to find the node's position in its _parent.tNodes array. It removes itself once found and sets its current coordinates to equal its ending translated coordinates. If you look back up to tree's translate method, you will see that the next thing that would occur is the rendering of the node. After that, since the node has now been removed from tNodes, it would be done translating.

That should take care of the translation, but what about attaching the children? Well, that's what the final method in this section does.

Place this method directly after the NodeClass's translate method:

```
NodeClass.prototype.showChildren = function() {
  var childrenNum = this.node.children.length;
  if (childrenNum < 1) { return false };
  if (this.children != undefined) { return false };
  this.children = [];
```

showChildren is what we called in our center method, that will – you guessed it – show the node's children. Before we do this, we need to make a few checks to make sure we have anything to show. The first thing we do is place the number of children the node has into a variable, childrenNum. If this number is less than 1, that means there are no children to show, and so we exit out of the function. Second, we check to see if the children are already expanded. You will see that as soon as we attach the children, we will store references to these children in this node's children array. If this array already exists, that means the children are attached and we do not need to continue, so we exit the function. If we have made it this far, we go ahead and create the children array and get ready to add the children.

Finish off the showChildren method with the following:

```
var i = 0;
while (i < childrenNum) {
  var angle = pi/(childrenNum+1) * (i+1) + this.angle;
  var distance = this.diameter*childDistance;
  var props = {};
  props.node = this.node.children[i];
  props.parent = this;
  props.angle = angle - pi/2;
  props.x = this.x;
  props.y = this.y;
  props.tX = Math.cos(angle) * distance + this.tX;
  props.tY = Math.sin(angle) * distance + this.tY;
  props.tZ = props.z = this.tZ - childDepth;
  this.children.push(this._parent.attachMovie("nodeSymbol",
  ➡ this.node.children[i].name + this._parent.depth,
  ➡ this._parent.depth--, props));
  i++;
  }
}
```

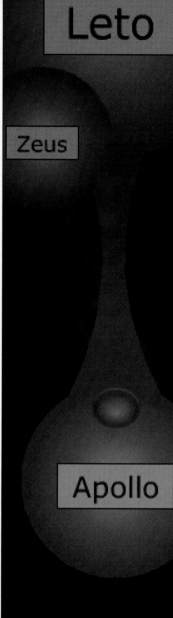

We must give a lot of information to the children at the outset, and this is where we do it. For each child, we first find the angle that we will be placing it at. The way I determined this was to take 180 degrees (or pi radians, half of a circle), divide that by the number of children plus 1 (so 3 children would divide 180 up 4 times, giving us 45 degrees for each), multiplying this by whatever iteration of the loop we are currently at (adding 1 so we don't place anything at 0 degrees), then adding the current angle of the parent node. Whew!

The rest of it is much more straightforward. After setting a variable to hold the distance of the node from its parent on the x and y axes, I've created a new object that I will pass with the attachMovie method, and attached to this object all of the properties I need to give the child node, including all of the node data (name, col, info, children and spouse), the node's parent node and the node's angle. For coordinates, I've placed it at the same x and y position as the current node, its parent, but I also gave it translated coordinates, which will be its ending position, that are outside of the parent, based on the angle I have determined multiplied by the distance I have determined. However, I went ahead and set its final z coordinate to simply be 100 less than the parent's z (100 since that was the value we gave childDepth above). Since we have given the child node different translated coordinates than its current coordinates, it will immediately upon creation move into its final position, giving us a nice birthing effect.

One last thing to add to enable this new functionality, and that's to tell Flash *when* to do all this. Jump back up to the init method of our NodeClass and amend it as follows adding in the extra lines:

```
label.text = " " + this.node.name + " ";
label._y -= label.textHeight/2;

var nb = this.nodeGraphic.nodeBack;
nb.onPress = function() {
this._parent._parent.center() };
nb.onRollOver = function() {
rollOver_txt.text =
➥ this._parent._parent.node.name };
nb.onRollOut = function() {
rollOver_txt.text = "" };
nb.useHandCursor = 0;

this.render();
```

nodeBack is the background graphic inside nodeGraphic. We need to add the button functionality to this interior movie clip since we will need separate functionality for the open button. Because of the movie clip's nested nature, when we call the center method that we created earlier we need to refer to _parent._parent to reach the node's timeline and the method. I've also taken this opportunity to add some rollover effects to the text field at the bottom of the interface.

Go ahead and test your movie and see what we've created so far. Not bad! We have a working, animating structure already! Now all we need to do is some optimization and enhancements.

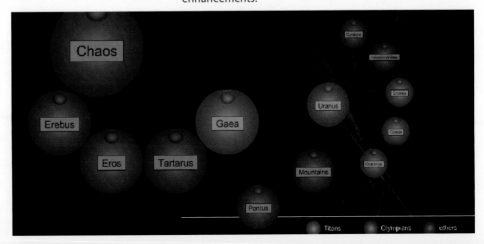

Masking backstage

One thing you might have noticed after the previous section is that we are continuing to show our nodes when they either move off the stage or when they are too small to be useful. We can take care of these problems quickly with a little visibility check. We already have our visibility range established by our `hither` and `yon` properties.

Still in our NodeClass layer, add this method to follow the `render` method:

```
NodeClass.prototype.checkVisibility =
➡ function() {
    this._visible = (this.z < this.yon &&
    ➡ this.z > this.hither && this.hitTest(window));
    return this._visible;
};
```

Remember adding the window movie clip at the start of our code? It was simply a box with an alpha fill of 0 so that it couldn't be seen. We used it initially to center our tree within the viewing area. We can also use it, though, to test whether our nodes are inside its boundaries or not. In this method, we make a quick check to see if not only our nodes are in `hither`/`yon` range, but also if the nodes are inside the window movie clip. We set the visibility of our node to be `true` or `false` based on these conditions and return this Boolean value to wherever we called the function. Now, of course, we need to call the function!

In the `render` method in `NodeClass`, add the following lines:

```
this._xscale = this._yscale = this.z *
➡ depthFactor*scaleFactor + 100;
    if (this.checkVisibility()) {
this.drawConnector() };
}
```

I went ahead and combined this new line with an additional method we will write in a moment. Basically, we call the `checkVisibility` method inside an `if` conditional check. If it returns `true`, we will draw the connectors for the node. If it returns `false`, meaning the clip is invisible, we do not need to waste processing power on the connectors.

Test your movie again to see the visibility check in action!

We're almost done with our masking, but we still are able to see clips as they move outside of the viewing window. They are not made invisible until they are completely outside, so let's make a quick mask to clean this up.

Go back to the code layer and add these new lines to our script:

```
this.createEmptyMovieClip("window", 1000);
window.beginFill(0, 0);
window.lineTo(windowWidth, 0);
window.lineTo(windowWidth, windowHeight);
window.lineTo(0, windowHeight);
window.endFill();
window.duplicateMovieClip("mask", 1);

this.createEmptyMovieClip("tree", 0);
tree._x = windowWidth*.5;
tree._y = windowHeight*.5;;
tree.depth = 15000;
tree.setMask(mask);
```

Since we already have a movie clip that's the same size as the viewing area, we quickly duplicate it for purposes of a mask (it doesn't matter that the alpha is 0 since alpha is not taken into account with masks). Once the tree is created, we use `setMask` to have the mask movie clip mask the tree movie clip. Short and sweet, and extremely effective! Test your movie once more to see the result.

Gooey connections

In the `render` method above, we called the `drawConnectors` method, which we will use to connect each of the nodes with its parent. This is my favorite part of this project as it adds a real organic feel to the system as well as taking advantage of dynamic gradient fills. (I just love that new drawing API – so many new toys!) To achieve this effect, we will need to add some variables in other parts of the code to help us out.

Go to the code layer and add these lines following the declaration of the pi variable:

```
connectorSin1 = Math.sin(-pi/3);
connectorCos1 = Math.cos(-pi/3);
connectorSin2 = Math.sin(-pi*2/3);
connectorCos2 = Math.cos(-pi*2/3);
```

Each of the nodes will use these values to find the x and y position of the corners of the connectors (which we will use the drawing API to create). Instead of having to calculate these values for each node, we place them in variables that we can access later. These hold the sine and cosine of angles -60 and –120 degrees, which is where we will place each corner of the connector in relation to the center of the node graphic.

With these values determined, we need to find the x and y points for each particular node. We will do this inside the `init` method for the `NodeClass`. Add the following lines to the end of the `init` method, but before the `render` call:

```
this.createEmptyMovieClip("connector", 1);
this.connX1 = connectorCos1 * this.radius;
this.connY1 = connectorSin1 * this.radius;
this.connX2 = connectorCos2 * this.radius;
this.connY2 = connectorSin2 * this.radius;

this.render();
```

You can see that first we add an empty movie clip named `connector` that will hold our drawing. Next we calculate the x and y positions of our connector's corners, based on our sine and cosine values multiplied by the radius of our graphic.

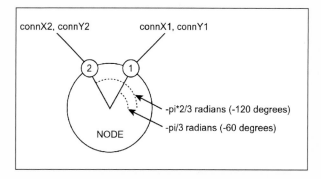

Now it's time to create the `drawConnector` method, which will take care of the drawing of our gooey connectors. Place the beginning of this new method after the `checkVisibility` method of our `NodeClass`:

```
NodeClass.prototype.drawConnector =
➡function() {
   var x = this._x - this.parent._x;
   var y = this._y - this.parent._y;
   this.connector._rotation =
➡Math.atan2(y, x) * 180/pi - 90;
   var distance = Math.sqrt(x*x +
➡y*y)*100/this._xscale - this.radius*.25;

   this.connector.clear();
   this.connector.moveTo(this.connX1,
➡this.connY1);
```

x and y are local variables that hold the distance of our node from its parent node on each axis. Using this, we can determine the angle at which we need to rotate our connector movie clip by sending the values to the `Math.atan2` method (which we multiply by 180/pi to convert to degrees, and subtract 90 from since Flash views 0 degrees as east and not north, which is what we need).

The distance is the Pythagorean theorem at work, which is adjusted for our node's current scale. Honestly, subtracting a quarter of the radius was a value I stumbled upon which worked perfectly. I spent a good deal of time racking my brain on *why* so I could provide you with an explanation, but sometimes you thank your good fortune and answer the question "Why does this work?" with the answer "Because it does."

The next two lines of code can be explained, though. We clear the connector of its previous drawing and move the "pen" to our starting x and y position.

These two lines help determine the height of our drawing, which we will need for our gradient parameters. Place these lines directly after the previous code:

```
y = -(distance + this.connY1);
var gradientHeight = y - this.connY1;
```

Our second y position is determined by adding the distance to the initial y position. We make this value negative as well, since the second corner of our connector is above the first corner.

gradientHeight is then easily calculated by finding the difference of our first and second y values. This will be the total height of our gradient.

Let's create the gradient now with the following code, which should directly follow the previous lines:

```
var colors = [this.node.col.connector,
➡this.parent.node.col.connector];
   var alphas = [100, 100];
   var ratios = [70, 220];
   var matrix = {matrixType:"box",
   ➡ x:this.connX1, y:this.connY1, w:50,
   ➡ h:gradientHeight, r:pi/2};

this.connector.beginGradientFill("linear",
➡colors, alphas, ratios, matrix);
```

beginGradientFill takes a number of parameters. First, we send the gradient type, which in our case is "linear" (you can also use "radial"). Next, we send three arrays of values. The colors array holds the colors of our node and parent node and the alphas array holds each color's opacity. The ratios array is the location on the gradient where each specified color is at 100%. These values will be between 0 and 255 (a hexidecimal percentage). I have placed the values to be 100% at 70 for the node's color and at 220 for the parent node's color. This will mean that the gradient will actually only occur between these two values, which is near the middle of the connector.

Finally, the matrix is an object containing a number of properties we need to send the beginGradientFill method. matrixType will always be box for this method of gradient (the alternative method to create a gradient would be a whole other lesson), the x and y are the starting point of the gradient in relation to the registration point of the movie clip (which we set at our connector's first corner), the w and h are the width and height of our gradient (the width makes little difference for the linear gradient we are creating), and r is the radians we wish to rotate the gradient at, which I set to 90 degrees to turn the gradient onto its side.

Wow! That's some method! But when it's all over and done we get a terrific effect. Speaking of all over and done, let's finish up this drawConnector method so we can see it!

The final lines draw the sides to our connector:

```
this.connector.curveTo(-10, -distance*.5,
this.connX1, y);
   this.connector.lineTo(this.connX2, y);
   this.connector.curveTo(10, -distance*
   ➡.5, this.connX2, this.connY2);
   this.connector.endFill();
}
```

The curveTo command accepts four parameters. The final two parameters are the actual coordinates we are drawing to, which you can see we have already determined with our connX1, connX2, connY2 and y variables. The first two parameters are the coordinates that the line curves *toward*. In our case, we pick a y position halfway up our connector and an x position on the opposite side of center from the curve, giving us a nice concave shape.

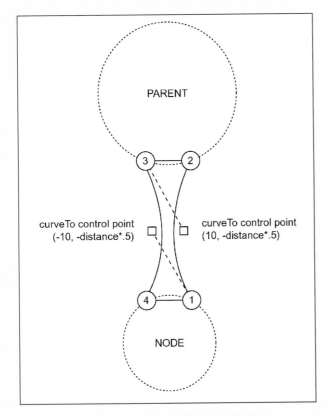

Test your movie to see what we have made. Fun!

You might notice an unwanted connector sticking out from our rootNode Chaos. Problem is, it doesn't have a node to connect to (poor Chaos!), so we need to make sure it doesn't try. We can fix it very quickly in our init method.

Add the following lines to our NodeClass's init method:

```
if (this._name == "rootNode") {
    this.render();
    return;
}

this.createEmptyMovieClip("connector", 1);
this.connX1 = connectorCos1 * this.radius;
this.connY1 = connectorSin1 * this.radius;
this.connX2 = connectorCos2 * this.radius;
this.connY2 = connectorSin2 * this.radius;
```

Here we have just done a quick check before we even add the connector movie clip. If the node is the rootNode, it renders itself and exits the method.

The rootNode will still run the drawConnector code unnecessarily, though, even if it has no connector movie clip, so let's add one more line to our drawConnector method:

```
NodeClass.prototype.drawConnector =
➥function() {
    if (this._name == "rootNode") { return
    ➥false };
    var x = this._x - this.parent._x;
    var y = this._y - this.parent._y;
```

Now the rootNode will immediately leave this function and not run the code. Test your movie to see everything in effect.

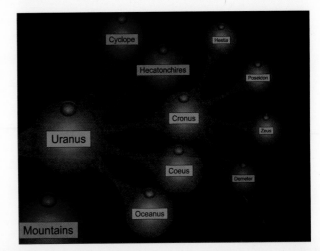

One branch at a time

If you have played with it a bit, you might notice that the system starts to slow down the more nodes you place on the stage. In addition to that, some nodes might block others when the branches start to get thick. To fix this problem, I decided to remove any "nieces" and "nephews" of nodes that were being clicked on. That way, you could see the direct lineage, but not the children of siblings. I felt this might speed things up as well (Flash doesn't like too many movie clips moving on the stage at once).

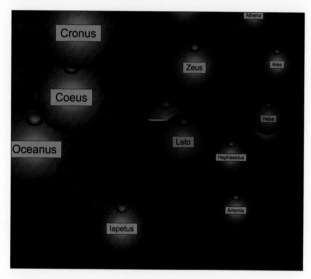

We are going to add another method to our `NodeClass` that will aid us in this extra functionality. Let's place the call to this new method inside our `center` method. Since that is where extra nodes are added as children it makes sense to remove the unnecessary nodes there:

```
NodeClass.prototype.center = function() {
    clearInterval(translateInt);
    this.parent.removeSiblings(this);
    this.showChildren();
```

So a node will actually tell its parent node to remove its siblings' children, which makes sense seeing as how a node really has no direct knowledge of its sibling nodes. Let's write the `removeSiblings` method to see how we accomplish this.

After the `NodeClass`'s `showChildren` method, add the following new lines of code:

```
NodeClass.prototype.removeSiblings =
function(skip) {
    var i = 0;
    while (i < this.children.length) {
        if (this.children[i] != skip) {
            this.children[i].collapseChildren()
        }
        i++;
    }
}
```

`removeSiblings` has a parent node run through its `children` array (skipping the child that called the method). If a child has a `children` array of its own, that means the children are currently on the stage. It tells the child to remove those children by calling its `collapseChildren` method, which we will write now.

Place this new method before our `removeSiblings` method:

```
NodeClass.prototype.collapseChildren =
➥ function() {
    var i = 0;
    while (i < this.children.length) {
        if (this.children[i].children !=
        ➥ undefined) {
            this.children[i].collapseChildren()
        }
        this.children[i].removeNode();
        i++;
    }
    delete this.children;
}
```

This is the function that we called in the previous method, which will remove the children of a node. You can see that it loops through its `children` array and calls the `removeNode` method (and if a child has children itself, then those children are removed as well). Once all of the children are removed, the `children` array is deleted, making way for the children to be attached again if the node is clicked.

The only thing left to write is the `removeNode` method we just called. Place it after the `removeSiblings` method:

```
NodeClass.prototype.removeNode = function() {
    var i = 0;
    while (i < this._parent.nodes.length) {
        if (this._parent.nodes[i] == this) {
            this._parent.nodes.splice(i, 1);
            break;
        }
        i++
    }
    this.removeMovieClip();
}
```

All this method does is loop through the tree's node array to find reference to itself. Once it is found, it removes the reference and removes itself from the stage using `removeMovieClip`. That's it.

Test your movie now to see how removing the siblings' children helps.

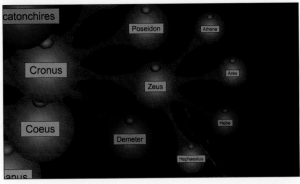

Spinning the tree

Now we have a pretty nice system as it is. Never satisfied, however, I wanted to add rotation to our tree. Thankfully, due to the way we have set this up, it's fairly easy. No need to use any 3D rotation math or transformation matrices – we have every node contained inside a movie clip and that means we only have to rotate the tree clip (thank goodness!). Since its registration point is at the center of the viewing window (where our clicked node is heading towards), it will look as though the tree is revolving around the node.

First, we need to decide where to call the rotation code. It makes sense to add it to our `center` method inside of `NodeClass`, since that is where the rotation will need to begin when a node is clicked. Here is the amended method:

```
NodeClass.prototype.center = function() {
    clearInterval(translateInt);
    clearInterval(rotateInt);
    this._parent.removeSiblings(this);
    this.showChildren();
    this._parent.tNodes = [];
    var x = -this.tX;
    var y = -this.tY;
    var z = -this.tZ;
    var i = 0;
    while (i < this._parent.nodes.length) {
        this._parent.nodes[i].setTranslate
    ➡ (x, y, z);
        i++;
    }
    translateInt = setInterval(this.
    ➡ _parent, "translate", intervalTime);
    this._parent.startRotate(-this.angle);
}
```

Pretty easy to start out with, no? At the top, we clear any interval if a rotation is already happening (remember it will be called `rotateInt`). At the bottom we tell the `_parent` (tree) to rotate and we send the negative of this node's angle property, which is basically the angle that tree will need to counter-rotate.

Go to the code layer where we wrote the `tree.translate` method and place this method beneath it:

```
tree.startRotate = function(amount) {
  this.rot = this._rotation;
  this.degrees = amount*180/pi;
  while (this.degrees < -180) {
  ➥ this.degrees += 360 };
  while (this.degrees > 180) {
  ➥ this.degrees -= 360 };
  if (Math.abs(this.degrees - this.rot) > 180) {
    if (this.rot > 0) {
      this.degrees += 360
    } else {
      this.degrees -= 360
    }
  }
  rotateInt = setInterval(this, "rotate",
  ➥ intervalTime);
}
```

This code looks more confusing than it actually is. Basically, I store the tree's current rotation in `rot` since we will be adjusting this number during our animation and it needs to remain separate from the actual property. This is because the value might need to go beyond 180 or −180, which `_rotation` is never allowed to do (for instance, -190 will automatically be converted to 170). I store the degrees to rotate to in the variable `degrees` (which I convert from radians). If the `degrees` value is outside the range of -180 to 180, I adjust it. Once both `degrees` and `rot` are within the same range, I find the shortest rotation amount between the two and adjust `degrees` again if necessary. The adjustment is required in order to spin in the right direction. For instance, if `degrees` is 170 and rot is -170, 20 degrees would be the shortest distance to spin to reach the proper angle, not 340 degrees. In this case, 360 would be subtracted from degrees, leaving an amount of -190, which would allow us to spin the 20 degrees from -170 to -190. With `rot` and `degrees` set to be in the form we need them, I set an interval to call tree's `rotate` method, which we will write now.

Place this method right after the previous code:

```
tree.rotate = function(amount) {
  this.rot -= (this.rot -
  ➥ this.degrees)/intervals;
  this._rotation = this.rot;
  if (Math.abs(this.rot - this.degrees) < 1) {
    clearInterval(rotateInt);
  }
}
```

Another easing, motion-tweened animation. We just adjust the rotation of our tree a little each interval call. Once we're close enough, we clear the interval. Test your movie now to see the result.

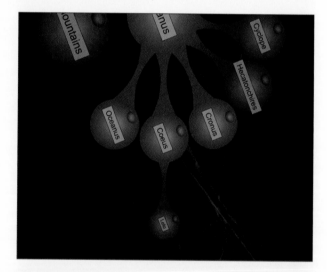

See the problem? By rotating the tree we are also rotating each node, which in turn causes the text to rotate into unreadable positions. What we need to do is rotate the node graphic in the opposite direction as the tree. We'll create one final method inside `NodeClass` to take care of this.

Add this method after `NodeClass`'s `drawConnector` method on the NodeClass layer:

```
NodeClass.prototype.rotateGraphics =
➥ function(degrees) {
    this.nodeGraphic._rotation = degrees;
}
```

Here we simply rotate the graphic of the node. Easy. Now to call this method, we could simply place a loop in the tree's `rotate` method that would run through its nodes. This would be the easy thing to do. What I want to do, however, is show you a new way of handling situations like this that perhaps is unnecessary in the current system, but you might find invaluable later. We are going to create a custom event.

There is an undocumented feature in Flash MX that will allow us to create our own custom events in our movies (events like `onEnterFrame` or `onMouseMove`), and then register objects to receive these custom events. For instance, you know that every instance of a movie clip automatically receives notification every time a frame is entered, and you can write a handler to run a function when that event occurs:

```
mcInstance.onEnterFrame = function() {};
```

In this case, the event is already defined and the movie clip is already set up to receive notification of the event. Now imagine if you could define your own events and decide which objects should receive notification when these events are fired. This is now possible, and it only takes a few lines of code. So let's give it a try!

Add this new line to the code immediately following the creation of our tree movie clip, on the code layer:

```
this.createEmptyMovieClip("tree", 0);
tree._x = windowWidth*.5;
tree._y = windowHeight*.5;;
tree.depth = 15000;
tree.setMask(mask);

ASBroadcaster.initialize(tree);
```

`ASBroadcaster` is an undocumented object that allows us to enable new objects to broadcast events, which is what we would like tree to be able to do. The `initialize` method gives this ability to tree. Now tree can define new events to broadcast to the Flash movie.

Now we need to actually broadcast our custom event, which we will do every time we rotate our tree. Place these new lines in our `tree.rotate` method:

```
tree.rotate = function(amount) {
    this.rot -= (this.rot -
    ➥ this.degrees)/intervals;
    this._rotation = this.rot;
    if (Math.abs(this.rot - this.degrees) < 1) {
        clearInterval(rotateInt);
    }
    this.broadcastMessage("onRotate", -
    ➥ this._rotation);
}
```

Since we have initialized this object with `ASBroadcaster`, we can use `broadcastMessage` to fire a custom event. Now every time the `tree.rotate` function is called, it will send out the custom event `onRotate` to any object registered to receive it. In addition, we send an additional parameter, `this._rotation`, that can be used by the objects receiving the event.

Two more lines will do everything we need for our new event to work. First, we need to have objects that will *receive* this new event, and will hopefully act upon it.

Go to the `NodeClass` layer and add the following lines to the `NodeClass`'s `init` method:

```
this._parent.addListener(this);
    this.onRotate = this.rotateGraphics;

    if (this._name == "rootNode") {
        this.render();
        return;
    }
```

addListener adds this object (this node) as a listener for any event that tree (this_parent) will broadcast. On the next line, we assign a function for this custom event, in this case the rotateGraphics method we wrote just a few moments ago. Now, in addition to receiving notification of all of the standard movie clip events (enterFrame, mouseMove, load, and so on), our NodeClass instances will receive notification when the tree rotates as well, and they will use the onRotate handler when this event occurs.

Test your movie now to see how the nodes know when to rotate their graphics. This ability to assign custom events can come in extremely handy – and is pretty fun to play around with, too!

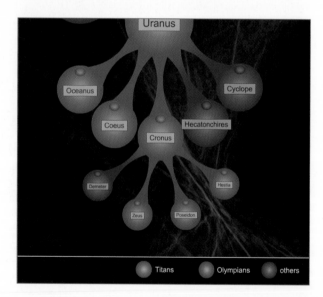

Taking it further

What I've shown you in this chapter is how to build, manipulate and animate a branching structure. The finished file as was presented in this tutorial can be found in the download files as gods_tree_book.fla if you want to look at the code in its entirety. As you saw in the initial gods_tree.swf, I went on to build another level of functionality for this system by allowing the user to click on nodes to access additional information (plus I added spouse nodes to the system). All the code is commented, and I encourage you to open it up and take a look at how certain things were accomplished.

In addition, imagine where you could take this concept and this file further. Although it works well to display branching information, and indeed that is what it was built for, I couldn't help but think of some great games that could be built from this system, from a more sophisticated Whack-a-Mole to a Choose Your Own Adventure type interactive story. Instead of loading a single interface full of information, perhaps you could set the system up as a gallery where selecting a low-res image on a node loaded the higher-res full screen version. How about making the gallery system respond to the types of images that a user has previously chosen, loading similar or complementary images in the next generation? Maybe you could remove the user entirely and use some random generation and funky math to animate the nodes and the colors of the system to create some surrealistic Web-art. Or maybe I should stop giving my ideas away and beat you to the punch!

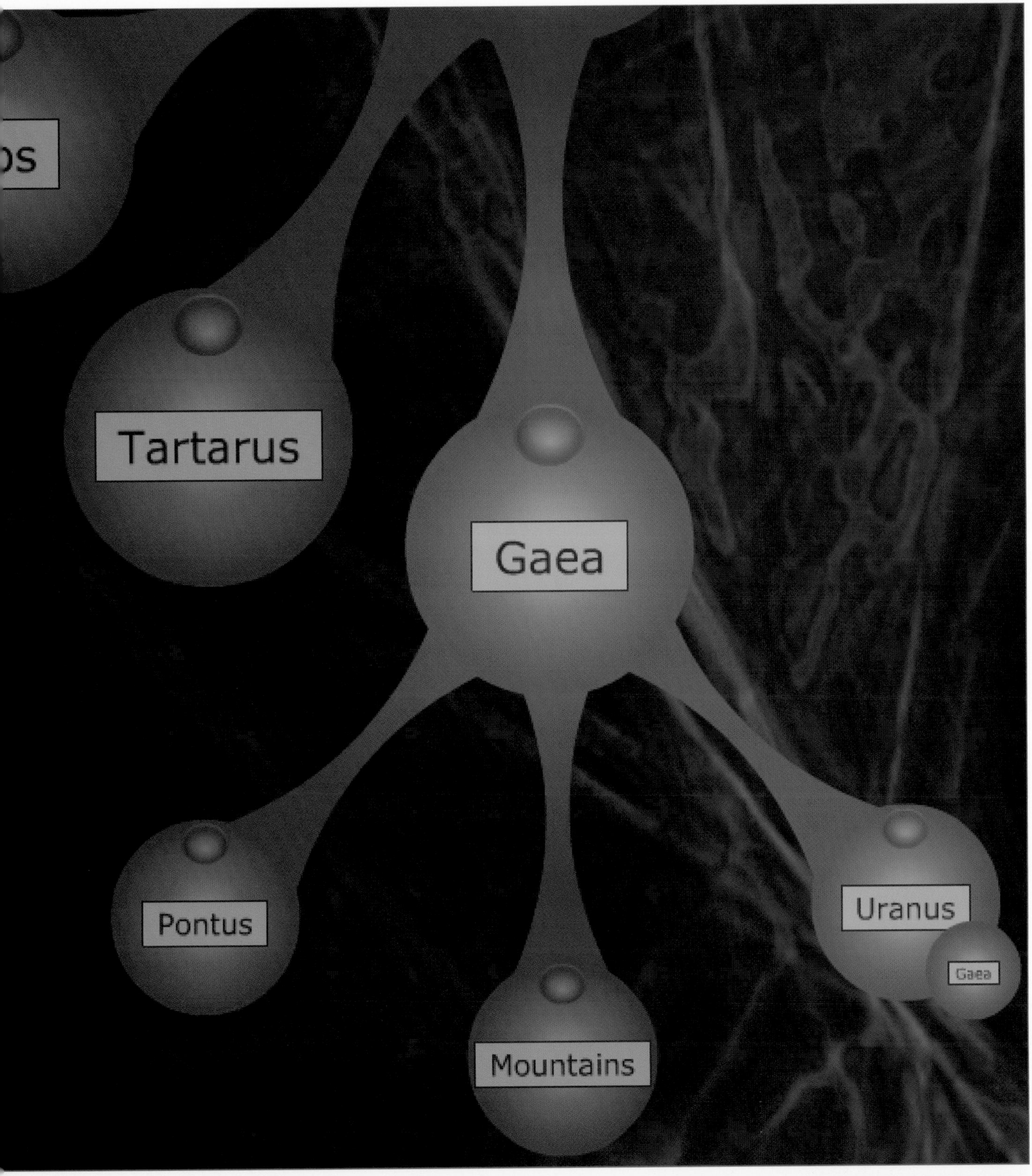

ps

Tartarus

Gaea

Pontus

Mountains

Uranus

Gaea

My final thought

Data. Boring, right? But why does it need to be? Often, the information that is being presented might be fascinating but it is being defeated by the way it is being presented. I encourage you to experiment with ways to better communicate your information, and more inventive and interesting ways to navigate through that information. We often learn by exploring, and Flash gives you amazing options to offer users an experience of accessing information in an incredible and enriching environment. Take advantage of it!

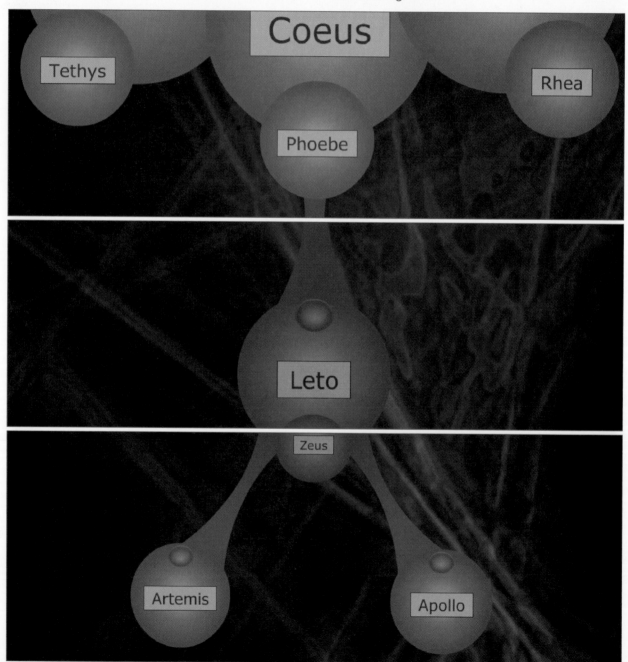

MAKING XML WORK FOR YOUR INTERFACE

Having looked at the use of Flash in presenting data graphically, it's a good idea to look at how other technologies can help Flash reach this end. This chapter is all about getting your interfaces fully intertwined with XML (eXtensible Markup Language) – something that's going to allow it to function in a simpler, more logical way.

The original idea I had for this interface was a kind of clustering application. The interface would bring in some XML data and then display that as a series of clusters, giving a graphical representation of the structure of the data. The difficulty with something like that is to provide an accurate representation of the structure while also maintaining legibility. It's one thing to draw a series of clusters of dots to highlight different concentrations of data, but quite another to turn this into an effective navigation. One solution to this problem is that implemented by Inxight, which can be seen at www.inxight.com/map/, in which the various branches of the tree span out as you drag across them in a kind of fisheye effect. I'm not sure whether one would be able to produce something similar within Flash, at least not with the same smoothness, and I'm not sure that I'd be capable of the mathematics involved.

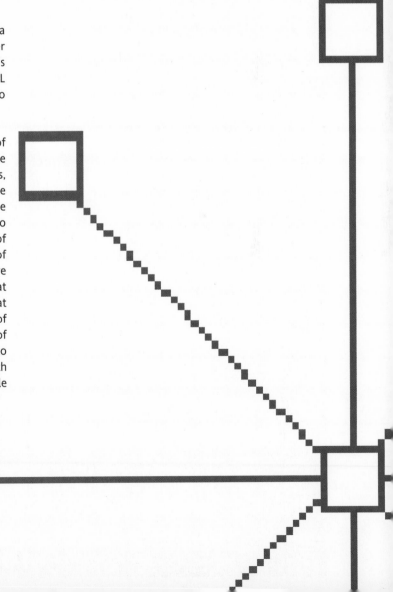

What I decided to go for instead was something perhaps a little more simple, but hopefully a bit more legible and usable. The basic premise I started with was that each node in the XML structure, each category if you will, would form the hub of a cluster, with each of the sub-categories grouped around the circumference. Rather than showing all of the nodes at once in a kind of fractal pattern this will show one path through the data at a time. While this means that we no longer have a picture of the overall structure of the data it will show us all of the alternate paths we could have taken while reaching a particular category. The following diagrams should make the process somewhat clearer. They demonstrate the thought process I went through in arriving at the final interface.

The diagram on the left is the first one I made of just one open cluster. I realized fairly quickly that the positioning of text would be a problem. If one were to position the text consistently on one side of the node graphic there would be overlap with the line connecting the node to its parent. Positioning the text differently depending on which direction the node was pointing in was a possibility but seemed somewhat clunky. The solution I came up with was to put each piece of text on top of the graphic, resizing the graphic to fit the proportions of the text.

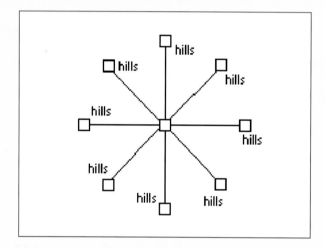

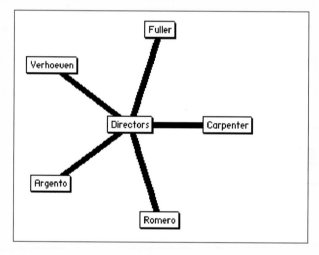

When the user wants to see the contents of one of the child nodes, they click that node and it becomes the centre of a new cluster. The first problem one encounters is how to plot this. As you can see in the following diagram there is an overlap between the two separate clusters.

The obvious solution to this seemed to be to move the sub-category away from its parent category before opening it. That way the two categories sit side by side without any overlap.

Looking at the diagram below you might be able to anticipate a problem. If one clicked Ghosts of Mars on the Carpenter cluster, then that cluster would shoot back into the original cluster, obscuring those original choices. It would really just end up as a mess.

One possible solution to this was to open up each node across a span of the circumference instead of distributing them around the whole circumference. For example, if the node was on the left of its parent, its children would open up on its left hand side across a small segment of the circle. This would be a similar sort of approach to the tree map discussed above. While this could be workable, I realized that overlap would again be a problem. If the nodes are plotted around a smaller portion of the circumference, they are quickly going to end up on top of each other.

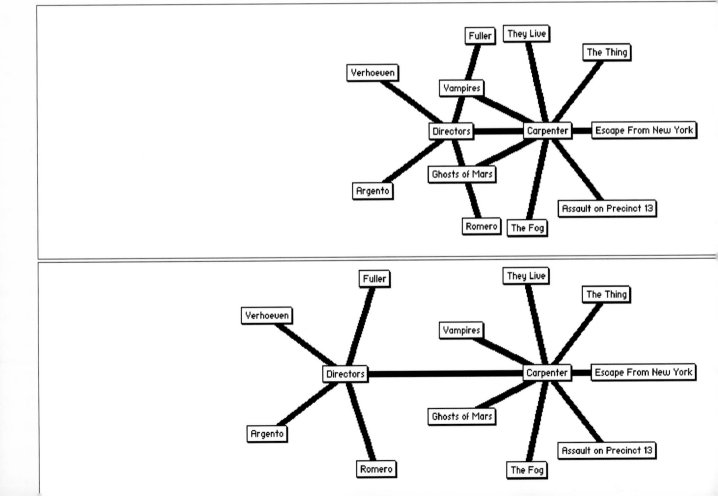

Instead of opting for that solution I decided on something different. What I hit upon was that overlap would not be a problem if the nodes all opened in the same direction. This could be achieved by rotating the cluster so that the node to be opened was always on the right hand side before opening it. This not only circumvents the overlap issue, but also gives more of a sense of direction – a sense of moving in one direction towards a goal. The movement from left to right could be seen to connote progression in western culture, echoing the way we read and write.

So in this case, the order of events that we have is as follows:

1. User clicks a node.

2. All the nodes rotate so that the selected category is on the right hand side.

3. The selected node shoots out to the right so that its children will be clear of its parent's children.

4. The children of the selected node appear around it.

We'll think more about the precise mechanics of that later – for example what to do if one of a node's children is open and we then click a different child. First we'll look at the code we need to import an XML structure to display.

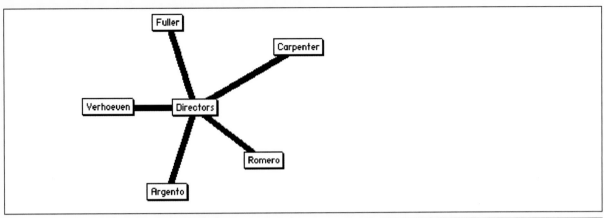

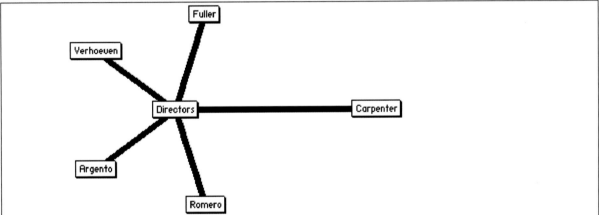

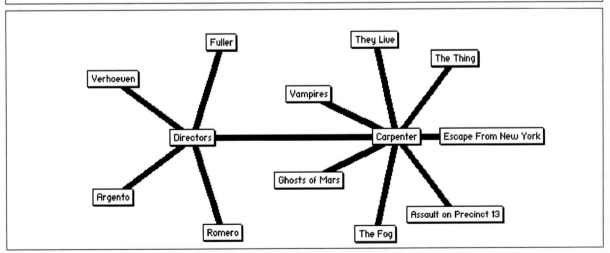

108

The XML

Before we look at the mechanics to display and navigate through the structure, we need to bring in the XML and convert it into an object structure. Here's the XML code that we'll be using:

```
<cat name="Directors">
  <cat name="Carpenter">
    <cat name="Escape From New York">
      <cat name="Kurt Russell"/>
      <cat name="Lee Van Cleef"/>
      <cat name="Ernest Borgnine"/>
    </cat>
    <cat name="Assault on Precinct 13">
      <cat name="Austin Stoker"/>
      <cat name="Darwin Joston"/>
      <cat name="Laurie Zimmer"/>
    </cat>
    <cat name="The Fog">
      <cat name="Adrienne Barbeau"/>
      <cat name="Hal Holbrook"/>
      <cat name="Janet Leigh"/>
    </cat>
    <cat name="Ghosts of Mars">
      <cat name="Natasha Henstridge"/>
      <cat name="Ice Cube"/>
      <cat name="Jason Statham"/>
    </cat>
    <cat name="Vampires">
      <cat name="James Woods"/>
      <cat name="Daniel Baldwin"/>
      <cat name="Sheryl Lee"/>
    </cat>
    <cat name="They Live">
      <cat name="Roddie Piper"/>
      <cat name="Keith David"/>
      <cat name="Meg Foster"/>
    </cat>
    <cat name="The Thing">
      <cat name="Kurt Russell"/>
      <cat name="Wilford Brimley"/>
      <cat name="TK Carter"/>
    </cat>
  </cat>
  <cat name="Romero">
    <cat name="Martin">
      <cat name="John Amplas"/>
      <cat name="Lincoln Maazal"/>
      <cat name="Christina Forrest"/>
    </cat>
    <cat name="Dawn of the Dead">
      <cat name="David Emge"/>
      <cat name="Ken Foree"/>
      <cat name="Scott H Reininger"/>
    </cat>
    <cat name="The Crazies">
      <cat name="Lane Carroll"/>
      <cat name="WG McMillan"/>
      <cat name="Harold Wayne Jones"/>
    </cat>
    <cat name="Day of the Dead">
      <cat name="Lori Cardille"/>
      <cat name="Terry Alexander"/>
      <cat name="Joseph Pilato"/>
    </cat>
    <cat name="Night of the Living Dead">
      <cat name="Judith O'Dea"/>
      <cat name="Duane Jones"/>
      <cat name="Karl Hardman"/>
    </cat>
  </cat>
  <cat name="Argento">
    <cat name="Suspiria">
      <cat name="Jessica Harper"/>
      <cat name="Stephania Casini"/>
      <cat name="Flavio Bucci"/>
    </cat>
    <cat name="Deep Red">
      <cat name="David Hemmings"/>
      <cat name="Daria Nicolodi"/>
      <cat name="Gabriele Lavia"/>
```

```
      </cat>
      <cat name="Tenebrae">
        <cat name="Anthony Franciosa"/>
        <cat name="John Saxon"/>
        <cat name="Guiliamo Gemma"/>
      </cat>
      <cat name="Phenomena">
        <cat name="Jennifer Connelly"/>
        <cat name="Daria Nicolodi"/>
        <cat name="Donald Pleasance"/>
      </cat>
    </cat>
    <cat name="Verhoeven">
      <cat name="Basic Instinct">
        <cat name="Sharon Stone"/>
        <cat name="Michael Douglas"/>
        <cat name="Jeanne Tripplehorn/>
      </cat>
      <cat name="Starship Troopers">
        <cat name="Casper Van Dien"/>
        <cat name="Dina Meyer"/>
        <cat name="Denise Richards"/>
      </cat>
      <cat name="Showgirls">
        <cat name="Kyle MacLachlan"/>
        <cat name="Elizabeth Berkley"/>
        <cat name="Gina Gershon"/>
      </cat>
      <cat name="Robocop">
        <cat name="Peter Weller"/>
        <cat name="Nancy Allen"/>
        <cat name="Ronny Cox"/>
      </cat>
      <cat name="Total Recall">
        <cat name="Arnold Schwarzenegger"/>
        <cat name="Sharon Stone"/>
        <cat name="Rachel Ticotin"/>
      </cat>
    </cat>
    <cat name="Fuller">
      <cat name="Shock Corridor">
        <cat name="Peter Breck"/>
        <cat name="Constance Towers"/>
        <cat name="Gene Evans"/>
      </cat>
      <cat name="Pickup on South Street">
        <cat name="Richard Widmark"/>
        <cat name="Jean Peters"/>
        <cat name="Thelma Ritter"/>
      </cat>
      <cat name="Underworld USA">
        <cat name="Cliff Robertson"/>
        <cat name="Beatrice Kay"/>
        <cat name="Larry Gates"/>
      </cat>
    </cat>
  </cat>
```

You'll see that each node has the node name `cat` and one attribute, `name`, which obviously refers to the name of the category. If a category has nodes nested within it, then they are its sub-categories. For example `Romero` has five sub-categories, `Martin`, `Dawn of the Dead`, `The Crazies`, `Day of the Dead` and `Night of the Living Dead`. Those five sub-categories each have three sub-categories. We're going to parse this structure and create an object for each category. Each of these objects will also have an array, `kidsArray`, which will contain the objects referring to their sub-categories. You will find this in the download files, saved as `structure.xml`, and it needs to be placed in the same directory as the Flash file we'll be using.

Importing and parsing the XML

I started by creating a new movie, with a white background. I set the stage dimensions to 750 pixels wide by 400 pixels high, and the frame rate to 31 fps. The background colour is dark gray (#333333).

I then began to place the code in the first frame of the timeline.

Before doing anything else, add this line of code to turn anti-aliasing off:

```
_quality="LOW"
```

This makes things perform better and I prefer the look of the lines without anti-aliasing.

Now we can begin with the code proper. First of all I created a constructor for a spinnerNav object, which would bring in the XML, parse it and then create the first of our clusters:

```
function spinnerNav(){
    this.init()
}


spinnerNav.prototype = new MovieClip()
Object.registerClass("spinnerNavSymbol",spinnerNav)
```

This code makes spinnerNav inherit from the movie clip object and then associates it with spinnerNavSymbol. When an instance of spinnerNavSymbol is attached to the stage, it will automatically become an instance of the spinnerNav class. At this point I also created a new movie clip symbol, setting the linkage to export for ActionScript and giving it the linkage ID spinnerNavSymbol. We'll just have this clip in the library, as we'll be attaching it dynamically.

I then added this code to create a new instance of spinnerNav:

```
var obj={
filename:"structure.xml",
    clusterRadius:100,
    separator:210
    }

_root.attachMovie("spinnerNavSymbol","spinnerNav",1,obj)
```

Here I create a generic object to pass to the spinnerNav as it is created. First is the filename for the XML document I'm using. Then I have two other parameters, the first of which, clusterRadius, is the radius of any particular cluster, and the second, separator, is the distance between any two open clusters. When the spinnerNav is created using attachMovie, obj is passed to it and all of the values inside obj are copied into it.

Now we continue with the methods for our spinnerNav class. These methods will be placed after the Object.registerClass line above. You may have noticed that in the constructor I created above, an init method is called. That method will call another method, importXml:

```
spinnerNav.prototype.init = function(){
    this.outputObject = {}
    this.importXml(this.fileName)
}
```

As well as calling importXml, the init method also creates a generic object, outputObject, which will hold the object structure created when parsing the XML. Next I created the importXml method, which goes directly after the code above. It creates a new XML object, called myStructure, and then assigns it various properties and methods:

```
spinnerNav.prototype.importXml = function(filename){
    this.myStructure = new XML()
    this.myStructure.ignoreWhite = true
    this.myStructure.onLoad = this.triggerParse
    this.myStructure.parseNode = this.parseNode
    this.myStructure.parent = this
    this.myStructure.load(this.filename)
}
```

The first property is ignoreWhite, which will make the XML object ignore any white space, or formatting, that might be present in our XML document. Then the triggerParse method is assigned to the XML object's onLoad handler. This will be called when the XML object has finished loading. The next method, parseNode, will be called to parse each individual node and give it a parent property so that it knows where it has been created and can send a message back when it has finished parsing. Finally it calls the load method of the myStructure object, passing it the filename.

The `triggerParse` method that comes next is called when the XML object has loaded:

```
spinnerNav.prototype.triggerParse=function(success){
    if(success){
      this.parseNode(this.firstChild,this.parent.outputObject)
      this.parent.create()
    }
}
```

As it is assigned to the `onLoad` handler it will be passed a parameter which will be `true` if the XML has loaded and `false` if not. This parameter is checked to see if it is true before proceeding. Although I didn't actually choose to, I could have displayed a message if the XML fails to load by adding in an `else` statement.

Once the file has loaded successfully we call the `parseNode` method, passing it the `firstChild` of the XML document (the `directors` node in our case) and the name of the object we are putting the results of the parse into. Here's the completed method, first storing the category name and then looping through the children, creating objects for them and storing them in `kidsArray`.

```
spinnerNav.prototype.parseNode=function(xmNode,currentObj){
    currentObj.catName = xmNode.attributes.name
    if(xmNode.hasChildNodes()){
      currentObj.kidsArray = []
      for(var i =0;i<xmNode.childNodes.length;i++){
        currentObj.kidsArray[i]={}
        this.parseNode(xmNode.childNodes[i], currentObj.kidsArray[i])
      }
    }
}
```

The `parseNode` method is what's known as a **recursive** function. What this basically means is that it's a function that calls itself. In practical terms what it does is to look at the children of the node it is parsing and then calls the same method for the children and so on and so forth. When it hits a node that has no children, it will slip back up to the parent and carry on. It can be slightly difficult to conceptualize what is happening here, so stepping through the process can help. Here's a small XML document:

```
<0>
    <0_0>
    </0_0>
    <0_1>
        <0_1_0/>
        <0_1_1/>
        </0_1>
    <0_2>
    </0_2>
</0>
```

Now here's how the recursive function would step through it. You can see how it's moving top to bottom through all of the nodes in the structure.

```
Parse node 0
Node 0 has 3 children.
Check node 0_0, the first child of node 0.
Node 0_0 has no children. Slip back to node 0.
Check node 0_1, the second child of node 0.
Node 0_1 has two children.
Check node 0_1_0, the first child of node 0_1.
Node 0_1_0 has no children, slip back to node 0_1
Check node 0_1_1, the second child of node 0_1.
Node 0_1_1 has no children. Slip back to node 0_1
Node 0_1 has no more children. Slip back to node 0
Check node 0_2, the third child of node 0.
Node 0_2 has no children. Slip back to node 0
Node 0 has no more children. End parse.
```

The benefit of using a recursive function is that it will cope with whatever we throw at it. We can use it to take whatever XML structure we want and parse it into an object structure containing all the information we need. One thing to be aware of whenever parsing XML like this is that the activity is all taking place in one frame. Flash will remain stalled on the frame until the loop finishes executing. With large data structures this can become a problem and is solved by breaking up the parsing across frames, but for our purposes here this is fine.

So basically each time the `parseNode` method is called we have to do a number of things:

- Retrieve the category name from the XML node and store it in the object we have been passed.

- Check if the XML node has any children.

- If it does have children, we create a new array in the object to store them in.

- We then loop through the children.

- For each child, we create a blank object to store the information in, and place it within the array of children.

- We then call `parseNode` for the next node in the XML structure, passing it both this node and the new object we have created to store the results in.

One thing to note is that I've used `var i` in the loop. The `var` is very important here as it means that each time the method is called, `i` is a local value and is not shared between calls. This serves as a marker so that after the method has been called for one of the `childNodes`, the value of `i` is still intact and the loop carries on from where it left off.

After the parse is complete we end up with an object structure containing all the information we need – the name of each category and which categories are within each other. For example with our original XML document, `outputObject` has the `catName directors`, and an array containing five objects. These five objects have their own `catNames` – `Carpenter`, `Romero`, `Argento`, `Verhoeven` and `Fuller`. They have their own arrays of children.

If you run your movie at this point, or `spinner001.fla` from the download files, and list variables (Debug > List Variables) you'll see the structure of nested objects that we've created.

Creating the clusters

Now that I have all of the pertinent information in a convenient format, I need to embark on displaying it.

After the parse completes I call a `create` method. This deletes the XML from the memory, and then attaches an instance of a new class `clusterNode`. It will finally call the `addKids` method of the `clusterNode`, which will create the children of the node and display them in a circle around the node.

```
spinnerNav.prototype.create = function(){
    delete this.myStructure
    var obj = {
      myObject:this.outputObject,
      _x:120,
      _y:200,
      separator:this.separator,
      clusterRadius:this.clusterRadius
    }
    var base = this.attachMovie("nodeSymbol","baseNode",1,obj)
    base.addKids()
}
```

As we attach the `nodeSymbol` we pass it a number of parameters. Firstly we pass `this.outputObject`, which will be placed inside a property `myObject`. The new node will use this to ascertain how many children it has. We also pass it an `_x` and `_y` position, the values for the radius of each cluster, and the distance between each cluster that we passed to the `spinnerNav` earlier.

Next we need to create the `clusterNode` constructor, and set it up to inherit from the `MovieClip` object. This is much the same as earlier:

```
function clusterNode(){
    this.init()
}
clusterNode.prototype = new MovieClip()
Object.registerClass("nodeSymbol",clusterNode)
```

We also need to create a new movie clip, `nodeSymbol`, which will be attached as an instance of our class. For now, you can just draw a small square in it to represent the node. Later we'll look at how to display the graphic and text for each node, but first of all we're going to get the nodes plotted correctly.

First we create the `init` function:

```
clusterNode.prototype.init = function(){
    this.catName = this.myObject.catName
    this.kidsArray = this.myObject.kidsArray
    this.segment = (2*Math.PI)/this.kidsArray.length
    this.kidMcs = []
}
```

In this function we retrieve some data from the object passed to it to allow easier access to the array of children and the category name. We create a property segment, which refers to the number of radians between each category plotted around the node. A radian is basically an alternative way of measuring angles. When Flash computes the cosine and sine of angles it uses radians, and so it's easier to just use radians than working in degrees and converting back and forth. A circle contains 2 times π radians, so to calculate the angle between n nodes around the edge of a circle we use $2*\pi / n$. Finally we create an array `kidMcs` which will contain the movie clips which instantiate each `clusterNode` that we create.

Now we write the `addKids` method, which will create all of the children of the current node. In a moment we'll adjust this so that the new nodes animate into position, but for now we'll just position them directly.

```
clusterNode.prototype.addKids = function(){
    for(var i =0;i<this.kidsArray.length;i++){
        var obj = {
            _x:Math.cos(this.segment * i)*this.clusterRadius,
            _y:Math.sin(this.segment * i)*this.clusterRadius
        }
        this.attachMovie("nodeSymbol","kid"+i,i,obj)
    }
}
```

If you run the code like that, you'll see that it draws the main node in the center, surrounded by five child nodes. We've plotted the nodes around the edge by using basic trigonometry. Each point is positioned on the edge of a circle with the radius `clusterRadius` at the angle `this.segment * i`. So on the x-axis we take the cosine of the angle and multiply it by the radius, and on the y-axis we do the same using the sine of the angle. The new movie clips are attached within the original node, so all of the co-ordinates are relative to the center point of the original node.

While this does get the job done, it's not very visually appealing. What we want instead is to create the nodes one at a time and have them move to their target position around the edge of the original node. We're going to need to write some more methods to do this.

- `addKids` – triggers the addition and initializes counter variables. Informs its parent node that it has opened. Sets the `onEnterFrame` handler to `addNextKid`.

- `addNextKid` – if it has not already created all of its children it calls `createChild` to create the next child.

- `createChild` – creates a new `clusterNode` object, passing it all the relevant data. Calls the `moveToPosition` method for this new node, passing the target radius to `moveto`.

- `moveToPosition` – stores the target radius. Sets the `onEnterFrame` handler to `rotateMe`.

- `rotateMe` – calls `moveToTarget` each frame. If `moveToTarget` returns true clears the `onEnterFrame` handler.

- `moveToTarget` – gradually shifts the node's radian and radius properties until they equal the target values, at the same time shifting the node's position on stage. Returns `true` when it has reached the target.

That looks like quite a lot of methods, but each one is a necessary part of the mechanism. Generally we have one method to initiate an action, and then another method that is called every frame to carry out that action over time and create the motion, the animation.

First of all we have the `addKids` method, new and improved to replace the one we wrote before:

```
clusterNode.prototype.addKids = function(){
    this.kidCount = 0
    this._parent.kidOpen = this
    this.opening = true
    this.onEnterFrame = this.addNextKid
}
```

This is fairly simple – we're really just initializing a number of things. We have `kidCount`, which is the number of children that have been created so far, `kidOpen`, which is set in the `clusterNode`'s parent to indicate that one of its children has sprouted its own children, and `opening`, which indicates that the node is busy creating its children. The importance of these latter two properties will become apparent later on, when we can click on nodes to open them – we will be performing different actions depending on what the state of the parent is. For example we don't want to be able to open a child node until its parent has opened all of the node's siblings. Finally we assign `addNextKid` to the `onEnterFrame` handler.

This method will move on to the next child and create it:

```
clusterNode.prototype.addNextKid = function(){
    this.g++
    if(this.g%2 ==0){
      if(this.kidCount<this.kidsArray.length){
        this.createChild(this.kidCount)
        this.kidCount++
      }else{
        delete this.onEnterFrame
        this.opening = false
      }
    }
}
```

All of the actions here are wrapped inside an `if` statement. What we're doing is incrementing a counter variable, `g`. If `g` is divisible by 2 we create the next child. This is just to create a slight delay between the creation of each node, every other frame rather than every frame, and is purely for aesthetic effect. We then check whether we have created all of the child nodes, comparing `kidCount` with the length of `kidsArray`. If we still have children to create we call `createChild`, if not we delete the `onEnterFrame` handler and set `opening` to false.

Then I created the `createChild` method, which sets up a number of properties for the new node and then creates it. When it has been created we call its `moveToPosition` method to send it to the correct position:

```
clusterNode.prototype.createChild = function(num){
    var obj = {
      myObject : this.kidsArray[num],
      separator : this.separator,
      clusterRadius : this.clusterRadius,
      kidNum : num,
      radianTarg : num * this.segment
    }
    var nooKid = this.attachMovie("nodeSymbol","kid"+num,num+1,obj)
    this.kidMcs[num]=nooKid
    nooKid.moveToPosition(this.clusterRadius)
}
```

We're using the value num, which was the value of kidCount passed to the method, to specify which entry in kidsArray contains the correct information for the new node and also to calculate its target radian value, radianTarg. Once we've attached the new clusterNode movie clip we put a reference to it, nooKid, in the current node's kidMcs array. We'll be using this later. The moveToPosition method is very simple:

```
clusterNode.prototype.moveToPosition = function(radius){
   this.radiusTarg = radius
   this.onEnterFrame = this.rotateMe
}
```

All we are doing here is storing the radius value passed to it as radiusTarg and then setting the onEnterFrame handler to rotateMe. It may seem that there's not a lot of point storing the radius as this will always be the same value, but we'll be using this later for when we want a node to shoot out and form the hub of its own cluster. We'll be able to re-use the methods we have already written, simply supplying a different radius value.

So now the new node will call rotateMe every frame. This is another simple function:

```
clusterNode.prototype.rotateMe = function(){
   if(this.moveToTarget(1)){
     delete this.onEnterFrame
   }
}
```

It will basically call moveToTarget until the node reaches the target radian and radius values. The method call is in an if statement. What this means is that if the method returns true then the actions within the if statement will be executed, if not they won't. So when moveToTarget returns true, the onEnterFrame handler will be deleted and the movie clip will stop moving.

You might have noticed the value 1 is passed to the moveToTarget method. This value is for tolerance. It represents the distance that the movie clip must be from its target before it snaps to it and the method returns true. This, again, is something we'll be using later, as we will not need as much accuracy when the clusters close as when they open.

Now for the method that actually executes the motion:

```
clusterNode.prototype.moveToTarget = function(tolerance){
   this.radian +=(this.radianTarg - this.radian)/3
   this.radius +=(this.radiusTarg - this.radius)/6

   this.xt = Math.cos(this.radian) * this.radius
   this.yt = Math.sin(this.radian) * this.radius

   this.x += (this.xt - this.x)/6
   this.y += (this.yt - this.y)/6
   this._x = Math.round(this.x)
   this._y = Math.round(this.y)

   if(Math.abs(this.xt-this.x)<tolerance && Math.abs(this.yt-this.y)<tolerance){
     this.radian =this.radianTarg
     this.radius =this.radiusTarg
     this.x = Math.cos(this.radian) * this.radius
     this.y = Math.sin(this.radian) * this.radius
     this._x = Math.round(this.x)
     this._y = Math.round(this.y)
     return true
   }
}
```

You could broadly see this method as containing four sections. Firstly we bring the node's `radian` and `radius` values towards their target values by adding a fraction of the gap between them. We then calculate x and y targets for the clip based on these values. Next we move the node's x and y properties towards those values in the same way. The final section of the method checks whether the x and y values are within the tolerance range of `xt` and `yt` – if they are, then the method returns `true`.

Note that rather than working directly with _x and _y movie clip properties, we're instead using x and y and then setting _x and _y as the rounded value of these properties. This is basically to deal with the problem that Flash has dealing with pixel fonts. If movie clips containing text fields are not placed on absolute pixels then the fonts blur, so we have to make sure that the _x and _y values we set are whole numbers. You might say that x and y are the **true** position of each node, whereas _x and _y are the **rendered** position of each node.

We use `Math.abs` to convert the distance, which may be positive or negative, into a positive (absolute) number to allow proper comparison. It should be noted that we could also implement different kinds of motion by altering this method. One could change it so that the nodes move to their targets with elasticity, or so that it uses the values determined from the radian and radius as the points to plot, rather than targets to move to. It would also be possible to have this method accept extra parameters to change the speed of motion under certain circumstances.

If you test this so far, (it's included in the download files as `spinner002.fla`), you should see the five children of the first node spiraling out from the center into position with a slight gap between them.

The next stage will be to sort out the graphics for each node before moving on to the interactive element.

Drawing the node graphic

For the node graphic we're going to create a new movie clip, which we'll call bg. We could use the drawing API to create this graphic, but I think it's generally quicker to make changes to graphics and try stuff out within the authoring environment. Within bg we're going to have three separate movie clips, left, right and mid. We'll be able to resize the graphic without distortion by stretching the mid movie clip and then positioning the right movie clip at its right hand edge.

So we have three new movie clips containing the following graphics:

left
- black rectangle, 1x19 px, placed with its top left at 0,0.
- black square, 1x1 px, at 1,0.
- pale green rectangle (#F1F4F0), 1x17 px, at 1,1.
- black square, 1x1 px, at 1,18.

right
- black rectangle, 1x19 px, placed with its top left at 1,0.
- black square, 1x1px, at 0,0.
- mid green rectangle, (#CFDACD) 1x17 px, at 0,1.
- black square, 1x1 px, at 0,18.

mid
- black rectangle, 50x1 px, at 0,0.
- pale green rectangle(#F1F4F0), 50x1 px, at 0,1.
- white rectangle, 50x15 px at 0,2.
- mid green rectangle (#CFDACD), 50x1 px, at 0,17.
- black rectangle, 50x1 px at 0,18.

Place these three movie clips inside bg and give them the instance names left, mid and right. You can place them adjoining each other at 0,0 if you like, but we're going to position them dynamically anyway so it doesn't really matter.

Next add another layer inside bg and create a text field, placing it at (0,0). I've used a pixel font from miniml.com. set to 8pt. If you want to use a device font then you should make sure that the font outlines are not embedded (Click on the Character button and choose Embed Font Outlines For No Characters) and set it to 9pt. An embedded pixel font is probably the best option, as motion tends to suffer a little when using a device font. Set the font to dynamic text and give it the instance name tf. Finally place an instance of the bg movie clip inside nodeSymbol and name the instance bg.

We're going to create a new draw method, which will put the category name inside the text field and then calculate the width of the text to determine the size and positioning of the background pieces. The draw method will be called from the init method:

```
clusterNode.prototype.init = function(){
   this.catName = this.myObject.catName
   this.kidsArray = this.myObject.kidsArray
   this.segment = (2*Math.PI)/this.kidsArray.length
   this.kidMcs = []
   this.draw()
}
```

Here's the draw method, I'll go through it section by section in a moment:

```
clusterNode.prototype.draw=function(){
   this.bg.tf.autoSize = true
   this.bg.tf.text = this.catName
   var wid = this.bg.tf.textWidth + 10
   this.bg.tf._x=this.bg.left._width + 2
   this.bg.left._x = 0
   this.bg.left._y = 0
   this.bg.mid._x =this.bg.left._width
   this.bg.mid._y = 0
   this.bg.mid._width = wid - (this.bg.left._width+this.bg.right._width)
   this.bg.right._x = wid - this.bg.right._width
   this.bg.right._y = 0
   this.bg._x = Math.round(wid/2)*-1
   this.bg._y = Math.round(this.bg.mid._height/2)*-1
   this.bg.swapDepths(1000)
}
```

So first of all I set the text field's `autoSize` to `true` so it will expand to accommodate any text we assign to it.

I then set the text property to `this.catName`, in order to make sure that the text field is filled with the name of the category.

I set a local variable `wid` to the width of the text in the text field plus 10 extra pixels as a buffer around the edge of the text.

I then position the text field just to the right of the `left` graphic.

Next I position and scale the left, mid and right graphics based on the `wid` variable

- The left graphic goes at (0,0)

- The mid graphic is placed at the right edge of the left graphic and scaled to take up the whole of `wid` minus the width of the left and right graphics.

- The right graphic is placed on the right hand side of the mid graphic, at `wid` minus its width.

Then I position bg itself so that it has its center at the node's center point. Note that we're using `Math.round` to ensure that it is on a whole pixel.

Finally I use `swapDepths` to position the graphic in front of any child nodes created. This becomes important when we draw lines from the children to the parent, which we'll cover next. Test this now, or look at `spinner003.fla` from the download files, to see our node graphics display.

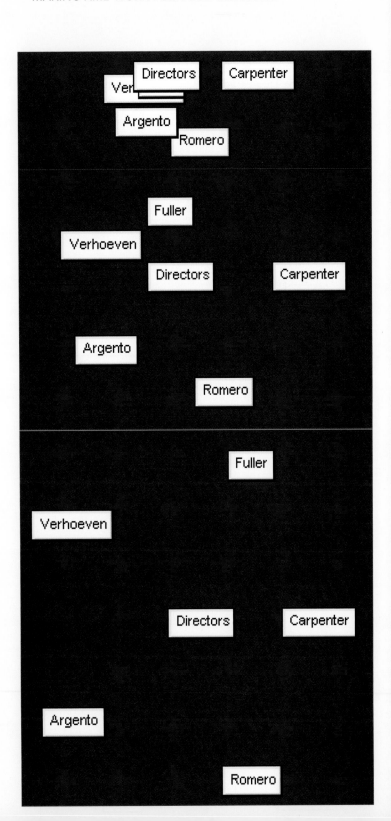

Connecting lines

Drawing lines connecting the children to their parents is an important visual cue to signify their relationship and is pretty simple to put in place. We're going to create a new method `connectToParent` to accomplish this. This method needs to be called whenever a node moves and so a call to it should be placed in the `moveToTarget` method:

```
clusterNode.prototype.moveToTarget =
➡ function(tolerance){
  this.radian +=(this.radianTarg -
  ➡ this.radian)/3
  this.radius +=(this.radiusTarg -
  ➡ this.radius)/6

  this.xt = Math.cos(this.radian) *
  ➡ this.radius
  this.yt = Math.sin(this.radian) *
  ➡ this.radius
  this.x += (this.xt - this.x)/6
  this.y += (this.yt - this.y)/6
  this._x = Math.round(this.x)
  this._y = Math.round(this.y)
  this.connectToParent()

  if(Math.abs(this.xt-this.x)<tolerance
  && Math.abs(this.yt-this.y)<tolerance){
    this.radian =this.radianTarg
    this.radius =this.radiusTarg
    this.x = Math.cos(this.radian) *
    this.radius
    this.y = Math.sin(this.radian) *
    this.radius
    this._x = Math.round(this.x)
    this._y = Math.round(this.y)
    this.connectToParent()
    return true
  }
}
```

All that `connectToParent` needs to do is clear any previous lines, set a `lineStyle` and then draw a line. We're using a fat green line:

```
clusterNode.prototype.connectToParent =
➡ function(){
  this.clear()
  this.moveTo(0,0)
  this.lineStyle(6,0xbac9b8)
  this.lineTo(-this._x,-this._y)
}
```

So first we clear all lines, then we move the drawing position to 0,0 and then set a `lineStyle`. We then move to the inverse of the node's current x and y position. This is basically because if the node is at (100,100), that is 100 to the right of and below the parent, then the parent is 100 to the left of and above the child, that is at (-100,-100). If you run that now, or test `spinner004.fla` from the download files, you'll see lines attaching each node to its parent. If you remove the `clear` statement, you actually get quite an interesting effect with the lines revealing the trajectory of the motion. If you then remove the `moveTo` statement you get a slightly different effect.

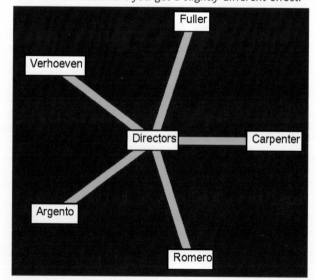

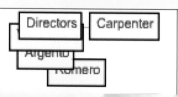
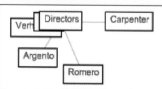

Building in interaction

Now that we have the basic mechanism for opening the children of a node and displaying with the correct graphics we can start on the interaction. The basics of this will be fairly simple. When the user clicks on a node, all of the nodes will rotate around their hub and the selected node will shoot out to the right. It will become more complicated when we have to deal with closing nodes, and in particular having to close one node before opening another, but first we'll just deal with the opening mechanism.

The first thing we need to do is add a button action to each node. We'll do this in the `init` method:

```
clusterNode.prototype.init = function(){
  this.catName = this.myObject.catName
  this.kidsArray = this.myObject.kidsArray
  this.segment =
  (2*Math.PI)/this.kidsArray.length
  this.kidMcs = []
  this.draw()
  this.bg.onPress = function(){
    this._parent.clickMe()
  }
}
```

When bg is clicked it calls `clickMe` in its parent, the node itself. For now this method will just call another method, but we'll be using it later to check a couple of conditions before acting:

```
clusterNode.prototype.clickMe=function(){
  this._parent.openChild(this)
}
```

So this calls the `openChild` method in the node's parent, passing the name of the movie clip as an argument. In the `openChild` method we first check if the node already has one of its children open. If it does we'll do nothing (for now). If not, we have to calculate the number of radians that the clicked node will have to rotate to bring it to the right hand side and adjust the radian targets of all of the child nodes accordingly. Once the radian targets have been adjusted we call `moveToPosition` for all of the child nodes. Note that the movie clip that was clicked, mc, passes `separator` as an argument, the variable we defined at the start for the distance between each cluster. This means that the node clicked will move further out to the right than the other nodes.

```
clusterNode.prototype.openChild=function
➡ (mc){
  if(this.kidOpen){
    //close kids first
  }else{
    this.redoRadians(mc)
    for(var i in this.kidMcs){
      if(this.kidMcs[i]==mc){
        this.kidMcs[i].moveToPosition
        (this.separator)
      }else{
        this.kidMcs[i].moveToPosition
        (this.clusterRadius)
      }
    }
  }
}
```

Fuller

Verhoeven

Directors

Carpenter

To calculate the number of radians that we need to rotate the nodes, we call another method, redoRadians. What this method does is calculates how far the clicked node's radian target is from the right hand side and then increments all of the nodes' targets by the same amount.

```
clusterNode.prototype.redoRadians=function
➡ (mc){
  var nearestHorizontal = Math.round
  (mc.radianTarg/(Math.PI*2))*Math.PI*2
  var difference = nearestHorizontal -
  ➡ mc.radianTarg
  for(var i in this.kidMcs){
    this.kidMcs[i].radianTarg +=difference
  }
}
```

The way the method is set up it will find the nearest horizontal — if the nearest horizontal is clockwise all the nodes will rotate clockwise, otherwise they will rotate counter-clockwise. Any radian on the right hand side will be a multiple of 2π, such as 4π, 8π, etc. If the clip's current target is 4.5π then the closest horizontal would be 4π, if it's 5.4π then the closest horizontal is 6π. So to calculate what the nearest horizontal for the clicked node is, we divide the current radian target by 2π, round the number, and then multiply by 2π.

Once we've calculated this figure, we loop through all of the current node's children and add that amount to their radian target (radianTarg) so that all the nodes are rotated by the same amount.

If you run the code like that, or test spinner005.fla, you'll see that as you click any node it will rotate its parent node, shooting out to the right, and then stop.

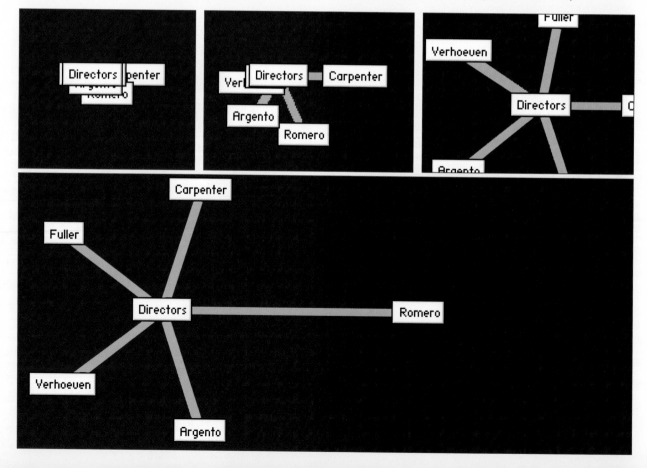

We can add a little extra code to make the sub-node open once it has reached its target. All we need to do to achieve this is add a few extra lines to the `rotateMe` method that controls the motion. Basically we just add a conditional which, when the node reaches its target, checks whether its target radius is equivalent to `separator` which indicates that it has been opened. If so, we call the node's `addKids` method. We could add a separate property to indicate that the clip is sprouting, but it's probably sufficient just to use the radius value for now:

```
clusterNode.prototype.rotateMe=
function(){
  if(this.moveToTarget(1)){
    delete this.onEnterFrame
    if(this.radiusTarg==this.separator){
      this.addKids()
    }
  }
}
```

If you run the code here, or check out `spinner006.fla`, you'll see that once each node has sprouted to the right it then opens its own children. You can navigate all the way down the tree doing this, but at the moment it's impossible to go back up. This is because the `kidOpen` property is set in the parent as soon as one of its child nodes opens its own children. Next we'll work on making the tree close as well as open.

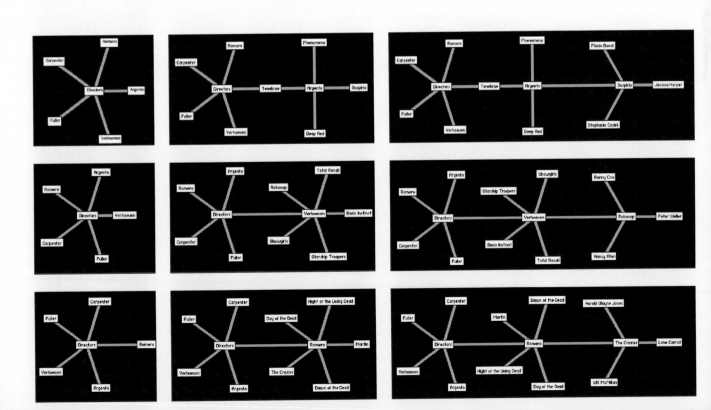

Queuing actions

The next stage in building this interface is to allow the user to move back up the tree to take an alternate path, to open a different set of branches. This complicates matters somewhat. So far we have been able to call open and have that branch open. What we need to implement here is a mechanism whereby one clicks a node and it then checks if any of its siblings are open. If they are open, then they must first be closed, and only when they are closed can the selected node open. This is complicated further by the fact that if the user has traversed far down the tree and then clicks to open a different top-level category, the interface might have to close two or three clusters before it can open the new top-level category.

To circumvent this situation we have to build in a series of checks. When the user clicks to open a category that already has one of its siblings open, we will have to first call a method closeKids that will close the open node. We will also queue an action in the parent node. When the child node has removed all of its children it will then call this method that's waiting in the parent. The same thing will apply when calling the closeKids method. If the child that is open has one of its own children open then that will have to be closed first, and so on until you reach a node with no open children.

First of all then, we need to make modifications to the openChild method:

```
clusterNode.prototype.openChild=function(mc){
  if(this.kidOpen){
    this.setWait(this,"openChild",mc)
    this.kidOpen.closeKids()
  }else{
    this.redoRadians(mc)
    for(var i in this.kidMcs){
      if(this.kidMcs[i]==mc){
        this.kidMcs[i].moveToPosition
        (this.separator)
      }else{
        this.kidMcs[i].moveToPosition
        (this.clusterRadius)
      }
    }
  }
}
```

Now when a node is told to open one of its children and it already has a child open, it will do two things. First of all it calls a setWait method, passing it three arguments. These correspond to an object, a method name and a parameter to pass. We'll write this method in a moment. After it has stored these, we then call the closeKids method in the child that is already open.

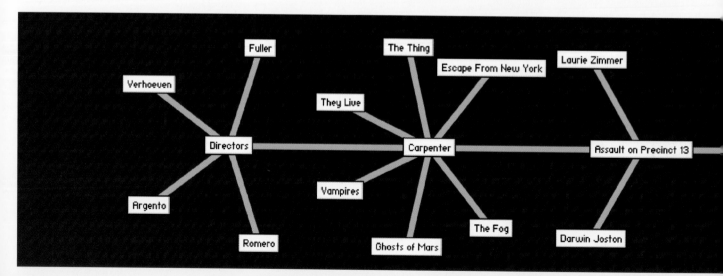

The setWait method just stores the arguments that it has been passed for later use:

```
clusterNode.prototype.setWait =
➥ function(obj,method,args){
  this.waitObj = obj
  this.waitMethod = method
  this.waitArgs = args
}
```

To go with this we also create a checkWait method. When a node closes, it will call this method in its parent. It basically checks if it has a method waiting to be executed, a waitMethod, calls it and then deletes the method, along with its corresponding object and argument:

```
clusterNode.prototype.checkWait =
➥ function(){
  this.waitObj[this.waitMethod]
  (this.waitArgs)
  delete this.waitObj
  delete this.waitMethod
  delete this.waitArgs
}
```

The procedure for closing a node's children will work in a similar way to the addKids method we created earlier, in that it is one method that calls a series of other methods:

- closeKids – initiates the closing. Checks if any of its children have sprouted their own children. If so, it calls closeKids for that node. If not, it checks that it has kids and then sets onEnterFrame to closeNextKid.

- closeNextKid – this method decrements a counter and calls closeMe for the next child node.

- closeMe – sets new targets for the radius and radians so that it will move back to its parent. Sets onEnterFrame to goClose.

- goClose – decrements alpha. Moves node towards its parent. Calls the parent's removeChild method when it is close enough.

- removeChild – this method is passed a number and the node removes the child corresponding to that entry in the array. It decrements its kidCount. When kidCount reaches zero, all the nodes have been closed and it calls allClosed.

- allClosed – deletes kidOpen in the node's parent. Calls the parent's checkWait method.

Austin Stoker

So to start with, we write the `closeKids` method:

```
clusterNode.prototype.closeKids =
➥function(){
  if(this.kidOpen){
    this.setWait(this,"closeKids")
    this.kidOpen.closeKids()
  }else{
    if(this.kidCount == 0){
      this.allClosed()
    }else{
      this.removeCount = this.kidCount
      this.onEnterFrame =
      this.closeNextKid
    }
  }
}
```

As you can see, the first conditional checks if any of its children has children open. If so, it calls `closeKids` for that child and stores `closeKids` as its own `wait` function. When its child has closed and removed its child nodes, it will then close and remove its own child nodes.

If none of its children has children open, we first check that the current node has children open, in case we click in the gap between a node starting to open and actually creating the movie clips. If it doesn't, we call `allClosed` straight away.

If the node does have children open, and none of its children has children open, then we can go ahead and close it, setting the remove counter to the value of `kidCount` and assigning `closeNextKid` to the `enterFrame` handler.

The `closeNextKid` method is quite simple. It just decrements `removeCount` and then calls the `closeMe` method for the next node in its `kidsArray`. When `removeCount` is less than zero, it removes the method from the `enterFrame` handler:

```
clusterNode.prototype.closeNextKid =
➥function(){
  this.removeCount--
  this.kidMcs[this.removeCount].closeMe()
  if(this.removeCount < 0){
    delete this.onEnterFrame
  }
}
```

The `closeMe` method will be called for each node to be closed. It basically sets new targets for the node's radian and radius values.

```
clusterNode.prototype.closeMe =
➥function(){
  this.radianTarg += 3
  this.radiusTarg = 0
  this.onEnterFrame = this.goClose
}
```

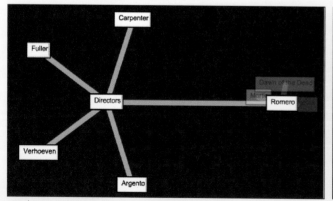
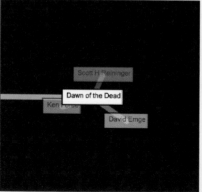
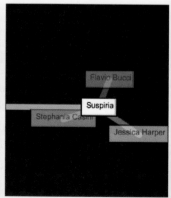

Setting `radiusTarg` is self-explanatory, while we add three to the node's `radianTarg` (roughly equivalent to 180 degrees) so that it rotates as it closes – purely an aesthetic consideration.

Once we've set the new targets, we set the `onEnterFrame` handler to `goClose` which will handle the actual closing:

```
clusterNode.prototype.goClose = function(){
   this._alpha-=10
   if(this.moveToTarget(5)||
   ➥this._alpha<=10)
   this._parent.removeChild(this.kidNum)
}
```

As we close each node we also reduce the alpha, making the effect slightly smoother. Next we call `moveToTarget` which handles the actual motion as earlier. Note that now we're passing it a value of 5 for tolerance, which means that it will be judged to have reached its target when it is within 5 pixels of it on the x and y axes. Once the node is either within 5 pixels of its parent node or its alpha is below 10, we call the `removeChild` method in the parent node, passing the current node's `kidNum`.

The `removeChild` method is straightforward. We remove the child node's movie clip and delete the corresponding entry in the `kidMcs` array. After that, we decrement the parent's `kidCount` value. When this value has reached zero all of its children will have been removed, and so we then call the node's `allClosed` method.

```
clusterNode.prototype.removeChild =
➥function(num){
   this.kidMcs[num].removeMovieClip()
   delete this.kidMcs[num]
   this.kidCount--
   if(this.kidCount==0){
      this.allClosed()
   }
}
```

Once all of the node's children have been closed, we then want to let the node's parent know that it can execute any queued actions. This is what is accomplished in the `allClosed` method:

```
clusterNode.prototype.allClosed =
➥function(){
   delete this._parent.kidOpen
   this._parent.checkWait()
}
```

So here we've done two things. Firstly we have removed the parent's `kidOpen` property, and secondly, we have called the parent's `checkWait` method, which executes any queued actions, either opening a different child or closing itself.

If you test the movie at this point, or `spinner007.fla`, you'll see that it's generally functioning correctly. The user can now click on any node, whether or not its parent already has open children, and the interface will go through the correct series of events to open the node.

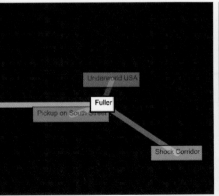
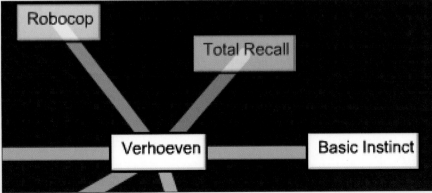

Final polishing

While in the course of most events this works fine, there are still a couple of problems we have to deal with. The first is that if the user clicks one of a node's children before all of the other children have been created, the positioning is messed up. This happens because the instruction to rotate all of the nodes is sent out before the final child / children are created and so the final child / children are left in their original positions. It's actually quite hard to do this, you would have to click just as the node is shooting out from its parent after being created, but it's still best to guard against this.

The second problem is something we have not addressed yet, what to do when a node has its children open and one clicks it. At present if you do this then it closes them and immediately opens them up again – a bit of a redundant exercise. It would be better if the open node closed its children and moved back towards its parent. We'll implement that as well. Both of these things are fairly simple, just a case of adding a couple of extra conditionals to the routines we already have.

Both changes are implemented in the `clickMe` method. To solve the first problem, we add a check to see if the parent node's `opening` property is true when the child node is clicked. If it is then we do not open the node, but set the parent's queued method to `openChild`:

```
clusterNode.prototype.clickMe=function(){
    if(this._parent.opening){
      this._parent.setWait
      (this._parent,"openChild",this)
    }else{
      this._parent.openChild(this)
    }
}
```

Currently nodes only check if they have queued actions when their children have closed. To deal with this we need to add another call to `checkWait`, this time after the node has created all of its children:

```
clusterNode.prototype.addNextKid =
➡ function(){
    this.g++
    if(this.g%2 ==0){
      if(this.kidCount<
      ➡this.kidsArray.length){
        this.createChild(this.kidCount)
        this.kidCount++
      }else{
        delete this.onEnterFrame
        this.opening = false
        this.checkWait()
      }
    }
}
```

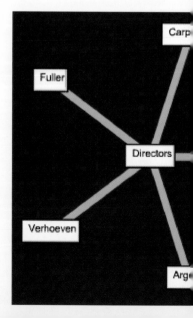

That's the first problem solved. To deal with the second problem, we need to add a second conditional to the `clickMe` method. This time we have to check if the node has one of its children open. If it does then we need to close the node and then queue an action to make the node move back into its parent cluster. We'll also add another conditional to check that the node is not already open before finally calling the `openChild` method:

So the `if` statement checks if the node has an open child, and if so tells it to close and then move back.

The `else` statement makes sure that the node does not already have open children before opening it.

If you run the movie now, or check out `spinner008.fla`, it should be more or less unbreakable.

```
clusterNode.prototype.clickMe=function(){
    if(this._parent.opening){
      this._parent.setWait
      (this._parent,"openChild",this)
    }else{
      if(this.kidOpen){
      this.setWait(this.kidOpen,
      "moveToPosition",this.clusterRadius)
        this.kidOpen.closeKids()
      }else if(this.kidCount<1){
        this._parent.openChild(this)
      }
    }
}
```

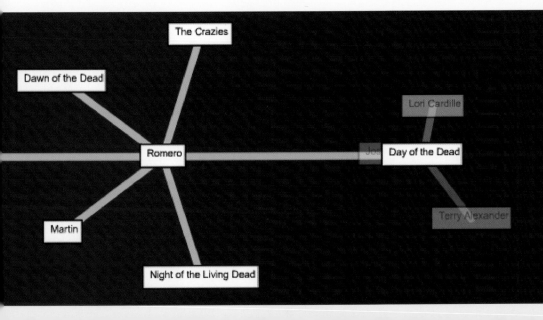

Further thoughts

So now we have a fully working interface. At this stage it would seem appropriate to discuss its strengths and weaknesses.

I would say that in a number of senses it is successful as a navigation device. It is easy to use while still providing novelty. While the user might at first be unsure of what is going to happen when they click on one of the tags, it *is* fairly apparent that that is what they have to do. Upon clicking, the motion that ensues might initially feel odd, but I think that the logic of it shines through. Motion is the key to this. The transition between states underlines the logic of the interface. It feels quite solid and predictable, like a machine. The user is generally aware of both where they are and the alternative routes they could have taken.

While looking at how the interface succeeds, it's important to also acknowledge where the interface fails. While the interface can cope with most structures, if you needed to include 20 categories within another category, you'd quickly encounter problems with the labels overlapping each other. Already one can see this with some of the longer category names. You could try and circumvent this by having each node `swapDepths` when the user rolls over it, but that might look slightly odd and would not meet our aim of legibility.

Also if the interface were more than four levels deep at any point, it would begin to move off the right of the screen. A fairly simple way of solving this would be to have whatever node is currently open centered on stage, and this might also be a fairly pleasing effect visually, adding to the sense of progression. I've included a basic file, called `spinner_centered.fla`, in the download files, demonstrating this with comments wherever I've added any code.

A bigger concern is perhaps the size of the interface. With any interface occupying that much space on the screen, you're in danger of detracting from whatever content there may be. This could possibly work if the content one was dealing with was in floating windows, or you could have the interface fold away when not in use. It would be possible, for instance, to have the subnodes that were not chosen fade out or retract when the navigation is not in use, leaving the nodes that were chosen as a breadcrumb.

The beauty of this interface, as it stands, is that you could easily modify it to suit your own purposes, and that the aesthetics are separate from the data content. It shows how the use of XML can bring data dynamically into your interfaces, allowing you to play with the structure as much as you want.

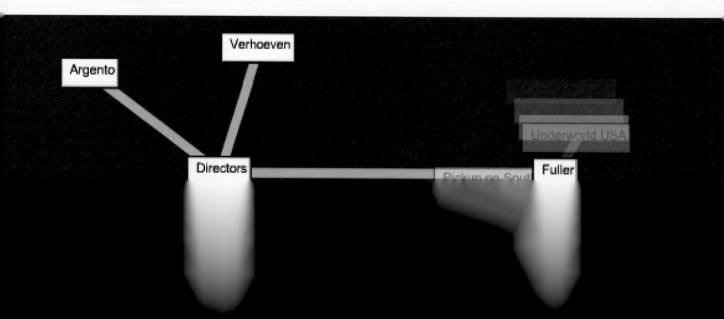

A PHP POWERED SITE

Creating a file browser

One of the greatest problems with web sites today is the lack of consistency in navigation. When we arrive at a site, there's no guarantee that we're going to know how to navigate around it. That's okay if you're willing to explore, but we have users out there who will run away screaming if they don't immediately, intuitively understand how to operate our site.

It was this thought that drove me to create the content of this chapter. I thought to myself, "most people know how to navigate the standard file system in most operating systems". Display of icons, double-click to activate, scroll up and down through the items, and we're set. It's simple.

So, I thought, why not bring that simplicity into a Flash movie? Why not set up my directory structures so that they're logical, clear and intuitive? Then, build a Flash movie that loads the directory structure somehow, and lets the user navigate freely in a way that they're used to.

I set about doing this, and here is the finished result:

This folder happens to be filled with JPG images, which, when double-clicked, open up a little JPG viewer within the window:

This is complete with zoom in / zoom out and download buttons.

Alternatively, we can navigate to a location containing MP3 files:

If we double-click on an MP3 file, an MP3 player opens:

And then of course, if we find any text files, (with the extension `.txt`), then Flash opens up the text file in a text reader window:

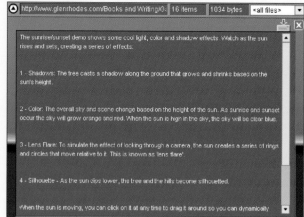

Any other file types, and by default, Flash will open them up in a blank browser window, via the `getURL` action.

Navigation is, of course, accomplished with the use of folder icons, like so:

Double-click on a folder, and we navigate into it, and its contents populate the window.

At the top of the screen is a status bar with several pieces of information, and interface items:

These are, from left to right:

- Navigate Up button – takes us up one level.

- Current location – where we are in the site.

- Number of items – tells us how many items (files/folders) are in this window.

- File size – tells us how big the currently selected item is, in bytes.

- File type – a filter for which type of files we're allowing Flash to show us.

This is, in effect, a complete file system-esque navigation interface, which can be intuitively understood by anyone with a basic understanding of computers. Of course, you can never quite account for every potential user out there, but in terms of my target audience, I'm confident that it is self-explanatory and simple.

Planning the interface

I designed this interface so that any aesthetic aspect can be modified – the design of the background image, the file type icons, the JPG and MP3 viewers and the text viewer can all be changed without affecting the way the interface works. It's also easy to add functionality in order to handle a new file type. It's as simple as adding to the double-click processing routine, which we'll look at in a minute. This means we can create our own types of files, icons and viewers, and the functionality of the entire site can be enhanced, without breaking anything.

So I started my planning by thinking about what function points would have to be added to Flash in order to make all this happen.

- Double-click functionality – Flash detects single-clicks (press and release) but I needed to find out when something had been double-clicked.

- The ability to read the contents of web directories – this would have to be accomplished using a PHP script on the Web server.

- The `FileInfoComponent` – this would be a generic component containing all the functionality and code for handling a particular file type. This object would have to be given a file name and location, and it must know how to respond to a double click, and what to do with the file.

- A general parser function – this would take the contents of a folder and create one instance of the `FileInfoComponent` per file/subfolder within that parent folder. This function must make all the `FileInfoComponent` instances respond, in some way, to a scroll bar, to facilitate scrolling through the files, should they be larger than one screen.

- File type functionality – this needed to be created so that our file types can be handled from within the interface. I would design this for MP3, JPG and TXT.

Double-clicking

Let's get right into it and take a look at how we will accomplish the double-clicking effect. This is a generic double-click handling function.

```
myMovieClip.onMouseDown = function()
{
    if (this.hitTest(_root._xmouse,
_root._ymouse, true))
    {
    this.g = getTimer();

        if (this.firstclick != true || this.g >
    ➥ (this.clicktime + doubleclickspeed))
        {
            this.firstclick = true;
            this.clicktime = this.g;
        }
        else
        {
            if (this.g < this.clicktime +
            this.doubleclickspeed)
            {
            }
            this.firstclick = false;
        }
    }
}
```

As you can see, this function is triggered when the user presses the mouse button, and what we're doing is performing a `hitTest`, to determine if the mouse is over the movie clip when the mouse button is pressed. We're using a movie clip as opposed to a button, as it's not really a button that we're clicking, but an icon (like a file), which is better represented as a movie clip.

When something is double-clicked, we essentially measure the time between the first mouse down and the second mouse down. If they fall within a certain range (defined in the variable `doubleclickspeed`), that's considered to be a double-click. If they fall outside that time range, then it was not a double-click, but two single clicks instead, which do nothing.

We then make sure that it's not the 'first time' clicking the button, or if it has been more than the defined amount of time since this button was last clicked. If so, then we set a flag, `firstclick`, to `true` and set the time of the current click in `clicktime`. If it *was* more than `doubleclickspeed` milliseconds since the last click, then we must consider the double-click to have timed out.

Otherwise, if this was not the first click, and it still falls within the range of `doubleclickspeed`, then we can perform the function or code that we want to have happen on double-click. Once this code has been executed, we must set `firstclick` back to `false` again, so our icon is reset to unclicked and is ready for double-clicking.

Reading the contents of a Web directory

One of the critical aspects of building this interface is actually reading the contents of a directory, or folder of some sort. When creating this interface, I wrote a PHP script, which reads the contents of a folder on a web site, and then returns that information as variables to Flash. Without this vital backbone, everything else would not run.

You can find the PHP script in the download files, called `dirstuff.php`, ready for you to put onto your server and use, plus a file called `script_expo.pdf` which contains a more detailed explanation of the code if you want to dig deeper into the PHP side of things. Obviously a really detailed discussion of the PHP is a bit outside the scope of this chapter, but to briefly understand some key points:

First, we must pass a few parameters to the script, and it will return to us a variable string of filenames, types and sizes.

The parameters that the script expects are:

- `matchDir` – this contains a relative directory from where we would like the file listings. If we specify images, for example, then all files returned by the script will be from the `/images` directory.

- `matchExt` – the file extensions that we would like to display. If we only wanted GIF files to be sent back, then we would send `matchExt` as `gif`.

For example, when we make a call to the script (which is called `dirstuff.php`), we pass parameters with a `LoadVars` object, like so:

```
myLoadVars.load(base + "dirstuff.php?
➡ matchDir=Tutorials&matchExt=*");
```

If we want all files to be returned, then `matchExt` can be set to `*`, or can be completely left out. When the files are returned, they'll be sent back in a string of text, which is divided into name/variable pairs, like so:

```
&file0=.&fsize0=512&file1=..&fsize1=
➡ 512&file2=High Score List.link&
➡ fsize2=48&file3=Hi Score Files.zip&
➡ fsize3=159583&file4=FlashintheCan Game
➡ Talk.pop&fsize4=56&file5=Motion and
➡ Collision slides.swf&fsize5=15499&
```

Each file is passed as a name, `file0`, `file1`, `file2`, and a size, `fsize0`, `fsize1`, `fsize2`. So, in this example, file 5 is called `Motion and Collision slides.swf` and it's 15499 bytes in size.

When this has happened, our directory contents, and the file sizes, have been successfully transmitted to Flash for use with our `FileInfoComponent`, and Flash file browser, which we will move on to building now.

MX specific items

So, now that we're able to load in the contents of a web directory, we need to do some things on the Flash MX side. We're going to be using a few important, and Flash MX specific items – **components** and the LoadVars object.

In our file browser, we're using a custom component called the FFileInfoComponent. Once instantiated and set up, each instance of this component is completely self-sufficient and will respond to double-clicks by performing a context-sensitive action, derived from the file extension of the attached file.

For example, if the instance we click on is representative of a JPG image on the web server, then the component will activate a built-in JPG viewer. When an MP3 file is double-clicked, then the component will activate a built-in Flash MX MP3 player. In fact, we can extend it to handle just about any type of file we wish. By default, if the file type is unknown, then it will be opened up in a web browser window.

To look at the FFileInfoComponent, let's open up filebrowser.fla. From within there, open up the library and scroll down until you see the FileInfoComponent component.

Double-click on the component in the library, or right-click and choose Edit. We'll be presented with something that looks like this:

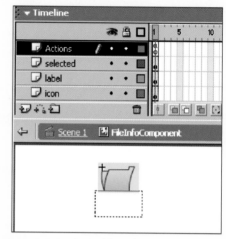

Our component consists of four layers:

- The **Actions** layer contains all the code that makes this otherwise regular movie clip into a component.

- The **selected** layer contains a semitransparent blue movie clip that is used to indicate when a file is selected. When a file is clicked on, it will become selected, and this box will be made visible.

- The **label** layer contains a text field with the instance name 'label'. This is where the filename is drawn.

- The **icon** layer contains a movie clip, or asset, which is simply a multi-framed movie clip. If you want to look at this without moving layers around or looking in the library then lock the selected layer first and then double click on the icon. Each frame contains a different icon that corresponds to a file type. As support for more file types is added, then more frames will be added to this movie clip. It has an instance name, fileInfoIcon.

The filetypes that this version has icons for are GIF, JPEG, MP3, PHP, HTML, XML, TXT, ZIP, FLA, SWF, AS (ActionScript file), and directory, which uses an icon of a folder. Any other file type uses a generic unknown icon.

The main magic comes from the code that's attached to the Actions layer. Once we have our directory read, and all our `FileInfoComponents` placed, it's up to each instance to handle its own behaviors. Let's look at the functionality of the `FileInfoComponent` itself, and then in the next section, we'll look at how it's all put together, and how all the instances are created from the directory information returned by the PHP script.

The FileInfoComponent actions

All the code in this section comes from the Actions layer in the `FileInfoComponent` component itself. Since we're creating a component, we need to define a base class that will handle all the methods and properties associated with each instance. We're going to tie this class to the physical `FileInfoComponent` movie clip, to ultimately create `FFileInfoComponent` – notice the extra F at the beginning to denote our entire component, rather than the instance.

The code begins like so:

```
#initclip
function FileInfoClass ()
{
    this.autoparse();
    this.update();
    this.amSelected = false;
    this.selectedBox._visible = false;
    this.doubleclickspeed = 300;
}
```

This is the constructor function, which is also used to define the name of the class that we're tying to our movie clip. In this case, the class is called `FileInfoClass`. Think of it like creating a new base object, like `String`, `Array`, or `Math` – this class is `FileInfoClass`. We're using the

`#initclip` action to specify that we only want this definition code to be run once, when the component itself is first loaded in the library, and not every time an instance is created.

We'll see later that when each instance of the `FileInfoComponent` is created, several variables are passed into it. These are:

- `xpos` – the x position of the instance.

- `ypos` – the y position of the instance.

- `filename` – the actual name of the file, for example `picture.jpg`, `mysong.mp3`.

- `filePath` – the absolute path of the file, for example `http://www.mysite.com/files/mysong.mp3`

- `fileSize` – the size of the file in bytes.

Since these variables are passed in when the instance itself is created, the variables therefore exist when the constructor function is called. There is also one more variable, `picFrame`, which is assigned by default when the instance is created. In fact, if we look at the library again, right click on the `FileInfoComponent` and choose Component Definition, we can see that four variables are defined by default.

The variables `filename`, `filePath`, `picFrame` and `fileSize` are set to `default.txt`, `/`, `1` and `0` respectively. However, these will not normally be used, as they're overwritten in the `attachMovie` code that is used to create each instance. We'll look more at this in the next section.

So, when an instance of the `FileInfoComponent` is created, there are several initialization steps that we must perform, as we saw in the constructor function.

First, we're calling an internal method called `autoparse`. This is responsible for analyzing the associated filename, and then setting the value of the `picFrame` parameter to the correct frame of the `fileInfoIcon` movie clip.

Once we've got a value for `picFrame`, we call `update`. This is a short function, and it simply tells the `fileInfoIcon` to `gotoAndStop` at `picFrame`. This function also tells the instance to set its `_x` and `_y` parameters to the `xpos` and `ypos` that were set upon initialization. This will physically move the instance on screen. Finally, `update` sets the value of the label to be the filename, stored in the `fileName` variable.

When a `FileInfoComponent` instance is clicked on, it becomes the selected file. We have a flag attached to each instance called `amSelected`. Here, we're setting it to `false`, indicating that it's not selected. This code will make more sense shortly. Next, we're setting the visibility of the `selectedBox` to `false`, and setting the parameter `doubleclickspeed` to 300. The `selectedBox` is used to indicate which file is currently selected, and the `doubleclickspeed` is used to indicate the maximum amount of time allowed for the second click to follow after the first click, in order for it to be considered a successful double-click.

The next line of code, after the `constructor` function, is this:

```
FileInfoClass.prototype = new MovieClip();
```

This is necessary in order for the class to inherit all the events of the `MovieClip` object. Without doing this, there'd be no tie between our class, and events like `onMouseDown`, and `onMouseMove`.

Next, we have the `autoparse` function:

```
FileInfoClass.prototype.autoparse = function ()
{
    this.fTypes = new Object();
    this.fTypes["BAK"] = 10;
    this.fTypes["JPG"] = 2;
    this.fTypes["JPEG"] = 2;
    this.fTypes["GIF"] = 2;
    this.fTypes["HTM"] = 3;
    this.fTypes["HTML"] = 3;
    this.fTypes["XML"] = 3;
    this.fTypes["TXT"] = 4;
    this.fTypes["PHP"] = 5;
    this.fTypes["SWF"] = 6;
    this.fTypes["AS"] = 6;
    this.fTypes["FLA"] = 7;
    this.fTypes["MP3"] = 8;
    this.fTypes["ZIP"] = 9;
    this.fTypes["FOLDER"] = 1;

    var tExt = this.fileName.toUpperCase().
    ➥ split(".")[1];
    if (tExt == undefined &&
    ➥ (this.filesize % 512) == 0) tExt = "FOLDER";

    this.picFrame = this.fTypes[tExt];

    if (isNaN(this.picFrame) ||
    ➥ this.picFrame == undefined)
    this.picFrame = 10;
}
```

This function creates an object called `fTypes` with several properties. Each property is actually a file extension (for example GIF, HTML, ZIP, MP3) and each one has a value that corresponds to a frame in the `fileInfoIcon` movie clip. (Note that I have included BAK for future compatibility – we may later decide to include a BAK icon). What we do here is set `tExt` to be the uppercase extension of the filename attached to this instance.

If the file has no extension, and its file size is an even division of 512, then it is most likely a folder. (This is to do with the way folders are stored...they're not files, so they need only a fixed amount of room. In cases like this, they're usually rounded up to the closest number that's a power of 2, such as 128, 256, 512, so that the storage takes up a whole even number of bytes.) In that case, we set the extension to `FOLDER`, so that we have something to compare with in the `fTypes` object.

We're then setting the `picFrame` property based on the extension with:

```
this.picFrame = this.fTypes[tExt];
```

In the case where there's no matching extension, we set the `picFrame` to `10`, because that's the general image we use for an unknown file type.

Next comes the other function we mentioned earlier, `update`:

```
FileInfoClass.prototype.update = function () {
    this.fileInfoIcon.gotoAndStop(this.picFrame);
    this._x = this.xpos;
    this._y = this.ypos;
    this.label.text = this.fileName;
}
```

The `update` function, as discussed before, simply tells the `fileInfoIcon` to `gotoAndStop(this.picFrame)`, sets the `_x` and `_y` position of the component, and sets the label to `this.fileName`.

These functions are only ever declared once, because of the `#initclip` action, and therefore, all our functions are declared on the prototype object of the `FileInfoClass` class, hence the `FileInfoClass.prototype` before each function name.

The next line of code, after this, is:

```
Object.registerClass("FFileInfoComponent",
 FileInfoClass);
```

This is where we tie our new class, `FileInfoClass`, to the actual component movie clip from the library. In the library, our component is configured to export with the linkage ID `FFileInfoComponent`. Here, we're tying the class and the movie clip together, by using the `registerClass` method of the `Object` object. This is an important line of code. Without this, none of our instances would be alive – their code would not work. They would merely be static movie clips.

Next, we have two functions, `doSelect` and `doDeselect`. As you might have guessed, these are responsible for setting the state of this instance to appear selected, or to remove this state by deselecting it:

```
FileInfoClass.prototype.doSelect =
 function ()
{
    this.amSelected = true;
    this.selectedBox._visible = true;
    _root.titleBar.fileSize.text =
     (this.fileSize) add " bytes";
}

FileInfoClass.prototype.doDeselect =
 function ()
{
    this.amSelected = false;
    this.selectedBox._visible = false;
}
```

We're simply making the `selectedBox` visible or invisible, and setting a flag called `amSelected` to `true` or `false`. One more thing – when a file is selected, we want to display its file size at the top of the window. For this, we have a movie clip called `titleBar`, on the main timeline. While it might not be ideal for a component to depend on a movie clip outside of itself, this seemed like the easiest way to do it here. We could, if we were so inclined, write a function on the `_root` called `updateDisplay`. This function would take the file size as a parameter. Then, once a file is selected, we could call:

```
_root.updateDisplay(this.filesize);
```

and our `updateDisplay` would handle the file size in whatever way our specific application deems fit. We would have to write the `updateDisplay` function, something like this:

```
updateDisplay = function(passedSize)
{
titleBar.fileSize.text = passedSize;
}
```

This way the component itself never has to refer to anything outside of itself except for the `updateDisplay` function. However, these improvements are up to you to take forward.

Within this movie clip, there's a text field with the instance name `fileSize`. We're setting that text to be the size of the associated file, followed by the word bytes.

Next, we have a series of 'getters' and 'setters'. These are functions, which have the sole responsibility of setting the value of certain properties, or getting and returning the value of those properties. They go like so:

```
FileInfoClass.prototype.setType = function (t)
{
    this.picFrame = t;
    this.update();
}

FileInfoClass.prototype.setFileName =
➡ function (n)
{
    this.fileName = n;
    this.update();
}

FileInfoClass.prototype.setFilePath =
➡ function (p)
{
    this.filePath = p;
    this.update();
}

FileInfoClass.prototype.getFileName =
➡ function ()
{
    return (this.fileName);
}

FileInfoClass.prototype.getFilePath =
➡ function ()
{
    return (this.filePath);
}

FileInfoClass.prototype.getType = function ()
{
    return (this.picFrame);
}
```

They should be fairly self-explanatory. For the most part, we don't call these functions directly – rather, methods of the `FileInfoClass` call these getters and setters for internal usage only. They're essentially private functions.

This next function is the core functionality center of the `FileInfoComponent`. This function, called `handleFile`, is responsible for performing the appropriate action associated with each type of file when it is double-clicked. In essence, this decides how to activate, or handle, the file when the user chooses to activate it.

```
FileInfoClass.prototype.handleFile =
➥ function()
{
    stopDrag();
    if (this.picFrame == 1)
    {
        _root.parentdir[_root.dirlevel++] =
        ➥ _root.matchDir;
        _root.matchDir += this.fileName add
        ➥ "/";
        _root.loader2.load (_root.baseURL add
        ➥ "dirstuff.php?matchExt=" add
        ➥ _root.matchExt add "&matchDir="
        ➥ add _root.matchDir);
    }
    else
    {
        var tname = this.fileName.toUpperCase();
        if (tname.indexOf(".JPG") > -1)
        {
            _root.viewwindow._visible = true;
            var destfile = this.filePath add
            ➥ this.fileName;
            _root.viewwindow.blankmc.
            createEmptyMovieClip("holdermc", 0);
            _root.viewwindow.blankmc.holdermc.
            ➥ _y = 14;
            _root.viewwindow.blankmc.holdermc.
            ➥ loadMovie(destfile);
            _root.viewwindow.destfile =
            ➥ destfile;
            _root.viewwindow.jpgtitle.text =
            ➥ this.filename;

            _root.busy = true;
        }
        else if (tname.indexOf(".TXT") > -1)
        {
            txt = new XML();
            txt.onData = function(dat)
            {
```

```
                _root.textfilecontentmc.
                ➥ textfilecontent.text = dat;
                _root.textfilecontentmc._visible =
                ➥ true;
                _root.busy = true;
            }
            var destfile = this.filePath add
            ➥ this.fileName;
            _root.textfilecontentmc.destfile =
            ➥ destfile;
            txt.load(destfile);
        }
        else if (tname.indexOf(".MP3") > -1)
        {
            _root.mp3player._visible = true;
            var destfile = this.filePath add
            ➥ this.fileName;
            _root.mp3player.streamSound
            ➥ (destfile);
        }
        else
        {
            var destfile = this.filePath add
            ➥ this.fileName;
            getURL (destfile, "_blank");
        }
    }
}
```

This function looks at the type of file associated with this `FFileInfoComponent` instance, and then responds to it accordingly.

The first type it looks for is a folder. If an instance is set to be a folder, then it's handled by forcing the entire window to be redrawn, with the new path. First, we check to see that the file type is a folder.

If it is, then we specify the new path by adding / and `this.fileName` onto the current path, which is stored in the variable `_root.matchDir`. We also store the name of the previous path (where we are moving from) in an array called `_root.parentdir`. As we navigate deeper, we need to always know the name of the previous path. So, we add it into this array, and then increment a counter called `_root.dirlevel`. This way, we're keeping a history of previous locations.

Here's the way that `_root.parentdir` would look after navigating in four levels.

`_root.parentdir[0]` : http://www.mysite.com/siteroot/

`_root.parentdir[1]` :
 http://www.mysite.com/siteroot/images/

`_root.parentdir[2]` :
http://www.mysite.com/siteroot/images/photos/

`_root.parentdir[3]` :
http://www.mysite.com/siteroot/images/photos/sunsets/

At this point, `_root.dirlevel` would be 4.

Later, we'll see that when the Navigate Up button is pressed, we decrement `_root.dirlevel`, and then get the contents of the directory at `_root.parentdir` of the new `_root.dirlevel`.

Once our new path is determined and placed in `_root.matchDir`, we call the PHP script to initiate the actual loading of the file structure data from the server, utilizing the parameters `matchExt` and `matchDir`.

We'll see later that `loader2` is a `LoadVars` object, which is responsible for handling incoming data, and then completely formatting and laying out the `FileInfoComponent` instances for the new folder.

Next, we have handlers for JPG, TXT and MP3 files.

- **JPG** – when we handle a JPG file, we're setting a number of properties of a movie clip on the `_root`, called `viewwindow`. This is a simple movie clip that has zoom in/out features, as well as panning of images within its window. We're using the `loadMovie` command to load the JPG directly, as Flash MX now supports this.

- **TXT** – when we double-click on a text file, we want to load the entire text file into a viewer window. This window is actually a movie clip called `_root.textfilecontentmc`. This contains a text field named textfilecontent, and a scroll bar so we can scroll through it. We're using the XML object to load in the entire file as raw text, and then we're displaying that text directly in the text field, without any parsing or processing.

- **MP3** – we have a simple movie clip called mp3player, which is a self-contained streaming MP3 player that has stop and play capability built in, as well as time, title and position display. The player can be dragged around, and there's a little hard-drive icon for people to click on if they want to download the MP3 file.

In all three cases, we're setting a variable called `_root.busy` to be true. This is required so that when the JPG, TXT, or MP3 windows are open, we cannot inadvertently click on a `FileInfoComponent` instance beneath it. The `_root.busy` flag is used in the `onMouseDown` function, as we'll soon see.

Lastly, there's a 'catch all', which handles any unknown file type by sending it to a blank web browser.

Next in our code, we have the onMouseDown function:

```
FileInfoClass.prototype.onMouseDown =
function()
{

 if (!_root.busy)
 {

  this.offx = _root._xmouse - this._x;
  this.offy = _root._ymouse - this._y;

  if (this.hitTest(_root._xmouse,
➥ _root._ymouse, true))
  {

   this.startDrag();
   this.doSelect();

   _root.mousepressed = true;
   _root.mousestartx = _root._xmouse;
   _root.mousestarty = _root._ymouse;

   this.g = getTimer();

   if (this.firstclick != true ||
➥ (this.g > (this.clicktime
➥+ this.doubleclickspeed)))
   {
    this.firstclick = true;
    this.clicktime = this.g;
   }
   else
   {
    if (this.g < this.clicktime +
➥ this.doubleclickspeed)
    {
     this.handleFile();
    }
    this.firstclick = false;
   }
  }
  else
  {
   this.doDeselect();
  }
 }
}
```

This handles the double-clicking that we discussed earlier. There are also a few key differences.

We're making sure that the _root.busy flag is not true – otherwise, this click must be ignored. We're checking to see if the file itself is being clicked on, via the hitTest method, and if so, we're calling our doSelect method. We're also making it draggable by calling the startDrag method. When we press the mouse button down, we want to also grab onto the file, and move it around, if we so desire. Finally, if this is a double click, then we call the handleFile method.

If the hitTest was false, then we call doDeselect. This means that only one file will be selected at a time, because unless we're clicking on a file, it'll deselect itself, and since we only have one mouse cursor on screen, we'll only ever be hitTesting with one file (unless they're stacked on top of each other, but then, startDrag will only drag one item at a time, anyway).

We then have one more function:

```
FileInfoClass.prototype.onMouseUp =
➥ function()
{
   this.stopDrag();
   _root.mousepressed = false;
}
```

When the mouse is released, we want to stop all dragging, and set the mousepressed flag to false.

Lastly, we finish off with:

```
#endinitclip
```

This indicates that this is the end of the class definition.

Now we've seen the code attached to the FileInfoComponent, and how to send the contents of a directory with PHP, let's look at how to tie it all together, and parse the variables to create the directory layout on screen.

Setting it all up

When the file browser first starts up, we initialize several variables and set properties about certain movie clips. Our initialization code, which is located on the Actions layer of the main timeline, looks like this:

```
numFilesLoaded = 0;
viewwindow._visible = false;
textfilecontentmc._visible = false;
mp3Player._visible = false;
parentdir = new Array();
dirlevel = 0;
filesPerRow = 7;
xspace = 75;
yspace = 80;
xadd = 8;
yadd = 49;
busy = false;
```

We're hiding the JPG viewer, text file viewer and MP3 player. We're also creating the parentdir array (discussed in the previous section).

In addition to this, we're setting five variables:

- filesPerRow – the number of file icons to display in one horizontal row on screen.

- xspace – the amount of horizontal space between each FileInfoComponent instance.

- yspace – the amount of vertical space between each row.

- xadd – the amount to add to the _x position of each instance. Used to offset the files from the screen edge.

- yadd – similar to xadd, but for the _y axis.

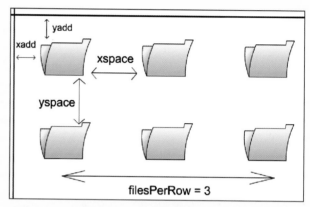

We're then setting the busy flag to false. This is used to determine when to ignore clicks, or process them.

Next, we start defining the variables and objects that are necessary in order to facilitate our server communication:

```
if (baseURL == undefined) baseURL =
➥ "http://www.mysite.com/";
rootDir = matchDir = "";
matchExt = "*";
loader2 = new LoadVars();
loader2.load (baseURL add
➥ "dirstuff.php?matchExt=" add matchExt
➥ add "&matchDir=" add matchDir);
```

Here, we're setting up the baseURL for our website, and defining the extension that we're going to be matching against. When we set matchExt to "*" by default, this means we want to request all files. We're also creating a LoadVars object, called loader2. Once it's created, we immediately initiate a load, calling our dirstuff.php script, with the necessary parameters – matchExt and matchDir. These are the same parameters mentioned in the section of this chapter in which we covered the PHP script.

When the data comes back from the server, the loader2 LoadVars object will trigger the callback function, onLoad. This is where all our component instances are created and laid out.

The function is as follows:

```
loader2.onLoad = function (success)
{
    for (var i = 0; i < numFilesLoaded; i++)
    {
        _root.anchor["file" add i].removeMovieClip();
    }

    var n = numFilesLoaded = 0;
    var numpassed = 0;

    while (this["file" add n] != null)
    {

        if (this["file" add n] != "." &&
        ➥ this["file" add n] != "..")
        {

anchor.attachMovie("FFileInfoComponent",
➥ "file" add numpassed, numpassed + 10, {
➥ xpos : (numpassed % filesPerRow) *
➥ xspace + xadd, ypos : Math.floor
➥ (numpassed / filesPerRow) * yspace +
➥ yadd, fileName : this["file" add n],
➥ filePath : baseURL add "site/" add
➥matchDir, fileSize : this["fsize" add n]});

            numpassed++;
        }
        this["file" add n] = null;
        n++;
    }

    numFilesLoaded = numpassed;

    filescroll.setScrollProperties(400, 0,
    ➥ Math.floor(numpassed / filesPerRow) *
    ➥ yspace + yadd - 300);

    anchor._y = 0;
    filescroll.setScrollPosition(0);

    titleBar.fileCount.text = numpassed add
    ➥ " items";
    titleBar.pathName.text = baseURL add
    ➥ matchDir;
}
```

This function is simple, yet it has the authoritative control over the entire bridge between Flash MX and the PHP script. The first thing we're doing is erasing any previously created instances of the FFileInfoComponent, with this code:

```
for (var i = 0; i < numFilesLoaded; i++)
{
    _root.anchor["file" add
i].removeMovieClip();
}
```

numFilesLoaded is a variable used to count how many files have been returned to us by the PHP script, and it's conveniently used later to indicate how many files are in the current display.

Once that's done, we have to zero a few counter variables (including numFilesLoaded).

At this point, we begin stepping through the returned variables, which, if we recall, will be in the form file0, file1, file2, file3, and fsize0, fsize1, fsize2, fsize3, and so on.

```
while (this["file" add n] != null)
{
```

Then, we ensure that the file is not a "." or a ".." – special files which mean self and parent, and are used for navigation in a FTP client, telnet or command prompt.

```
if (this["file" add n] != "." &&
this["file" add n] != "..")
{
```

If this is the case, then we proceed with the big command:

```
anchor.attachMovie("FFileInfoComponent",
➡ "file" add numpassed, numpassed + 10, {
➡ xpos : (numpassed % filesPerRow) *
➡ xspace + xadd, ypos :
➡ Math.floor(numpassed / filesPerRow) *
➡ yspace + yadd, fileName : this["file"
➡ add n], filePath : baseURL add "site/"
➡ add matchDir, fileSize : this["fsize"
➡ add n]});
```

What does all this mean? It's quite simple really. We have a movie clip on the main timeline called anchor, and we're using the attachMovie command to attach all our instances of the FFileInfoComponent to it. This way, when we move anchor around the stage, all the files will move with it – a convenient scrolling tool.

We're creating instances of the FFileInfoComponent, with the names file0, file1, file2, file3, and so on. The next parameter is the depth level, which we're setting to numpassed + 10, which means that the depth will be 10, 11, 12, 13, and so on.

The third parameter in the attachMovie function is an object that contains initial values to be set in the new instance. We're setting their initial xpos and ypos essentially like so:

```
xpos = (numpassed % filesPerRow) * xspace + xadd;
ypos = Math.floor(numpassed /
➡filesPerRow) * yspace + yadd;
```

We're also passing in the filename, file path and the file size. Once the instance is created, we continue on until all the incoming data has been parsed. Then, we set numFilesLoaded to be numpassed, which will actually be the number of files passed in.

We're then setting the scroll properties of the scrollbar called filescroll, which will be used to move the files up and down, should the file list be longer than one screen. The setScrollProperties method takes three parameters:

- pageSize – this defines how big the 'thumb' is (the square that we slide up and down). Its size depends on a ratio of the next two parameters.

- minPos – this is the value of the minimum location of the scrollbar. Usually, this is 0. This means that when the scrollbar is at the absolute top, and we use the getScrollPosition method, it's this value that will be returned.

- maxPos – the opposite of minPos. This is the value at the absolute bottom of the scrollbar.

If the minPos was 0, and the maxPos was 1, then the scrollbar would only have two possible values, 0 or 1, depending upon where the thumb was. In this case, we could say that the scrollbar itself is '2' in length. So, if we set the pageSize to be 1 then the thumb will take up exactly 50% of the scrollbar. If our minPos was 0 and our maxPos was 100, on the other hand, and our pageSize was still 1, then the thumb would be a hundredth of the size of the scrollbar.

So, we set our scroll properties like so:

```
filescroll.setScrollProperties(400, 0,
➡Math.floor(numpassed / filesPerRow) *
➡yspace + yadd - 300);

anchor._y = 0;
filescroll.setScrollPosition(0);

titleBar.fileCount.text = numpassed add
➡" items";
titleBar.pathName.text = baseURL add
➡matchDir;
```

We're then setting the scroll position to be 0 (so the scrollbar is scrolled to its absolute top). Then finally, we're setting two things in the title bar; the number of files visible (`items`) and the path of that particular folder, like in the top of this image:

That's the end of the `loader2.onLoad` function.

When the Navigate up button is pressed, to take us back up a level, the following code, attached to the Navigate up button, is run:

```
_root.matchDir = _root.parentdir[–
➥_root.dirlevel];
_root.loader2.load (_root.baseURL add
➥"dirstuff.php?matchExt=" add
➥_root.matchExt add "&matchDir=" add
➥_root.matchDir);
```

This code moves back in the `parentdir` array, to the previous directory, and then reissues the `loader2.load` function.

Now, back to the scrolling. In order to facilitate this – to bring it to life – we use the following code:

```
filescroll.setChangeHandler ("scrolling");

scrolling = function()
{
   _root.anchor._y = -
➥filescroll.getScrollPosition();
}
```

It's very simple, thanks to the use of `anchor`. We're telling the scrollbar to call the function `scrolling`, whenever the thumb is moved, or 'scrolled'. By taking the current scroll position (the value returned by the scrollbar) and applying it to the `_y` parameter of the anchor, all our files will move up or down, as the scrollbar is moved.

The rest

The remaining interface items consist of the JPG viewer, the text file viewer and the MP3 player. As cool as they are, however, they're not the focus of this chapter, which is supposed to illustrate the cool file interface, and not get into players and viewers as well. Feel free to explore and learn the code – it's all very simple. The most complicated code is the MP3 player, which handles streaming and time display in order to play properly. The other two – JPG and text file – are actually controlled, for the most part, by the `handleFile` function in the `FileInfoComponent` itself.

One of the nice things about this interface is that it's really quite easy to change the graphics as we see fit. As we saw earlier, each frame of this movie clip corresponds to a different file type icon.

Changing the images is as simple as editing the `fileInfoIcon` movie clip within the `FileInfoComponent` assets folder in the library.

The interface can be expanded as desired, and possibly integrated with other elements on the stage. To see this in action, take a look at my site, www.glenrhodes.com. Although the engine is the same as that presented here, I have recently updated it to change the aesthetics, as seen here.

Rather than making graphics that are reminiscent of files and computer systems, perhaps we could use an image of a cookie jar, or any other item to represent 'folders'. Within those, rather than have file icons, we could change the icons to cookies, so that our file browser consists of cookies within cookie jars. The iterations are endless – here is another version I came up with.

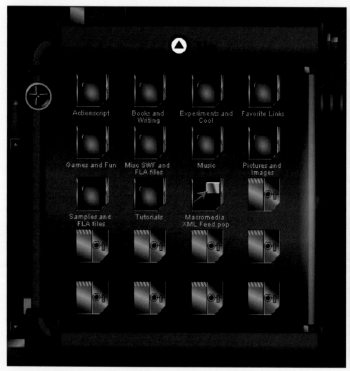

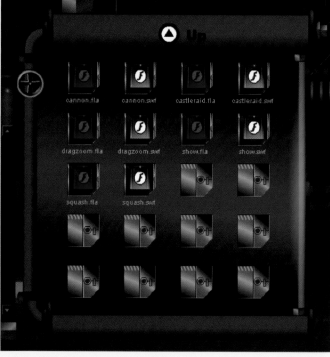

PLANNING SITE STICKINESS

We've had a look at a few methods of creating inspiring sites and interfaces, but "inspiring" can really only go so far in keeping your visitors interested. How do we go beyond that? One of the most desirable tricks in web design is how to make people come back to a site on a regular basis. In this chapter we're going to look at creating a feature that is responsive to each individual user.

Now of course there are lots and lots of ways that we could choose to represent this in our Flash movies, such as the simple but rather dry method of displaying a text field that says "It has been X days since your last visit". However, I decided that I would be a bit more creative here, and use an organic concept, something that grows and shrinks according to environmental conditions, to show how often a user is coming back to your site.

We're going to use the idea of a houseplant that will start out with small brown leaves. If the user visits the site every day, their plant will grow and become a nice healthy green. In the course of creating this, we'll look at some exciting new features of Flash MX that make our programming job a lot easier, some of which aren't well documented (heck, some of them weren't even mentioned in the original MX Help files at all!).

User information and the shared object feature

So, the problem: we need to track how often a user is coming back to our site. We can then use the drawing API to make a plant that will grow or shrink in size and change color, depending on how frequently the site is visited.

So, how do we track and store this information? Well, I could batter you with a host of workable solutions: PHP, ASP, ColdFusion MX, PERL, or MySQL. While these could provide a very solid and robust solution to the problem at hand, it would in most instances require a whole lot more learning, and the possibility of having to install and configure some daunting server software in order to make the idea work.

So why make things complicated and difficult for yourself when there's an easier road to take? Follow me now, intrepid reader, into the mysterious world known as the **shared object**...

This awesome new feature of Flash MX is hardly known about at all, much less written about in practical ways. You won't find it in the documentation that came with the early releases of MX, and it's because of this that you won't find too many examples out there on how to use it either.

Shared objects allow you to store data in several different forms in a special location on the user's computer so you can easily retrieve that information at a later date. It's the same as a cookie, only much, much more powerful.

Now, one thing you should be aware of: when a user first encounters your site, the Flash Player alerts the user to the fact that the SWF wishes to save data to their machine with a shared object, and prompts the user to allow or disallow this to happen. If the user disallows it, you won't be able to store and retrieve any information in your Flash movie. It's not advisable to make your movies critically reliant on the shared object – ensure that if a user disallows the use of them on their machine your movie will still work alright.

The movie we're going to make will run ok without permission to use the shared object, but the plant won't grow or shrink in size – the user will always just have a small brown plant on the stage of the movie. And, quite frankly, it's all they deserve, after my hard work.

Saving information using shared objects

By using ActionScript to create a shared object, the Flash Player saves a small file on the user's computer with a `.sol` extension. This file can be used to store all manner of information in the form of variable strings and numbers, arrays, and even objects like XML.

At a glance, both saving and retrieving data from a shared object looks much the same. To save data to a shared object file, we write some ActionScript that looks like the following:

```
savedObj = sharedObject.getLocal ("myFirstFlashCookie");
savedObj.data.storedVariable = "hello world!";
savedObj.data.storedNumber = 123456;
savedObj.data.storedArray = myArray;
savedObj.flush();
```

You can replace the name of the `sharedObject` instance with anything you like, in this case it's `savedObj`, and you can also replace the name of each property of the `sharedObject`, which in our case is `storedVariable`, `storedNumber`, and `storedArray`. What you cannot change is the `sharedObject` method named `data`, which appears in the middle part of each line. If you do change this, your `sharedObject` simply will not work.

The last little line of code as seen above – `savedObj.flush();` tells the Flash Player to write the properties we specified and their values into the `sharedObject` file called `myFirstFlashCookie`. As you can see, you can store strings, numbers, arrays, almost anything you like inside the shared object. Cool, huh?

To retrieve the information we stored using the previous piece of code, we write the following:

```
retrievedObj = sharedObject.getLocal("myFirstFlashCookie");
_root.myVar = retrievedObj.data.storedVariable;
_root.myNumber = retrievedObj.data.storedNumber;
_root.myArray = retrievedObj.data.myArray();
```

Simple! First we save a property of the shared object called `storedVariable` to the `sharedObject` file on our computer, then when we retrieve the information from the file, we create a new variable called `_root.myVar`, whose value we make equal to `retrievedObj.storedVariable`.

Starting on the code

As a good start-out example, we're going to use this idea to store the time and date at which a user last visited the site, and display our plant graphic growing or shrinking in size depending on how frequently the user visits our site.

Open the file `stickiness.fla` from the download files and select the empty movie clip named **plant** at the top left of the stage. Go into Edit in Place mode. This movie clip (with an instance name of plant or _root.plant) contains three layers, two of which actually contain code. Let's look at the shared objects by taking a look at the ActionScript on the layer named Date Actions. This layer is the one we'll use to store all the code required to send and retrieve information about the visitor frequency.

We start with the following piece of code on the Date Actions layer:

```
myDate = new Date();
currentTime = myDate.getTime();
```

Using the built-in `Date` object, we create a new instance of the `Date` object and call it `myDate`. We then create a variable called `currentTime` and give it a value equal to the `getTime` method of the `Date` object. The `getTime` method gets the current UTC (Universal Time, or Greenwich Mean Time) time – the number of milliseconds that have elapsed since January 1, 1970. We're going to use this number to compare the time in milliseconds between any two consecutive visits, in order to tell how long it has been between visits for a user.

Normally you would save data to a `sharedObject` file before retrieving it, but in our particular case, we want to retrieve the information from the shared object before we write to it, otherwise we'll keep overwriting the old date data with the new date data before we've had a chance to make a comparison of the two. First we create a function called `getLastVisit` which we execute to see when the user was at our site last:

```
function getLastVisit() {
    retrievedObj = sharedObject.getLocal
➡ ("timeHolder");
    lastVisited = retrievedObj.data.lastVisit;
    plantSize = retrievedObj.data.plantSize;
    firstVisit = retrievedObj.data. firstVisit;
    timeDifference = Math.round
➡ ((currentTime-lastVisited)/3600000);
    daysSinceLastVisit = Math.ceil
➡ (timeDifference/24);
}
```

The function begins by creating a new instance of the shared object. This instance has the name `retrievedObj`. So we create a new instance of the `sharedObject` object, and get information from the `sharedObject` file called `timeHolder`.

We then create some variables to temporarily store information from the retrieved `sharedObject`. These are:

- `lastVisited` – used to tell us in milliseconds the time of the last visit.

- `plantSize` – a number used to represent how big or small the plant will be.

- `firstVisit` – a Boolean used to tell us whether this is the very first visit or not.

- `timeDifference` – gives us the number of hours in total since the last visit.

- `daysSinceLastVisit` – rounds up the number of days since the last visit.

After this, we call the function `getLastVisit`:

```
getLastVisit();
```

Now that we've retrieved the information from the shared object with our function, it's time to do some calculations based on the numbers we've received.

First we need to check to see if our shared object file exists, confirming whether or not the user has visited our site before. We do this using an `if` statement:

```
if(!firstVisit){
  plantSize = 0;
  daysSinceLastVisit = 0;
  firstVisit = 1;
}
```

It checks to see if a variable named `firstVisit` has any value at all, rather than being undefined. In the function `getLastVisit`, we tell `firstVisit` to equal `retrievedObj.data.firstVisit`. If the user has never been to the site before, the shared object file `timeHolder` won't exist on their computer, and so when we try to retrieve the value of `retrievedObj.firstVisit`, it will be undefined. If this is the first visit by the user, we set the variable `plantSize` to 0, set the variable `daysSinceLastVisit` to 0, and the variable `firstVisit` to 1.

The second `if` statement in our code on the Date Actions layer checks to see how long it has been since the user's last visit, if they have been to the site before:

```
if((daysSinceLastVisit == 0) &&
➥(plantSize < 50)){
  plantSize ++;
} else if ((daysSinceLastVisit > 0) &&
➥(plantSize > 0)){
  plantSize -= daysSinceLastVisit;
}
```

It allows us to make the plant either grow or shrink depending on when the user was here last. If the number of days since the last visit was 0 (meaning the user was here in the last 24 hours), we'll make the plant grow in size by a factor of 1 by saying `plantSize++`, with a maximum size of 50. Otherwise, if the number of days since the last visit is greater than 0 (meaning it's been more than one day or 24 hour period since the last visit), we're going to penalize the user for not visiting often enough and make their plant wilt in size and color by setting the variable `plantSize` to decrease by one for every day it has been since they were here last.

Now that we have used all the information about the user's last time of visit to set the size of the plant accordingly, it's time to save the current time and a few other variables to the user's `sharedObject` file so it can be accessed the next time they visit our site. We do all this by writing a very short and neat function called `saveTime`:

```
function saveTime() {
  savedObj = sharedObject.getLocal
  ➥("timeHolder");
  savedObj.data.lastVisit = currentTime;
  savedObj.data.plantSize = plantSize;
  savedObj.data.firstVisit = firstVisit;
  savedObj.flush();
}
```

Again, just like we did with the function `getLastVisit`, we create another instance of the `sharedObject` object. To save confusion with the first instance we created in `getLastVisit`, we'll call this one `savedObj`. We're going to set three custom properties for the `savedObj` instance:

- `savedObj.data.lastVisit` – the current UTC (Universal Time) time in milliseconds.

- `savedObj.data.plantSize` – a number representing the new size of the plant.

- `savedObj.data.firstVisit` – tells us that the user has visited the site before.

The last line inside the function:

```
savedObj.flush();
```

saves the data to the `sharedObject` file on the user's computer for retrieval the next time they come back. We then execute the `saveTime` function by writing on the next line:

```
saveTime();
```

Watering the leaves (or: Converting RGB colors to Hex values)

The last function on this layer, `convertColors`, is a neat little piece of code you might find useful in many other projects as well. Let's take a look at the code and then talk about what it does:

```
function convertColors(varName, varR,
➡ varG, varB) {
  newR = varR.toString(16);
  if (newR == 0) { newR="00" };
  newG = varG.toString(16);
  if (newG == 0) { newG="00" };
  newB = varB.toString(16);
  if (newB == 0) { newB="00" };
  this[varName] = ("0x" add newR add newG
➡ add newB);
}
```

This function allows us to dynamically create variables whose values are equivalent to hex values – the letter / number combinations used on the web when referencing colors. For example, #000000 is black, #FFCC00 is orange, and #FFFFFF is white. By passing the RGB values of the colors we want to convert into the function, we can output the hex value equivalent of those same RGB numbers and use them in the drawing API. Doing this will allow us to dynamically change the color of the plant from brown to green. Lush!

Into the function `convertColors` we'll pass a name for the variable we'll create, as well as three numerical values representing the red, green, and blue values ranging between 0 and 255 that make up the color we want. Inside the function we create a temporary variable for the red, green, and blue values, and convert them to base 16 using the `toString(16)` method. Doing this converts the number to a string.

For example if we pass the number 200 into the `string(16)` method for the variable `newR`, the string `c8` is returned, and if we do the same for `newG` by passing in the number 150, we get back the string `96`, and lastly of course we need a hex string value for blue, so we pass a value of 0 into the function for `newB`, and we get back `0`. Now seeing as we need a six character string for the hex color, we do a small check on each new variable to see if the string returned equals 0, and if it does we make it equal to 00.

Lastly we dynamically create the variable to store the final color.

We want our plant to start as a fairly unhealthy looking brown color, and it's rather fortunate for us that the RGB values for brown and the RGB values for a bright healthy green can be easily transformed into a neat little formula that allows us to dynamically change the color of the plant based on the frequency of user visits.

The RGB values of the brown that we'll use are:

- Red: 200
- Green: 150
- Blue: 0

And the RGB values for the healthy bright green are:

- Red: 150
- Green: 200
- Blue: 0

As you can see, reducing the Red value and increasing the Green value of our plant by the variable plantSize as the user visits the site will conveniently turn the plant from brown to green!

To execute the function and create a variable whose value is a hex string representing a color that we'll use to color our plant, we write:

```
convertColors("fillColor", (200-plantSize),
➥ (150+plantSize), 0);
```

We end up with a variable named fillColor that has a string value of 0xC39B00. Then we do the same again to store the color for the outline of the plant:

```
convertColors("outlineColor",(150-
➥ plantSize),(100+plantSize),0);
```

which gives us a variable named outlineColor, which has a string value of 0x906A00.

So now we've created some variables to store the value of the outline and fill colors of the plant, and seeing as we've created this neat little function already, we may as well use it to create the colors for the pot that the plant sits in, by dynamically creating the variables potFill and potColor:

```
convertColors("potOutline", 0, 102, 255);
convertColors("potFill", 0, 153, 255);
```

Animating the plant

Now we have set all this up, we can go ahead and animate our plant. The very last line of code on the Date Actions layer tells Flash to make the plant using a function called (funnily enough...) makeThePlant. The code looks like:

```
makeThePlant();
```

This invokes a function on the Plant Actions layer which uses the drawing API to draw and animate our plant.

We now move up to the code on the Plant Actions layer in our plant movie clip. This might look complicated, and well... it is. Sort of. The reason some of the code looks verbose is that the plant movie clip is made to simply drag and drop on to the main timeline of any movie that you might be making, and it will work. Not only that, you can add or remove individual leaves on the plant in very little time at all, and as such the code can be said to be scalable and dynamic – all the things we like in an efficient piece of code. That's not to say that the ActionScript on the Plant Actions layer couldn't be further refined (I'm fairly certain that it can), but I wrote it like this so it could be understood in a logical way and you'd learn about some great new features in MX ActionScript.

First up inside the Plant Actions layer, we create a two-dimensional array – an array whose elements are made up of a series of other arrays. Think of it as a nested array, if you will. Our array map, or two-dimensional array looks like this:

```
leafMap = new Array( ["leaf0", "left", 1,
➥ 130, 300, 75, 200, 130, 230, 10], ["leaf1",
➥ "right", 2, 130, 300, 180, 225, 130,
➥ 200,20], ["leaf2", "right", 3, 130, 300,
➥ 140, 170, 130, 200, 20], ["leaf3", "left",
➥ 4, 130, 300, 115, 180, 130, 200, 10],
➥ ["leaf4", "left", 5, 130, 300, 80, 200,
➥ 135, 155, 20], ["leaf5", "left", 6, 130,
➥ 300, 70, 230, 130, 200, 10],
➥ ["leaf6", "right", 7, 130, 300, 170,
➥ 200, 130, 200, 20]);
```

Let's take it apart and see what makes it tick. Take a look at the first element of the array. If we were to do a trace on the first element, it'd look something like:

```
trace( leafMap[0] );
```

and it would output:

```
"leaf0", "left", 1, 130, 300, 75, 200,
➥130, 230, 10
```

As you can see from this, the value of the first element in the array is... another array! That's all there is to it. If we wanted to get the first element out of the sub-array that makes up the first element of our array, we'd do this:

```
trace(leafMap[0][0]);
```

and it would output:

```
leaf0
```

To get the next element in the first sub-array, we'd type:

```
trace(leafMap[0][1]);
```

and it would output:

```
left
```

What we're effectively doing here is using an array to store a bunch of other sub-arrays containing unique information about each leaf inside it. So in this way, we have a "map" of what our plant is going to look like. The number of elements in the main array tells us how many leaves we're going to make, and each element contains a sub-array which stores information about the name for each leaf move clip we're going to generate, as well as the starting position of that leaf, the end point for each curve of the leaf, and so on.

The next piece of code takes us into Object-Oriented Programming territory. It's beyond the scope of this chapter to go too far in-depth about OOP in Flash. Suffice to say you're probably used to using built-in objects in Flash already. One of the more common built-in objects that you might be using is the `MovieClip` object, which has "properties" like `MovieClip._x` and `MovieClip._y` and `MovieClip._name`, and its own "methods" such as `MovieClip.gotoAndPlay` and `MovieClip.stop`. Some other objects that we've used so far in this movie are the `sharedObject` object, whose properties we define when we say `savedObj.data.firstVist = "something"`. We also used the `Date` object at the very beginning of this chapter when we got the time in milliseconds by calling the date method `myDate.getTime()`.

To expand OOP principles a little further, I'll explain some of the more important terminology associated with OOP by once again using the `MovieClip` object as an example:

- We have the predefined **Object** itself, called the `MovieClip` object.

- When we create a new movie clip, we are actually making a new **instance** of that `MovieClip` object (hence why we give movie clips instance names).

- When we create a new movie clip, whether by duplicating one that already exists, or using the `attachMovie` command or the `createEmptyMovieClip` action, the code used to create the new `MovieClip` instance is called a **constructor**.

- The `MovieClip` object that is already built in to Flash has pre-defined **properties**, such as `_x`, `_y`, `_name`, `_xscale`, and `_alpha`.

- The `MovieClip` object also has its own **methods**, such as `play`, `stop`, `startDrag`, and `loadMovie`.

As well as the built-in objects like `MovieClip` (buttons and text fields are now also objects in MX, each with their own properties and methods), we can also create our own custom objects to act as storage containers. Looking at our plant, we can see that the plant is made up of seven leaves, with each leaf having its own unique values in its properties. Let's look at how we can take an object-oriented approach to storing information about a particular leaf instance.

We start by writing down the type of information that we want to store for each leaf. We want to store things like:

- The name for the leaf instance.

- The direction the leaf curls in – whether left or right.

- The level that the movie clip for each leaf is sitting on.

- The thickness of the leaf.

Now because there is no built-in object in Flash that stores this specific information about each leaf, we are going to create our own custom object. How do we do this? By writing, or **defining**, our own **class** which will act as a constructor for the object we are creating.

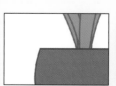

8

Looking at the ActionScript on the Plant Actions layer, the next piece of code that we have in our movie creates our own custom class called Leaf, which in turn creates a custom instance of the `Leaf` object when we call the class function further on in the code. Inside the class constructor function we also define which properties belong to the `Leaf` object as well. Let's look at the code:

```
Leaf = function ( name, dir, levelNum,
➡ originX, originY, stopX, stopY,
➡ controlX, controlY, thickness) {
  this.name = name;
  this.dir = dir;
  this.levelNum = levelNum;
  this.originX = originX;
  this.originY = originY;
  if (dir =="left") {
    this.stopX = stopX - plantSize;
  }else if (dir =="right") {
    this.stopX = stopX + plantSize;
  }
  this.stopY = stopY - plantSize;
  this.controlX = controlX;
  this.controlY = controlY;
  this.thickness = thickness;
  this.numStepsX = Math.abs(((originX-
➡ stopX)/100));
  this.numStepsY = Math.abs(((originY-
➡ stopY)/100));
  this.ID = setInterval(drawLeaf, 10,
➡ this.name, this.dir, this.levelNum,
➡ this.originX, this.originY, this.stopX,
➡ this.stopY, this.controlX,
➡ this.controlY, this.thickness);
};
```

Even though the first line of the above code looks like a function, it is actually a class definition which in turn constructs a custom object when the class is invoked. The first line of code starts the class which will make the Leaf object, and the following lines of ActionScript underneath declare and define the properties that the `Leaf` object will have. We start each property declaration with a `this` to denote that the property exists for each unique instance that is being created – in other words, this instance that is being created.

Take a look at the arguments inside the class function (`name`, `dir`, `levelNum`, and so on). Each one of these arguments represents an element in the sub-array which in turn makes up our `leafMap` array. Let's look again at the first element in the `leafMap` array:

```
["leaf0", "left", 1, 250, 400, 195, 300, 250,
➡ 330, 10]
```

and another look at the arguments (or parameters) in our Leaf class constructor function:

```
(name, dir, levelNum, originX, originY, stopX,
➡ stopY, controlX, controlY, thickness) {
```

You've probably already guessed by now that each element inside the `leafMap` sub-array corresponds exactly to an argument inside the `Leaf` class definition. `leaf0` corresponds to `name`, `left` corresponds to `dir` and so on. Here is what all of these arguments are for and why they're there.

- `name` – the name of the movie clip we're going to draw inside with the API.

- `dir` – whether the leaf curls out to the left or to the right of its starting point.

- `levelNum` – the level that each leaf movie clip is going to be on.

- `originX` – the starting x position of the leaf movie clip.

- `originY` – the starting y position of the leaf movie clip.

- stopX – the end x point for the tip of each leaf.

- stopY – the end y point for the tip of each leaf.

- controlX – the x position of the control point for the curved outline of each leaf.

- controlY – the y position of the control point for the curved outline of each leaf.

- thickness – a number used to make each leaf thinner or thicker.

We're going to leave the Leaf class for a moment and skip to the next function, called makeThePlant. This is where we call the Leaf class constructor function to make new instances of the Leaf object:

```
function makeThePlant () {
    movieHeight = _parent._height;
    makePot();
    for (x=0; x<(leafMap.length); x++) {
      temp = "leaf"+x+"Obj";
      this[temp] = new Leaf(leafMap[x][0],
    ➥ leafMap[x][1], leafMap[x][2],
    ➥ leafMap[x][3], leafMap[x][4],
    ➥ leafMap[x][5], leafMap[x][6],
    ➥ leafMap[x][7], leafMap[x][8],
    ➥ leafMap[x][9], leafMap[x][10]);
    }
}
```

The makeThePlant function firstly sets a variable called movieHeight, which we'll use at the very end of the movie, then executes another function called makePot, which creates the pot our plant sits in. We'll talk about that function a bit later. As you can see, the next few lines of ActionScript inside the makeThePlant function consist of a simple for loop that executes or loops for as many elements as there are in the leafMap array. In this case there are seven elements in the array. We can tell how many elements there are by accessing the array method called length. If we do a trace on leafMap.length; a value of 6 would be displayed in the output window.

(Remember that arrays start counting at 0, so the length of the array is actually 7 even though it outputs 6).

The code inside the for loop is where the object-oriented approach all starts to come together and hopefully makes some sense. To start with all we do is create a temporary variable to store the instance name of the Leaf object we're going to create. To avoid any confusion between the instance name of the Leaf object we're creating, leaf[x]Obj, and the name of the movie clip leaf[x] we'll need to create to draw the leaf in, we use the variable temp to store a string that will look like leaf0Obj the first time the loop is run, and leaf1Obj the next time, and so on.

The next line is where we create the instance of the Leaf object by calling the Leaf class constructor, and we use the variable temp to give that instance a name.

To summarize, what we've done is made a new instance of the Leaf object, and called the first one in the loop leaf0Obj, the second one leaf1Obj and so on until we have seven unique instances of the custom Leaf object. When we say inside the loop:

```
this[temp] = new Leaf(leafMap[x][0],
```

what we're actually doing is creating a new instance of the Leaf object called leaf0Obj, and by passing in all of the elements from the corresponding sub-array in our leafMap array into the Leaf constructor function, we give Leaf0Obj a whole bunch of properties with unique values. After doing this, we could do a trace on any or all of these properties like so:

```
trace(leaf0Obj.name + "," + leaf0Obj.dir);
```

This would output:

```
leaf0, left
```

Hopefully now you can see how the combination of storing all the data about each leaf in an array and passing that same information into a custom class allows us to easily make new instances of a leaf each with its own unique properties simply by adding more information to the `leafMap` array. Adding new properties for each leaf also only requires changes to just a few lines of code inside the class constructor function.

To finish up this part of the code, we now go back and look inside the `Leaf` class constructor to see what makes it tick. It's pretty straightforward. Looking at the first argument, `name`, that we passed into the constructor function, when we create our instance of the `Leaf` object we give it a property called `name`, with a unique value, by saying something like:

```
this.name = name;
```

What the above line of code does is say to the `Leaf` object instance create a property for me (`this` – meaning this instance) called `name`, and give it a value equal to the `name` argument that was passed into the `Leaf` class constructor function when the instance is created. Based on this principle, the rest of the code inside the `Leaf` class constructor should be quite easy to understand and follow.

Notice how we can also create properties that are defined by mathematical calculations based on the various arguments that we pass in, such as:

```
this.stopX = stopX - plantSize;
```

As you'll see later on, we'll use the `stopX` property to help determine the size of each leaf. We'll also increment the value of the variable `plantSize` so that when we repeatedly call the function named `drawLeaf`, the plant will grow in size and so appear to animate.

The last piece of code that I'd like to talk about in the `Leaf` class constructor is the one that looks like:

```
this.ID = setInterval(drawLeaf, 10,
➡this.name, this.dir, this.levelNum,
➡this.originX, this.originY, this.stopX,
➡this.stopY, this.controlX,
➡this.controlY, this.thickness);
```

You can get away without specifying `this` before all the arguments in this `setInterval` function, but it might help you to remember that those properties now actually belong to the `Leaf` object instance we created, and also to show that the set of arguments inside the `setInterval` function are slightly different in order and value from the arguments we originally passed into the `Leaf` class constructor function.

What does the above line of code do? It creates a `setInterval` action, which in turn executes a function we define in the parameters of the `setInterval`, and it will do this every `x` amount of milliseconds.

Remember that each instance of a leaf on our plant is an object that we created when we called the `Leaf` class constructor. We can see that for each leaf instance, we create a property called `ID`, and the value of this property is a `setInterval` action that executes a function named `drawLeaf` every 10 milliseconds and passes a whole bunch of arguments into that function. Too easy!
The reason for using the `setInterval` in this way is that by giving it a name, or identifier, we can destroy or stop it when we no longer need it.

I use `setInterval` here rather than `onEnterFrame` because with an `onEnterFrame` method you can't accurately control when you want a function to be called each time, and you can't always easily delete the `onEnterFrame` action once it's no longer needed. For these reasons using `setInterval` saves on processor usage, ensuring that the code runs as smoothly as possible.

The next big chunk of code is where we actually draw each leaf on the plant. We know that we now have seven instances of the `Leaf` object called `leaf0Obj`, `leaf1Obj`, through to `leaf6Obj`. Each of these instances has a group of properties (`name`, `dir`, `levelNum` and so on) with values unique to each instance. We're going to use the values of those properties inside the function named `drawLeaf` to actually draw each leaf.

But instead of diving headlong into the `drawLeaf` function and hopefully make some sort of meager sense from the rather complex code, I thought we'd take a rest from the plant movie for a few minutes and make another FLA that will serve two purposes:

- to demonstrate a simplified version of how we use the drawing API to make our leaf.

- to make a mini application that will automatically generate the parameters that make up each `child` array in our `leafMap` parent array.

You don't seriously think I sat down and mathematically calculated all those numbers by hand did you?

The drawing API in a mini-application

We're now going to leave our plant for a little while and make our mini-application to generate the sub-arrays that store the data about each leaf, and take a look at how the drawing API works. Open the file named `leafmaker.fla` from the download files. On the stage in the main timeline, you'll see three small movie clips that are colored red, yellow, and green – red to represent the stop point for the curve, green to represent the start point, and yellow to represent the control point for the curve.

The code on each movie clip and the buttons inside each movie clip are fairly basic and should be familiar to you. Suffice to say that all the code inside each movie clip's button does is drag the movie clip and run the `drawCurve` function via a `setInterval` action when pressed, and stop the drag action when the movie clip is released. We also make sure that each movie clip sits on a whole pixel number when released, just so it makes our array output look tidier. The function named `drawCurve` inside the `leafmaker.fla` looks like:

```
function drawCurve(){
_root.createEmptyMovieClip("arc", 1);
   thickness = 10;
   with(_root.arc){
   beginFill(0x33CC00, 60);
   lineStyle(1, 0x000000, 100);
   moveTo(_root.startMov._x, _root.startMov._y);
   curveTo(_root.cntrlMov._x,
   ➥ _root.cntrlMov._y, _root.endMov._x,
   ➥ _root.endMov._y);
   curveTo((_root.startMov._x-thickness),
   ➥ (_root.startMov._y-(100+thickness)),
   ➥ (_root.startMov._x),(_root.startMov._y));

   endFill();
   }
_root.myData = _root.leafName + ", " +
➥ _root.leafDir + ", " + _root.leafNum + ", " +
➥ _root.startMov._x + ", " + _root.startMov._y
➥ + ", " + _root.endMov._x + ", " +
➥ _root.endMov._y + ", " + _root.cntrlMov._x
➥ + ", " + _root.cntrlMov._y + ", " +
➥ _root.thickness;
}
```

The first line of code inside the function creates an empty movie clip called `arc` on the main timeline on level 1, so we can draw inside it with the drawing API. To draw anything in Flash with ActionScript, you have to provide a movie clip for Flash to draw into, and an empty one made for just this purpose is generally considered best practice. When you create an empty movie clip, its x and y are set to 0,0 relative to the timeline that it exists in. In our case the timeline the empty movie clip exists in is the `_root`, so the movie clip will exist at 0,0 of the main stage as well.

To draw a curve using ActionScript in Flash, the line has to have six parameters to begin with, and four for every line you draw in the clip after that. We're going to be able to drag our curved leaf around the screen to change its shape, so we're going to use the draggable movie clips' x and y positions as the parameters to pass into the `drawCurve` function and thereby draw the curved line.

Using a `with` action (similar to the old `tellTarget` action), we tell the `_root.arc` movie clip that we're going to draw a line that is 1 pixel in width, with a line color that is black (0x000000 is Flash's way of saying #000000 – the hex value of black), and the alpha for the line will be 100 percent. We then tell the movie clip to begin coloring in the leaf with `beginFill`, specifying the color and alpha of the fill.

We then tell the drawing API to start at a specific position (relative to the 0,0 of the movie clip being drawn in) by telling it to move to the x and y position of the green movie clip on the stage.

Then we actually draw our first curved line. As we have already specified the starting place to draw the line by using the `moveTo` action, now we're going to draw a curve to the point specified in the last two parameters, using the first two parameters in the `curveTo` action as the control point.

We then draw our second curved line by using a little math to offset the control point by an arbitrary amount (you could probably tweak this line to achieve different results) and draw the line from the end point (the red movie clip) back to the start point (the green movie clip). After this, we end the fill.

The last line of code outputs a string into a selectable text field on screen by concatenating the x and y positions of the green, red, and yellow movie clips, along with the other information we typed into the input fields. Just be sure to hit the button marked Generate Array whenever you make any changes.

Once we have our leaf in the shape that we'd like to see it when it's at full growth, all we have to do is copy the contents of the text field and paste it into the `leafMap` array in the appropriate place. You've then got the coordinates for every leaf that you want to make, without having to sit down and try work out in your head how and where each leaf will be and what it will look like.

The values in the array that are outputted to screen in our mini-application are those of the leaf as you'd see it when the plant is fully grown (when the variable `plantSize` is equal to 50). For our leaf to start out smaller and grow to the finished size as we see it in the mini-application, you should do the following:

- If the leaf curls out to the left, you must manually add 50 to the value of `_root.endMov._x`. For example if `_root.endMov._x` is 200 in the full-grown leaf, you must change the value of it to 250 in the `leafMap` array for that leaf.

- If the leaf curls out to the right, you must manually remove 50 from the value of `_root.endMov._x`. For example if `_root.endMov._x` is 350 in the full-grown leaf, you must change the value of it to 300 in the `leafMap` array for that leaf.

We're going to use the above code as a basis for drawing and animating each leaf back in our main plant movie.

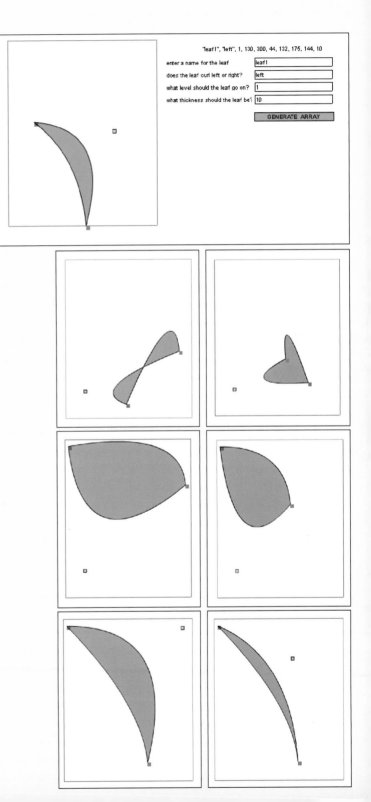

Planting the plant!

Let's go back to `stickiness.fla` and open up the movie clip on the stage where all our code is. Click on the Plant Actions layer and view the code there. Now to explain the `drawLeaf` function. It begins:

```
function drawLeaf (name, dir, levelNum,
➡originX, originY, stopX, stopY,
➡controlX, controlY, thickness) {
```

Remember when we created the instances of the `Leaf` class how we created a `setInterval` property called `[objectName].ID` that would call the `drawLeaf` function every 10 milliseconds to pass a whole bunch of arguments into the function every time it was called? Each leaf instance is executing this function every 10 milliseconds and passing its own values into the function each time as well. In this way we can re-use the one function to make all seven leaves do slightly different things depending on the arguments that are passed into it.

The first line of ActionScript inside the function simply says:

```
clear();
```

This action tells Flash to clear anything previously drawn with the API. If you commented this line out you'd see that every time the function is called, Flash keeps drawing new lines as we'd expect, but it leaves on the stage any lines it has drawn previously. You end up with some very weird looking leaves and a Flash movie that runs rather slowly because of the amount of vector data it's constantly trying to render.

The second line of code inside the function executes another function called `moveLeaf` that is outside of `drawLeaf`:

```
moveLeaf((name+"Obj"));
```

We'll talk about what `moveLeaf` does closer to the end of the chapter.

Following this are two `if` statements that are very similar except for a few mathematical calculations that are performed in each statement:

```
if (dir == "left") {
    endX = originX - stepArray[0];
    endY = originY - stepArray[1];
    if ((endX <= stopX) || (endY <= stopY)) {
        temp = eval(name + "Obj").ID;
        clearInterval(temp);
        if(plantSize > 25){
            makeFlower("flower" add name,
            ➡ levelNum, endX, endY);
        }
    }
}
if (dir == "right") {
    clear();
    endX = originX + stepArray[0];
    endY = originY - stepArray[1];
    if ((endX >= stopX) || (endY <= stopY)) {
        temp = eval(name + "Obj").ID;
        clearInterval(temp);
        if(plantSize > 25){
            makeFlower("flower" add name,
            ➡ levelNum, endX, endY);
        }
    }
}
```

Just to recap on the OOP theory that we touched on earlier, we are passing arguments into `drawLeaf` via the `setInterval` action which was created when we made an instance of the `Leaf` object. The first instance we created is called `leaf0Obj`. This instance has a property named `dir` (or `leaf0Obj.dir` in this example), which has a value that came from an element in the `leafMap` array. The `leaf0Obj` instance also had a property called `ID` (`leaf0Obj.ID`) which is a `setInterval` action. So by tracing back the arguments and variables we're using inside the `drawLeaf` function, we can see that:

- The sub-array elements of the `leafMap` array are passed into the `Leaf` class constructor function.

- The `Leaf` class constructor uses those elements passed into it as arguments to dynamically create properties that exist in each unique instance of the `Leaf` object, created when the class constructor is invoked.

- Those same properties are then passed into the `setInterval` action for each object instance as arguments, which are in turn passed into the `drawLeaf` function.

Why am I explaining this? So you know that when the object instance named `leaf0Obj` calls the `drawLeaf` function and passes a whole bunch of properties belonging to `leaf0Obj` into `drawLeaf` as arguments, what looks like a variable like `dir` inside `drawLeaf` – for example:

```
if(dir=="left")
```

is really in actual fact referring to the `dir` property of `leaf0Obj`, or `leaf0Obj.dir` – the object that called the `drawLeaf` function in the first place via the `setInterval` action. It is important to understand this in order to know how the function works.

Because the math required to animate a curve that curls out to the left is slightly different to a curve that curls out to the right, we need these two `if` statements to make it all work properly. Inside each `if` statement we declare two new variables, `endX` and `endY`, which are used to make the end point in our curve (the same point that corresponded to the x and y of the red movie clip in our mini-application). Every time the function `drawLeaf` is called, it also calls the function `moveLeaf`. This new function returns into `drawLeaf` two variables in the form of an array with two elements – `stepArray[0]` and `stepArray[1]`. Every time `moveLeaf` is called, it increases the value of the `returned` array so that when we subtract these numbers from the starting point (`originX`) in the `drawLeaf` function, the leaf will appear to animate out to the left. In the case of a leaf whose direction is right, we add the values of the `returned` array so that the leaf appears to animate out to the right.

After we declare the new end point for the leaf by making `endX` and `endY` equal values returned from the function `moveLeaf`, we have another `if` statement that checks to see if the end point of the curve (`endX` and `endY`) has reached the stop point for curve. If it has, we then clear the `setInterval` for the `leaf` object that is calling the `drawLeaf`.

We also have another `if` statement inside the previous ones, that checks once the leaf has stopped animating to see if the variable `plantSize` has reached a value greater than 25. If it has, we reward users for sticking with us, by making our plant grow some flowers.

Here we call the function `makeFlower` and pass some arguments into it. Essentially what we're doing is a cut-down version of `drawLeaf` in that the function `makeFlower` also creates some empty movie clips and draws a flower in each one. The function also puts the flower at the end point of the curve for the leaf that executed the function in the first place.

Now that we've gotten all those `if` statements out of the way, let's take a look at the next chunk of code:

```
createEmptyMovieClip(name, levelNum);
with (_root.plant[name]) {
        beginFill(fillColor, 100);
        lineStyle(1, outlineColor, 100);
        moveTo(originX, originY);
```

Does this look familiar? In essence this code is the same as the code that appeared inside the `drawCurve` function in our mini-application, with two minor differences. The first difference is that instead of hard-coding the colors for the fill and the outline of the leaves, we're using the variables `fillColor` and `outlineColor` – variables that we created in the `convertColors` function on the Date Actions layer way back at the beginning of this chapter. The math required to draw the curves for each leaf are slightly different, so we then have an `if/else` statement that draws the curves differently depending on whether the leaf curls out to the left or the right. The statement looks like:

```
if (dir == "left") {
    curveTo(controlX, controlY, endX, endY);
    curveTo((originX+thickness),
    ➥ (originY-(100+thickness)),
    ➥ originX, originY);
  } else if (dir =="right") {
    curveTo(controlX, controlY, endX, endY);
    curveTo((originX-thickness),
    ➥ (originY-(100+thickness)),
    ➥ originX, originY);
  }
```

The very last bit of code for this function stops the fill for the leaf by saying:

```
        endFill();
    }
    updateAfterEvent();
}
```

Notice the line `updateAfterEvent();` – this wasn't required in our mini-application but we use it here for the following reason. The function `drawLeaf` is being executed by every leaf object instance every 10 milliseconds – much much faster than the frame rate of our movie. The built-in function `updateAfterEvent` tells Flash to update the screen every time this line is executed, so our animation will display much more smoothly. Try commenting out the line and run the movie again. You'll see that it runs much differently, most likely a lot faster, but a lot less smoothly because the screen is only updating in time with the movie frame rate. Using the `updateAfterEvent` function in this particular movie will most likely use up a fair bit of processor power, so if you're at all concerned about users viewing this movie on low-end machines, you might want to comment out this line of code, or adjust how often the `setInterval` actions for each leaf are run. The animation of the plant will be more jumpy, but you'll save on processor power.

So that's really the meat and potatoes of the project. Here's a quick run down of the other functions that appear at the end of the Plant Actions layer.

Moving down through the code after the `drawLeaf` function, we come across a small but very important function called `moveLeaf`. The code looks like:

```
function moveLeaf(leafObject) {
    this[leafObject].stepX +=
    ➡ this[leafObject].numStepsX;
    this[leafObject].stepY +=
    ➡ this[leafObject].numStepsY;
    stepArray = Array(this[leafObject].stepX,
    ➡ this[leafObject].stepY);
    return stepArray;
}
```

This function is actually called from inside `drawLeaf`. The name of the leaf object instance (for example `leaf1Obj`) that is executing `drawLeaf` and therefore executing `moveLeaf` is passed into `moveLeaf` as an argument. Once this happens we modify some of the properties of the leaf instance, these being `stepX` and `stepY` (for example `leaf1Obj.stepX` and `leaf1Obj.stepY`). We increment each of these values by the value of another property of the leaf instance, namely `numSteps`. Back when we created each leaf object instance, on line 44 of the Plant Actions layer, using the `Leaf` class, we added some properties to each instance called `numStepsX` and `numStepsY`. The value of these variables was in effect a ratio between the x position of the leaf when it was at its smallest, and the x position of the end point of the leaf when it finished animating, and the same for the y positions of where the end point for the leaf started and finished. What the value of `numStepsX` and `numStepsY` allows us to do then is to move the x and y of the end point of a leaf each time the function `drawLeaf` is executed in proportion to each other, so that by the time the x position of the end point for a leaf reaches its final resting place when the animation finishes, the y position for the end point of the leaf is in the right place as well.

Now because we want to pass the new `stepX` and `stepY` properties of the leaf object back into `drawLeaf`, we combine the two variables into a new array called `stepArray`, and pass the values back into the function by writing:

```
return stepArray;
```

Why do we need to put the two variables into an array before passing them back into the `drawLeaf` function? Because you can only pass or 'return' one variable or object with the return action. So we can't write:

```
return this[leafObject].stepX;
return this[leafObject].stepY;
```

as it would only return `this[leafObject].stepX` to the function that called it. We sidestep this limitation by putting everything we want to return to `drawLeaf` into an array, which is after all only one object.

The second last function we come to in our code is a function called `makePot`, and it looks like:

```
function makePot() {
    createEmptyMovieClip("pot", 10);
    with (pot) {
        beginFill(potFill, 100);
        lineStyle(1, potOutline, 100);
        moveTo(220, 360);
        lineTo(280, 360);
        curveTo(290, 390, 270, 400);
        lineTo(230, 400);
        curveTo(210, 390, 220, 360);
        endFill();
    }
}
```

When we first execute the function `makeThePlant`, the next line of code in that function executes the function `makePot`. And the function does exactly that – it makes the pot that our plant sits in. We start by creating an empty movie clip, give it an instance name of pot and put it on level 10, so that it sits well in front of the seven leaves we made, which sit on levels 1-7. We then begin to fill the pot based on the color `potFill` we created with the `convertColors` function on the Date Actions layer. After this we draw a combination of curved and straight lines to form our pot, and end the fill at the end of the function.

The very last function in our code is used to draw the flowers that go on the end of each leaf once the variable `plantSize` reaches a value greater than 25.

Even though this function is quite long, if you break it down into its subcomponents, there's not much in it that we haven't already talked about. We start by creating an empty movie clip to draw the flower in, and set the x and y position of the flower to be the same as the end point for the leaf that called this function:

```
function makeFlower
➡ (name, levelNum, xPos, yPos) {
    this.createEmptyMovieClip(name,
    ➡ 20+levelNum);
    this[name]._xscale = this[name]._yscale = 1;
    this[name]._x = xPos;
    this[name]._y = yPos;
    this[name]._rotation =
    ➡ Math.round(Math.random()*360);
    with(this[name]){
      beginFill(0xFFFF00, 100);
      lineStyle(1, 0xFFCC00, 100);
      moveTo(-2, -9);
      curveTo(-20, -17, -10, 1);
      curveTo(-19, 24, 0, 9);
      curveto(22, 18, 8, -2);
      curveTo(18, -26, -2, -9);
      endfill;
    }
}
```

Then we use the drawing API to draw the flower (note that the colors are hard-coded in this function – you can just as easily go back to the Date Actions layer and create some variables to color the flowers just as we did for the leaves and the pot). We then scale the flower down to 1 percent, so that we can make it grow when the movie clip loads, and randomly rotate the flower movie clip just to give the finished plant a bit of randomness.

After this we create an `onLoad` method for the flower movie clip that we just made:

```
this[name].onLoad = function() {
    this.startX = this._x;
    this.num = 0;
    this.clicked = false;
}
```

This is effectively telling the movie clip that when it loads, it makes a variable named `startX` to remember where the movie clip's x position is when the flower first loads, and another variable named `clicked` that is set to `false` to denote that the flower hasn't been clicked on yet (we're going to make the flower do something when you click on it).

In Flash MX you can assign an `onRelease` action or an `onRollover` action to a movie clip, just as you would with a button, so this is what we do next:

```
this[name].onRelease = function() {
    this.clicked = true;
}
```

In a nutshell, this tells the movie clip to do something when the movie clip is clicked on with the mouse – in this case change the variable named `clicked` from `false` (which we set when the movie clip first loaded using the `onLoad` method) to `true`.

The next piece of code creates an `onEnterFrame` method for the flower movie clip:

```
this[name].onEnterFrame = function() {
    if(this._xscale < 50) {
        this._xscale = this._yscale ++;
    }
```

Inside this `onEnterFrame` method we then write an `if` statement that says to the flower: if the `_xscale` of the movie clip is less than 50%, make both the `_xscale` and the `_yscale` 1% larger, so that the flower will appear to grow in size over a few seconds in time.

The original code used to draw the flower with the API makes the flower quite large, as it was simply too difficult working out the curves for the flower petals on a really small scale, so we make the flower start out at a scale of 1% of what it really is, then make it grow from within the `onEnterFrame` method up to 50%.

A quick note on the `onEnterFrame` method as it's being used in this example – those of you who are upgrading your skills from Flash 5 will recall that `onEnterFrame` clip events had to be written on the movie clip itself. This method is discouraged in MX, as you can now more conveniently put all of your code within the one frame on your timeline, and not on the individual symbol. This allows us to put all the ActionScript for an entire movie on one location on the timeline, and it saves us from having to click all over the stage on different buttons and movie clips in search of code that we want to change.

Back to the `onEnterFrame` method of our flower movie clip, we then have another `if` statement that looks like:

```
if (this.clicked == true) {
    this._x = xPos + (this.startX + (30 *
➥ Math.sin(this.num)));
    this.num += 0.1;
    this._y += 2;
    this._rotation += 2;
}
```

What this little piece of code does is waits until the flower is clicked on, then moves the x position of the flower to the left or right of its original starting position. The code

in the second line of this `if` statement keeps generating a series of numbers that varies between a negative and a positive number, which we add to the original x position of the flower, thereby making it sway from left to right.

As we do all this, we increase the y position by 2 pixels each time, so that the flower appears to fall down to the bottom of the stage. We also increase the `_rotation` property of the flower by 2 degrees, just to create a slightly more organic motion as the flower falls.

The next `if` statement in our `makeFlower` function is written like so:

```
if (this._y > (movieHeight-6)) {
    this.clicked = false;
    this.enabled = false;
    }
  }
}
```

All this does is tell the flower that if its y position is greater than the height of the plant movie clip, it should stop falling and stay still. It does this by changing the value of clicked back to `false` again. Remember that all the code responsible for making the flower fall is inside the previous `if` statement that only executes if the value of clicked is set to `true`. If you made your movie so that the plant looked like it was sitting on a ledge or table, and the ground was a lot further down than the height of the movie clip, just simply add the extra distance from the ledge to the ground to the variable `movieHeight`. By setting `this.enabled` to `false` in the last line of the above `if` statement, we effectively stop the flower from having the ability to be clicked on any more so that it can't try and move again. Once a flower has come to rest you'll see that it can't be clicked on any more.

After the `makeFlower` function, there's an action that looks like:

```
stop();
```

Now let me tell you all about the stop action... only joking! That's it, we're done. Our plant grows smoothly, elegantly, and changes size and color according to how often we visit the site, and we've built it in such a way that we can easily change the colors of all the parts of the movie and add or remove leaves as we see fit. Nice work all round I say!

A note about testing and debugging this movie

You may or may not have noticed that inside the plant movie clip where all our code is, there is a layer called debug between the Plant Actions layer and the Date Actions layer, and that the layer has been turned into a Guide layer. To better understand what I'm about to talk about, un-check the guide layer option by right-clicking/CTRL-clicking the layer and un-checking the Guide option.

If you run your movie again, you'll see several text fields on the stage that display some pertinent information. Of course I'm well aware that the trace action can be used to display the output of variables, and also that MX has some very complex debugging devices built in to the Player in the authoring environment – but none of these options work when viewing a SWF in a browser window or an .exe file. I like to output variables I want to watch into dynamic text fields on screen so I can trace the variables in a browser window. And once I've finished debugging my movie, all I have to do is turn the layer with the text fields into a Guide layer and the movie displays as per normal. This way I don't have to keep adding and removing text fields every time I want to debug the movie.

One more thing. If you wish to avoid opening, closing, and re-opening the plant movie in order to see it grow, there's a line of code in the Date Actions layer on line 55 (//plantSize=26;) which you can uncomment and change the value of plantSize to between 0 and 50 if you want to see how the plant looks when it starts out and when it is at full growth. This won't affect any of the values inside your stored sharedObject as the line is written after the sharedObject data is stored on your computer.

There's also some code on line 20 (//daysSincelastVisit = 2;) that you can uncomment and change to force your plant to shrink in size (this will affect the data written to the sharedObject file on your computer). Doing this simulates not visiting the site for the amount of days you specify as the value of

the variable daysSinceLastVisit. Just make sure line 55 is commented out if you do this, otherwise there might be some conflict in what you are hoping to see.

Other things to do with this concept

This book is all about providing some inspiration when you design your interfaces. So please take some time after you've read this chapter to let all the code and concepts sink in, and try to come up with some of your own ideas about how to represent user-stickiness in your movies.

One idea I had while building this FLA for the book was to use the plant not to represent individual user stickiness, but use it as a kind of graph that represented overall viewer statistics. Flash MX has some awesome new built-in features that allow you to easily detect all sorts of information about a user viewing your site. Using the built-in System Object, you can detect such things as: the language installed on the users' computer (to give you a rough idea of what country users are coming from), the operating system they're using, their screen resolution (very handy, that one), and many other user settings.

You could also use a PHP script to fairly easily tell which browser and version that a user is running, as well as the URL they came from before visiting your site and a whole host of other information relevant to collecting global user statistics about your site. Your Flash movie could call the PHP script to retrieve this information in combination with settings gathered from the Flash System Object, and then send that information to a database for permanent storage on the server-side. Your plant could then retrieve this global information and act as a graph to display the statistics.

If you ever decide to build something like this based on what you've learned in this chapter, please let me know as I'd love to see what you've done with the concept.

A T-SHIRT DESIGNER

All people can be creative, but I think a lot of people are scared to be. When faced with a blank canvas, a brush, and a selection of paints, a lot of people just freeze up. There's something intimidating about the purity of a white page, and the permanence of putting paint on it.

I wanted to create an application that would encourage people to play around with design in an informal environment. Rather than start from a white square then, I decided to begin with the familiar shape of a t-shirt, on which users could experiment with drawing a design of their choice. I chose a t-shirt because it's somewhere where you often see photos, patterns, and logos, and it just happened to make nice pictures too.

The end result is an application that I'm extremely proud of, providing the ability for all to create, and an interface that doesn't take a manual to learn (of course, I could have included a manual...). The simplicity of the interface was one of the key considerations here, as I wanted it to appeal to a wide web audience of varying ability.

Interface inspirations

Here are some of my favorite programs and interfaces that have been an inspiration to the t-shirt application.

I ♥ BBC

Yes, it's true. Not the whole of the British Broadcasting Corporation (although I do love them dearly too), but the microcomputer model 'B' released in 1982 as part of their Computer Literacy Project. It was one of the many early computers that I cut my teeth on, and brings back many fond memories. Although I of course spent the majority of my time hard at work in Wordwise +, or typing in those beautiful BASIC programs, I also played a game or two every now and then. One of my favorite game series on the BBC was Repton by Superior Software. The game itself was an addictive puzzler starring a weird green lizard, but that's not what I'm here to talk about. Each game in the series came with its own character editor and map designer, and these were worth the price of the software alone. The limitations imposed by the pixel grid led to some pretty strange sprite interpretations of photocopiers and Coke cans, but somehow they always looked OK when you saw them in the game. Of course we didn't have a mouse at the time, so the cursor you can see in the screenshot was controlled purely by the keyboard. It just led to even more joy:

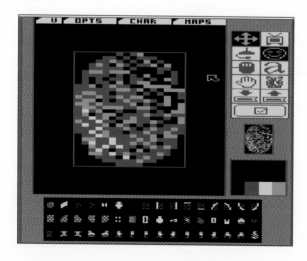

Another fun thing in Repton was drawing pictures in the map designer. You could do a self-portrait out of boulders and diamonds, and watch the whole thing fall apart in real-time when you played the level. Great days.

The beeb was used for much more than gaming though. It also had some pretty sophisticated graphics commands, and image-programming abilities that are still better than what Flash has only just achieved. PLOT, MOVE, and GCOL, were my first experiences with the world of vectors, but to be perfectly honest, I don't think I ever called them vectors back then. To me they were just lines. I actually made a pretty complicated (for me) drawing program with both line and pixel capabilities – admittedly it started off as an example program that came with a mouse, but I altered it enough to make it my own. Unfortunately, I can't get a screenshot of this in the book because my beeb only works nowadays if I open it up and hold down the BASIC ROM when I turn it on, and even then it sometimes decides to just sit and beep at me instead of booting up. If anyone out there has a beeb in good working order that they want to get rid of, then I'll be more than happy to give it a good home.

My drawing app (Spectrum ZX+)

The affectionately titled Speccy was superbad for graphics. In essence, it is the lo-fi graphic lover's dream, with it's clashing colors and limited color palette.

To say I pushed these graphic capabilities to their limit is talking rubbish. The best I could come up with (besides dodgy moiré patterns) was a drawing application, minus an interface. The drawing program resembled the classic etch-a-sketch tool: pen down… and still down. It was impossible to take the pen off the paper, but it had a groovy feel all the same, because sometimes limitations are good.

It also tests your memory, guesswork and keypressing, when you try to calculate where you are going over a previously drawn line.

For those of you who don't fancy clearing the cobwebs of the attic, here is a modern Flash interpretation (with nearing resolution and all – see SpecDraw.fla):

```
1  // speccy draw by ken jokol / pinderkaas.com
2  // movieclip inits
3  _root.createEmptyMovieClip("lines", 1);
4  lines.lineStyle(1, 0x000000, 100);
5  inc = 10;
6  rightBound = 250;
7  downBound = 190;
8  currentX = 130;
9  currentY = 80;
10 lines.moveTo(currentX, currentY);
11 // keys code
12 checkDir = new Object();
13 checkDir.onKeyDown = function() {
14     if (Key.isDown(Key.LEFT)) {
15         yAdd = 0;
16         xAdd = -inc;
17     }
18     if (Key.isDown(Key.RIGHT)) {
19         yAdd = 0;
20         xAdd = inc;
21     }
22     if (Key.isDown(Key.DOWN)) {
23         yAdd = inc;
24         xAdd = 0;
25     }
26     if (Key.isDown(Key.UP)) {
27         yAdd = -inc;
28         xAdd = 0;
29     }
30     currentX += xAdd;
31     currentY += yAdd;
32     if (currentX>rightBound) {
33         currentX = rightBound;
34     }
35     if (currentX<0) {
36         currentX = 0;
37     }
38     if (currentY>downBound) {
39         currentY = downBound;
40     }
41     if (currentY<0) {
42         currentY = 0;
43     }
44     lines.lineTo(currentX, currentY);
45 };
46 Key.addListener(checkDir);
```

Line 46 of 46, Col 27

The Spectrum program had a pretty amazing way of saving the drawing with the `SAVE "" SCREEN$` command, which saved the current screen to cassette. The image was then reloaded, and redrawn bit-by-bit during loading, accompanied by the amazingly evil spectrum loading din. This made for one heckuva slideshow for the family.

"Hey look Mom, another drawing of buildings," I said.

"WHAT'S THAT SON?" she yelled over the racket.

"NEVER MIND!" I screamed.

(repeat until tape needs turning over or smell of dinner burning in oven starts filtering into the living room)

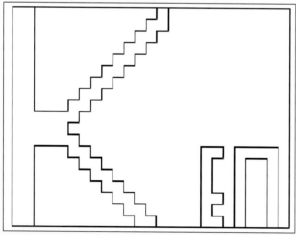

Degas Elite (Atari ST 520FM)

Around the time of STOS, my joystick-controlled File Management system, and a friend's (partially random and looped) INXS offering to the Public Domain, was a paint program called Degas Elite on the Atari ST.

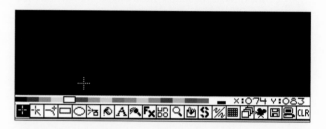

The thing that I remember most about Degas Elite wasn't the interface itself, but the fact that my brother and I massacred the OutRun loading screen with it. It truly defined an era.

The loading screen was littered with profanities and various other things, making OutRun impossible to play when our parents were around (ST games did take a pretty long time to load after all).

"Where did you learn such words?" they might've asked, or "Where did you get such an awful game?" more likely, curbing all future software purchases.

Deluxe Paint (Amiga 1200)

Deluxe Paint felt unique because of its frame-by-frame animation capability, which basically stinks in retrospect (compared to the mighty powers of Flash anyhow), but was liberating at the time.

One highlight that sticks with me, purely for extreme effort and completeness, was my friend Mark's rendition of his dog Jess catching a fly with her 30-inch tongue. It was truly swell seeing the eyes follow the fly round and round, before the tongue came out in a swift motion.

MacPaint (Macintosh)

MacPaint has to win hands down for the interface, mad bitmap texture fills and for being in black & white (partly due to the Mac System 6 environment but more in the way of aesthetics – or so I like to believe).

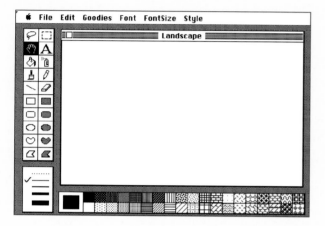

Not only did it define a generation for Mac users (like 'The Grouch' trash extension), but it had the most useable and spacious interface of any application of the time (MacPaint v2 didn't have the same appeal though).

I am impressed that the filetype is still supported nowadays, and I occasionally open it up when I can to fill random shapes with obscure textures.

Making a t-shirt app in Flash

Apart from the beauty of the aforementioned technologies, this application was inspired by the Flash MX ability to dynamically import JPGs. Although the application uses a lot more of MX's functionality – the drawing API for one – the original premise was to allow JPG manipulation on the fly.

Before you start: Yes, I know you can do something more advanced than this if you use Photoshop, Illustrator, or even Flash. Not only does this SWF make the ability to design more accessible to John Doe web user, but it also strips us of the comforts of corporate-developed applications and takes us back to the basic toolset where design and composition are the most important assets.

This is back to pen and paper stuff.

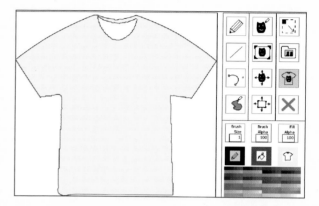

When it came to selecting the tools, I started with a huge list, and broke it down as time permitted. The application was made over a few busy days, and although it seemed to be a constantly fluxing idea, I knew from the start what I wanted to do. I suppose the tools that made the application are rudimentary, but this is also part of the appeal – stripping away any complexity and letting the user be creative and unrestricted by the application. The beauty of it from an application point-of-view is that it can always grow in functionality and complexity.

The application itself was built with modularity and expandability in mind, but could have been improved on given a little more time. The order of creation follows:

- I built in the drawing capabilities first, so that I had a very rough drawing application.

- I then added the colors, brush and fill options to complete this, adding essential interface elements as necessary.

- The next step was to add the JPG and masking functionality, so all the creative capabilities were live.

- I then finished up by adding the t-shirt mask, and the interface functionality.

The result is as you can see, fully formed, but highly expandable with respect to tools and further options.

Making the application

The application is made up of a fairly basic interface on the right-hand side, and a large drawing space on the left with a t-shirt shape on it. There is also a 'help' area beneath the interface that displays information on the tool that you're currently using, and displays the purpose of a tool when you roll-over its button in the interface. Let's take a quick look at the screen layout, and what each button does.

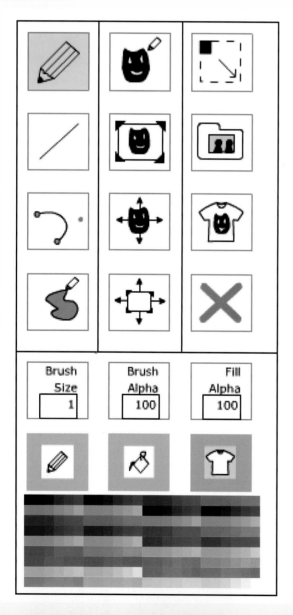

Pencil tool – the standard free-draw tool for pencil lines. This is also the default tool.

Line tool – similar to the pencil, but for drawing straight lines.

Curve tool – for drawing Bezier curves, click and drag three points to define the shape.

Fill draw tool – for drawing filled shapes. Rather than a paint bucket, if you want to fill a shape then you have to draw that shape as you would with the pencil, and then release the mouse to fill the shape. If you don't want a line around the fill, then either set the line to be the same color as the background, or set its alpha to zero.

Mask draw tool – this is similar to the fill draw tool, but it defines the shape for the mask that you will see the JPG through. You can draw more than one shape with this tool to create numerous windows into your image. The color and alpha settings of this tool make no difference to its effect.

JPG mask toggle button – this button simply toggles the JPG mask on and off. When it's on, only the masked parts of the image are shown, and when it's off, the complete image and mask are shown.

Mask move tool – this allows you to click on your JPG mask and drag it around to another position.

JPG move tool – this is similar to the mask move tool, but you move the JPG rather than the mask.

JPG scale tool – this tool allows you to click and drag on a JPG to resize it. You can also hold the SHIFT key down while you're dragging to constrain the proportions of the image.

 Load JPG button – this button will open up another box that allows you to enter the URL of a picture that you want to load into your image. You can only load one image per picture. When they are loaded in, the pictures are automatically resized to a square in the center of the t-shirt. Use the JPG scale tool to alter their size and proportions if needs be.

 Toggle t-shirt mask button – this toggles the main t-shirt mask on and off, hiding any extraneous elements that may have strayed over the edge of the shirt.

 Brush size – allows you to change the size of the stroke/brush lines. 1 is normal, 100+ is big... very big

 Brush and fill alpha – both of these boxes allow you to enter a percentage of opacity for strokes or fills respectively. Try layering large brush strokes with low alphas... mmmm...

Brush, **fill**, and **t-shirt color chips** – click once on these to select them (the selected one has a yellow center), and then click on a color in the palette to change to it. Changing the t-shirt color will have an immediate effect, the brush and fill colors will only come in to effect the next time you use one of the appropriate tools.

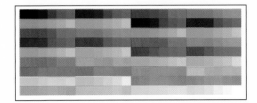

The **color** palette – this is where you choose the colors to draw with. Make sure the right color chip is selected first, then choose a color and start drawing.

The best way to look at how the application was made is to break down each individual tool and element of the interface. We'll start with a few basics about the whole application.

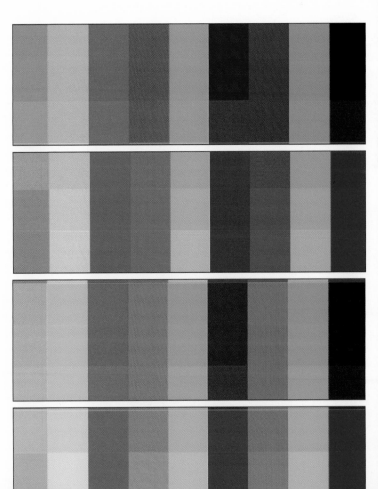

Initializing the movie

Before we look at the rest of the movie, there are a few fundamental variables and movie clips that need to be initialized first.

This drawing boundary is defined at the start of the whole code and is used by all of the drawing tools. Here are the global declarations:

```
_global.tabletleft = _root.square._x-(_root.square._width/2);
_global.tabletright = tabletleft+_root.square._width;
_global.tablettop = _root.square._y-(_root.square._height/2);
_global.tabletbottom = tablettop+_root.square._height;
```

The tablet or drawing boundaries are defined as the space of the square movie clip, located on the main stage. The equations here simply calculate the boundaries of square, and store them in four global variables. You'll see these used throughout the code.

The `tempLayer` global variable references the movie clip that is used for previewing some of the drawing tools.

```
_root.createEmptyMovieClip("temporaryDrawLayer", 8000);
_global.tempLayer = _root["temporaryDrawLayer"];
```

We are using global variables to hold references to our main objects, so that we can quickly and easily refer to them in the code without having to type out full paths every time, and so that if we change the set up of the layer structure, or its name, at any time, then we only need to do so in one place in the code, rather than every single time the layer is referenced.

`drawPad` stores all of the drawn elements created using the interface:

```
_root.createEmptyMovieClip("drawingPad", 45000);
_global.drawPad = _root.drawingPad;
```

`hitArea` tells `drawPad` to use the square movie clip from the stage as a hit area:

```
drawPad.hitArea = _root.square;
```

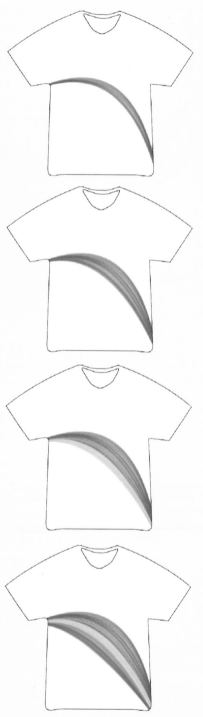

`jamJar` stores a reference to a movie clip that holds the mask and JPG movie clips:

```
_root.createEmptyMovieClip("JPGAndMaskHolder", 501);
_global.jamJar = _root.JPGAndMaskHolder;
```

Why `jamJar` you may well ask? Well, `jam` stands for JPG And Mask, and a jar is a holder. It's a little bit esoteric, but it was originally `jamHolder` and `jamJar` seemed so much nicer.

`JPGContainer` is the parent of the movie clip that loads in the JPG graphic:

```
jamJar.createEmptyMovieClip("JPGHolderHolder", 502);
_global.JPGContainer = jamJar.JPGHolderHolder;
```

`JPGHolderHolder` may seem like a daft name, but logically this movie clip is the holder of the movie clip that holds the JPG, so it kinda makes sense. Luckily, this name is only mentioned here, and from here on in, it's the much more palatable `JPGContainer`. The JPG graphic is nested within this movie for scaling and JPG manipulation. More on this later.

`JPG` is the movie where we load JPG images:

```
JPGContainer.createEmptyMovieClip("JPGHolder", 500);
_global.JPG = JPGContainer.JPGHolder;
```

`JPGM` stores a reference to the movie clip where a mask is drawn:

```
jamJar.createEmptyMovieClip("masker", 503);
_global.JPGM = jamJar.masker;
```

More on this later.

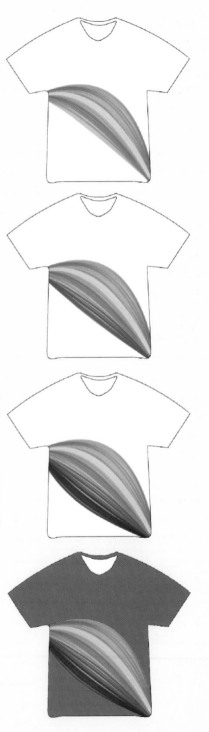

Interface elements

Buttons

All of the main buttons in the interface are based upon the same model, and are made to work with the same code. Each button is made up very simply of two frames, with a stop action on the first frame to stop it running away. The first frame is the normal button state, and has a white background, and the second frame is the button 'pressed' state, and has a yellow background.

The buttons all use the same code, so it makes sense to have the same function attached to them in the initial set up function, rather than repeating the same code in separate functions for each button. The way to do this in Flash is to use the `call` action. Here's the free draw tool function call as an example:

```
mainButCall.call(mainButDraw,
➡ funcFreeDraw, undefined, "Click and drag
➡ to draw pencil lines", "Pencil Tool");
```

`mainButCall` is the name of the button initialization function, and we'll look at how it works in a second. We then pass five parameters to this function – let's just have a quick look at what they mean:

- `mainButDraw` – this is the name of the movie clip on the stage that the function is going to be attached to.

- `funcFreeDraw` – this is the name of the function that we want that button to run when it is clicked.

- `undefined` – this is an extra parameter that we can pass to a function that will be called by the button. In the majority of cases in this FLA this is undefined, and we only really use it with the `fillDraw` function to tell it where to draw to.

- `"Click and drag to draw pencil lines"` – this is the help text that will be displayed at the bottom of the screen when the tool is being used.

- `"Pencil Tool"` – this is the help text that will be displayed when the user rolls the mouse over the button.

Now we know what we'll be passing to the function, let's take a look at the function and see what we do with each parameter. (Remember the first parameter called above is the name of the movie clip that the `call` action uses to attach the function to, therefore this parameter is not passed on to the function itself).

```
mainButCall = function (funcName, pass,
➡ helpText, rollText) {
    this.onRelease = function() {
        allButsOff();
        this.gotoAndStop(2);
        funcName(pass);
        _root.help.text =
        ➡ _root.help.prev=helpText;
    };
    this.onRollOver = function() {
        _root.help.prev = _root.help.text;
        _root.help.text = rollText;
    };
    this.onRollOut = function() {
        _root.help.text = _root.help.prev;
    };
};
```

When you click a button, the first thing that happens is that a function is called to turn off all of the buttons. This is just a lazy way of not having to store the previous tool that was used, and I'll explain how it works in a bit. The next thing that happens is that the current button goes to its second frame (with the yellow background) to show that it's been clicked. It then calls the relevant function that's associated with it, and finally sets the help text that will be displayed at the bottom of the screen while the tool is being used. The help text is just a dynamic text box that is set whenever a button is clicked or rolled over.

We also set `onRollOver` and `onRollOut` states for each button. These just display tool tips at the bottom of the screen whenever you roll over a button so that you can see what it does. The original help text is stored in a temporary variable, and then reset when the user rolls off the button.

Now for a quick look at the super-complicated function to turn off all of the buttons:

```
allButsOff = function () {
    mainButDraw.gotoAndStop(1);
    mainButLine.gotoAndStop(1);
    mainButCurve.gotoAndStop(1);
    mainButFill.gotoAndStop(1);
    mainButClear.gotoAndStop(1);
    maskDrawBut.gotoAndStop(1);
    mainButScale.gotoAndStop(1);
    applyMaskBut.gotoAndStop(1);
    moveMaskBut.gotoAndStop(1);
    moveJPGBut.gotoAndStop(1);
    mainMaskBut.gotoAndStop(1);
    loadJPGBut.gotoAndStop(1);
    tempLayer.clear();
    drawPad.onPress = drawPad.onRelease =
➥ drawPad.onReleaseOutside = undefined;
    _root.a1.removeMovieClip();
    _root.a2.removeMovieClip();
    _root.ctrl.removeMovieClip();
};
```

This basically just runs through every button and sets it to frame 1 – its off state – and then clears the temporary drawing layer, and makes sure there are no actions attached to the `drawPad`. The last thing that it does is to remove the three point clips that we'll be using for the curve tool from the stage.

The color chips for the brush, fill, and t-shirt background work on exactly the same principle. When they're clicked on, they turn themselves on, and the other color chips off. They then set a variable on the root to let the color code know which chip it is affecting.

Brush sizes

The brush size, brush alpha, and fill alpha tools are very simple. Each is basically just a holder for an input text box. Each text box has a variable attached to it, so that whenever a new value is typed into a box, the appropriate variable is updated. This variable is then called upon by the code whenever the brush size or one of the alpha values needs to be known.

The color palette

Colors are required in this drawing application for three things – the brush color, the fill color and the t-shirt color. The neatest and most intuitive way of displaying the available colors is by drawing a palette. Let's look at how it was done here.

Making the palette

When I've worked with color in a similar way to this before, I used bitshifting and found the whole process a little laborious. So, I decided to cheat this time, and use a simple procedure that I came up with when working with JavaScript rendered HTML tables (inspired by the graphci.com 2002 tableart competition, www.graphci.com/tableart, which I was asked to judge).

The full color range produced with this method is the standard web-safe palette of 216 colors. I'm not saying that I necessarily conform to this palette all the time, but it makes the coding a little easier here because the range of colors to reproduce is smaller.

Here's the palette (I always find these rather fetching):

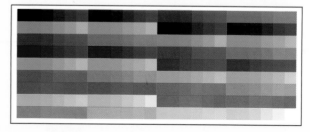

Firstly, a function to define before we get down to the meaty stuff.

```
function setHex(hexColor) {
    this.col = new Color(this);
    this.col.setRGB(hexColor);
}
```

This function is used throughout the code, for setting the color of the aforementioned tools. It is quite simple but can be used for almost anything. This function is used with the `call` command, so `this` applies to the object calling it. We'll see the practical use of it in the next section of code.

The function sets up a new `Color` object, for the object requesting it, and then sets its color to `hexColor`.

So where does `hexColor` come from? Well, this is where the cheating comes in, and the next bit of code comes into use. Let's look at it bit by bit.

OK, the first thing I wanted to do was to limit the color scheme to a web-safe palette, limiting the input to certain hex values. For those of you not versed in these values, these are 00, 33, 66, 99, CC and FF, and by taking any three of these to create a combination, you know you'll have a web-safe color. Pure red, for example, has a hex value of #FF0000 (made up of FF Red, 00 Green and 00 Blue).

With this considered, I started by setting up an array, containing all the web-safe hex values:

```
colors = new Array("00", "33", "66", "99",
➥"CC", "FF");
colorLen = colors.length;
```

The second line of code here simply gets the amount of elements in the array. This is used with the following loops.

Next we set up some variables:

```
rows = 0;
columns = 0;
count = 0;
columnCount = 24;
```

To understand these variables, it's important to know how the grid is made. It's drawn from top left to bottom right, writing row by row. `columnCount` represents the amount of columns or cells in each row, and is used later to check whether we should shift onto the next row. `count` is used as a standard variable to add to the instance name of each attached square, whereas `columns` and `rows` are used for drawing positions.

We then set up the three `for` loops:

```
for (redi=0; redi<colorLen; redi++) {
    for (greeni=0; greeni<colorLen; greeni++) {
        for (bluesi=0; bluesi<colorLen; bluesi++) {
```

We use the length of the `colors` array, set as `colorLen` (6 for each in this case) as the maximum amount. These three loops will run the code 6x6x6 times, giving us the magic number of 216.

After this comes the code executed in the `for` loops:

```
attachMovie("sq", "sq"+count, count);

if (columns == columnCount) {
    columns = 0;
    rows++;
}
columns++;
```

Remember that this code is run 216 times – it might sound like a lot, but it's instantaneous.

OK, the first line here doesn't require much explanation – it just fetches a tiny square from the library. Be sure to change the shape of this if you want to spice up the appearance of the palette, or if you just want bigger icons.

The conditional `if` statement on the next line performs a check to see if the current `columns` variable (aka the current column position) is the same as `columnCount`. If they are the same, then `columns` is reset, and `rows` is incremented. This is the equivalent of the typewriter reaching the end of the line, and that pleasurable 'bing' before you shift it to a new row. Lastly, `columns` is then incremented.

Then we have three lines to perform the all important positioning of the `current` square:

```
current = _root["sq"+count];
current._x =columns*(current._width)+530;
current._y = rows*(current._height)+380;
```

The x and y positions are set according to the variables `columns` and `rows`, multiplied by the width or height of the `current` square. The added figures at the end of each equation are just a manually calculated amount to place the grid at a certain place on the stage.

We then call the `getMeColor` function to set the `current` square as a button, and then store the hex value for this `current` square:

```
getMeColor.call(current);
current.hexy = "0x"+colors[redi]+
➥ colors[greeni]+colors[bluesi];
```

`getMeColor` is applied to every cell in the color palette, and depending on which element is requesting a color – be it brush, fill or t-shirt – it simply changes the chip color for that option and stores these colors on `_root`.

The next line uses the aforementioned arrays to create a color, and stores it in a variable called `hexy` within the current instance. One color is made of a value of red, green and blue, each extracting a value from the arrays, dependent on the position within the nested `for` loops. The color is prefixed by `0x`, to define it as a hex value.

`hexy` is used importantly later on, to get the color of a square from the palette.

The next line uses the `setHex` function to set the color of the `current` square:

```
        setHex.call(current, current.hexy);
        count++;
      }
    }
  }
```

Once all the `for` loops have run, the whole body of this code creates our web-safe color palette. As you can see, the code here isn't that difficult, and although the palette creation is incredibly simple, it is also extremely neat and efficient. Sure, it's cheating (because a more professional way would be to numerically calculate the colors, and then bitshift them along rather than piecing together the numbers in an array), but it saves all those painful conversions from one format to another, and evil math.

The tools

The pencil tool

The pencil tool is the standard scribble based-tool – no frills, no nothing. Put the pencil onto the paper, scribble, and if you can muster up the will power, take the pencil off the paper.

I like to think of this pencil tool as the equivalent of what most people do to post-it notes on the telephone – the creative action of drawing a continuous line, which creates random shapes and ever increasing complexity.

It will not come as a surprise that the pencil tool – aka the FreeDraw tool – is easily the most basic to code.

The general principle from a Flash and usability perspective is:

```
    Press mouse button to begin drawing,
    Draw a continuous line,
UNTIL....
    The mouse button is released,
    Stop drawing.
```

Not exactly rocket science, for sure.

Let's break it down into tasty chunks. Starting at the top:

```
funcFreeDraw = function () {
    _root.freeDraw = function() {
        if (_root._xmouse != oldX &&
    ➥ _root._ymouse != oldY) {
```

After the function declarations is a conditional to check whether the last `xmouse` (`oldX`) and `ymouse` (`oldY`) readings are any different to the current ones. This check is performed just in case the user continues to hold down the mouse button without moving the cursor, and it saves Flash drawing on the same spot unnecessarily.

If the last and current readings are different then the code begins:

```
if (_root.penDown == 0) {
    drawPad.moveTo(_root._xmouse,
    ➥ _root._ymouse);
    _root.penDown = 1;
} else {
```

This code checks firstly to see if the pencil is not already held down. This is performed because we need to know if the user is already drawing, or has their pencil off the paper. If the pencil is off the paper, then it will start drawing from where the user clicks the mouse. From then on, you can draw freeform.

The `penDown` state tells Flash if the pencil is currently touching the paper. Before you click to draw, it is set to 0, and after you've clicked it is set to 1. From now on, whilst the pencil is down, the following code will be run:

```
if (_root._xmouse>tabletleft &&
➥_root._xmouse<tabletright) {
    oldX = _root._xmouse;
}
if (_root._ymouse>tablettop &&
➥_root._ymouse<tabletbottom) {
    oldY = _root._ymouse;
}
```

The `if` statements on lines 1 and 4 here check to see if the pencil is drawing within the given area. (Remember that the global variables for the drawing boundary were defined at the start of the code.)

If the pencil is within these constraints, then `oldX` and `oldY` are updated to reflect the current mouse position on both axes.

If the readings suggest that the positions are outside either axis, then `oldX` and/or `oldY` aren't changed.

We then need to draw the line itself:

```
        drawPad.lineStyle(
➥ _root.mainButBrushSize.bSize, _root.col,
➥ _root.mainButBrushAlpha.bAlpha);
        drawPad.lineTo(oldX, oldY);
    }
  }
};
```

The first line here simply sets the `lineStyle` for drawing, taking attributes written from the brushes input boxes.

The second line draws a line from the current mouse position to the end of the last line (`oldX` and `oldY`).

The last section of code sets the functions to run on mouse button activity:

```
drawPad.onPress = function() {
    _root.penDown = 0;
    freeDrawInterval = setInterval
    ➥ (function () { freeDraw();}, 10);
};
```

The `onPress` code here simply defines the code that is carried out when the mouse button is pressed. The first thing that happens is that the `penDown` flag is set to 1, and this, if you remember from the start of the function above, tells Flash to perform a `moveTo` to the current mouse position.

After this, a `setInterval` action is set, telling Flash to run the `freeDraw` function every 10 milliseconds. This is used as opposed to the `onEnterFrame` code because it runs a little more regularly. Sometimes `onEnterFrame` is affected by the frame rate and we want this to run regularly.

Here's the last of the code for the pencil tool:

```
    drawPad.onRelease =
➥ drawPad.onReleaseOutside=function () {
        clearInterval(freeDrawInterval);
    };
};
```

This batch of code is set to run in the event of an `onRelease` or `onReleaseOutside`.

A word of warning here. When you write code like this using double declarations...

```
me.onRelease = me.onReleaseOutside = function () {
    doThis();
    nowThis();
}
```

... make sure you don't reformat your code, as Flash tends to stick all the function code in one line and you end up with unreadable code like this:

```
me.onRelease = me.onReleaseOutside = function () {doThis();nowThis();}
```

It's super-annoying, believe me...

Anyway, back to the code. When the mouse is released, the `setInterval` method is cleared, and the drawing is stopped.

That concludes the pencil tool, as I said, it's not tricky to understand. It doesn't use the preview instance, like the line or curve tools, and just draws straight onto the pad. If anything the pencil tool is incredibly crude and unsophisticated, but it is one of the tools that I'm more likely to use.

It also rocks when you play with the brush thickness and alpha.

You might find yourself using a virtual pad when you run out of paper, or if you suddenly become worried about the decline of the rainforests. See post_it.fla for the pencil tool in a post-it stylee. Paul Davis eat your heart out.

Line tool

There are two standard line drawing methods in drawing applications. The first is to click on a point to start the line, and then drag and release to fix the point where you want the line to end. The second method (sometimes called rubber-banding) is to click once to fix the first point, then click again to fix the second point, again to fix the third, and so on drawing out a continuous line. We chose to use the first method, but it would be a simple task to change the code to the second method if you preferred.

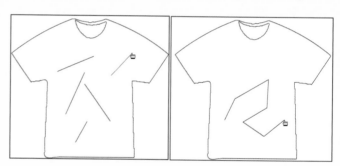

The line drawing tool is similar in execution to the freehand drawing tool, but with an important difference – instead of drawing directly onto the drawPad layer, we instead draw onto a preview layer first, and then fix the line onto the drawPad when the mouse is released.

The main line draw function is split into two parts, what happens when you press and drag the mouse on the drawPad, and what happens when you release it. Let's look at the onPress actions first.

The initial thing we do is record the x and y positions of the mouse, and store them as startX and startY:

```
funcLineDraw = function () {
    drawPad.onPress = function() {
        _root.startX = _root._xmouse;
        _root.startY = _root._ymouse;
```

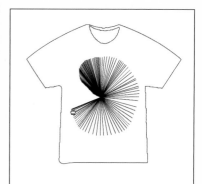

We then set up an onEnterFrame action on the root so that we can update the position of the preview line every frame. We place the event handlers on the root to ensure that they overwrite each other and there's no chance of two being run at the same time. We defined a global variable (tempLayer) for the position of the temporary layer earlier in the code, so we'll use that throughout this function. The first thing that we need to do every frame is to clear whatever was previously in the temporary layer so that there's only ever one line on it:

```
_root.onEnterFrame = function() {
    tempLayer.clear();
```

If you remove this line you can make some lovely patterns, but they're not really the effect we're after here:

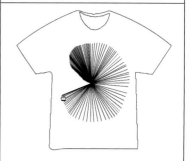

After clearing the layer, we define the lineStyle according to the current settings, and move the drawing position to the original coordinates set when we clicked the mouse:

```
tempLayer.lineStyle(_root.mainButBrushSize.bSize,
➥ _root.col,_root.mainButBrushAlpha.bAlpha);
tempLayer.moveTo(_root.startX, _root.startY);
```

We now run through a bit of boundary checking code to make sure that we don't draw outside the drawPad. This code is the same as it was for the pencil drawing tool – it checks to see if we're over the boundaries, and if we're not then it sets a variable (_root.xM & _root.yM) to hold the new mouse position, but if we are then it keeps the old position. We then draw a line from the original coordinates to the new ones:

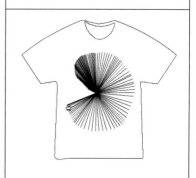

```
        if (_root._xmouse>tabletleft && _root._xmouse<tabletright) {
            _root.xM = _root._xmouse;
        }
        if (_root._ymouse>tablettop && _root._ymouse<tabletbottom) {
            _root.yM = _root._ymouse;
        }
        tempLayer.lineTo(_root.xM, _root.yM);
    };
};
```

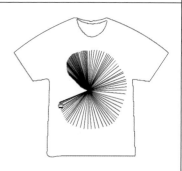

This line is redrawn every frame, and we get a nice smooth line from the start point to wherever we move the mouse.

When we release the mouse, we run through a similar set of actions, but we draw to the `drawPad` instead of to the `tempLayer`. First of all, we clear the `tempLayer` to delete the temporary line that we'd been using:

```
drawPad.onRelease = drawPad.onReleaseOutside=function () {
    tempLayer.clear();
```

We then set the `lineStyle` of the `drawPad`, and draw a line from the original start point to the last mouse position points. We also set the `_root.onEnterFrame` handler to be undefined, as we've finished with it until next time we click the mouse.

```
        drawPad.lineStyle(_root.mainButBrushSize.bSize,
        ➥ _root.col, _root.mainButBrushAlpha.bAlpha);
        drawPad.moveTo(_root.startX, _root.startY);
        drawPad.lineTo(_root.xM, _root.yM);
        _root.onEnterFrame = undefined;
    };
};
```

And that's all there is to the line tool. It's very simple, but you can make some great effects with it:

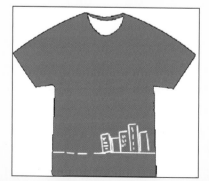

Curve tool

The curve tool is a little more complicated than the other drawing tools, but it's still fairly straightforward. The actual drawing method is similar to the line tool, in that we draw onto the same temporary layer first, and then fix it to the `drawPad` when we're done. The main difference comes with the way curves are actually drawn in Flash. For a straight line we only have two points, the start and the end, but for a curve, we have three points, the start anchor, the end anchor, and the control point. Flash uses a Bezier drawing system, but for ease of understanding we can substitute this for a trajectory metaphor.

Imagine that you're standing in a big field with an unlimited pile of metal balls by your side. About 20 feet away from you is a large and powerful magnet, and whenever you throw a ball, it is pulled onto the magnet. You and the magnet represent the anchor points of the curve, and the trajectory of the ball when you throw it describes the shape of the curve. Now, to make this example even weirder, imagine there's an annoying bird hovering in the air and squawking at you. You throw a ball with the perfect power and accuracy to hit the bird, but before it gets there, the magnet pulls the ball back to the ground:

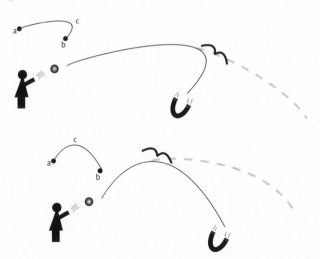

The bird then, is our control point. Whenever it moves and starts squawking again, you throw another ball, the magnet pulls it in, and the shape of the curve changes. As I said, this isn't exactly what happens in Flash but it should give you a bit more of an understanding of why the curve is the shape that it is. The best way to really understand it is to run the program and have a play with it.

OK, that's the theory dealt with, now on to the code. The first thing that we do is to define a couple of functions, but I'm going to explain it in the order that it happens, rather than the code order, so bear with me. The first thing that happens when you click on the curve tool button is that you are asked to click three points to set the initial positions of the anchor and control points.

There are three movie clips in the Library with the linkage names, a1, a2, and ctrl – these are the simple circles that will represent our anchor and control points. We first initialize the `clickedPoints` variable at 0, and then set up an `onRelease` handler on `drawPad`. We then run through a simple series of `if` statements to check if we're on our first, second, or third click. The actions we take for each are pretty similar, so I'll only run through the first one:

```
if (clickedPoints == 0) {
    _root.attachMovie("a1", "a1", 222220);
    _root.a1._x = _xmouse;
    _root.a1._y = _ymouse;
    clickedPoints++;
}
```

Here, we attach the appropriate clip from the library and set its depth level. We then position it according to the mouse position and increment the `clickedPoints` variable to move on to the next one.

Next, we draw the initial call onto the `tempLayer`, and change the help text to explain what to do next:

```
drawCurve.call(tempLayer, a1, ctrl, a2);
_root.help.text = "Drag green anchor
➥ points to position curve, then drag and
➥ release control point to fix curve and
➥ color";
```

Finally, we increment `clickedPoints` once more, so that we don't create any more circles when we click, and attach the `previewCurve` function to each of the movie clips:

```
        clickedPoints++;
    }
    previewCurve.call(_root.a1);
    previewCurve.call(_root.a2);
    previewCurve.call(_root.ctrl);
};
```

OK, that's all of the initialization done – now we move on to updating the preview curve each frame. Much of this code is similar to the line tool code, so I'll skip over some of it and focus on the parts that have changed. We set up the anchor points to be draggable, but constrained to the square drawing tablet:

```
previewCurve = function () {
    this.onPress = function() {
        tempLayer.clear();
        if (this != ctrl) {
            this.startDrag(true, tabletleft,
            ➥tablettop, tabletright,
            ➥tabletbottom);
        }
```

The control point is slightly different though:

```
else {
    this.startDrag(true);
}
```

If we constrained that to the square then you wouldn't be able to draw very big curves. To get around this, we'll allow the control point to be dragged anywhere on the stage. The curve itself will still be masked within the square so that it doesn't get all over the interface, but you can now have a lot more control over the shape of your curves. We'll get to what happens when you release it in just a second.

First though, we'll set an `onEnterFrame` handler on the `root` to redraw the curve every frame:

```
_root.onEnterFrame = function() {
    tempLayer.clear();
    tempLayer.lineStyle
➥ (_root.mainButBrushSize.bSize, 0x000000, 100);
    _root.point1x = _root.a1._x;
    _root.point1y = _root.a1._y;
    tempLayer.moveTo(_root.point1x,
    ➥ _root.point1y);
    tempLayer.curveTo(_root.ctrl._x,
    ➥ _root.ctrl._y, _root.a2._x, _root.a2._y);
};
};
```

This code is the same as that we used for the line tool, the only difference being that we're using `curveTo` instead of `lineTo`, and feeding it our extra set of coordinates. We set the preview curve to always be black and 100% alpha so that you can clearly see the shape of the curve that you're drawing.

When we release the mouse, we also want different actions for the points. The anchor points will just stop dragging, as they are already constrained to the square, but the control point has some extra code:

```
this.onRelease = this.onReleaseOutside =
➥ function () {
    this.stopDrag();
    if (this == ctrl) {
        drawCurve.call(drawPad, a1, ctrl, a2);
        tempLayer.clear();
        if (_root.ctrl._x>tabletright) {
            _root.ctrl._x = tabletright;
        }
        if (_root.ctrl._x<tabletleft) {
            _root.ctrl._x = tabletleft;
        }
        if (_root.ctrl._y<tablettop) {
            _root.ctrl._y = tablettop;
        }
        if (_root.ctrl._y>tabletbottom) {
            _root.ctrl._y = tabletbottom;
        }
    }
    _root.onEnterFrame = undefined;
};
```

When we release the control point, we first fix the curve onto the `drawPad` and clear the `tempLayer`, but we then snap the position of the movie clip back so that it's inside the square. We do this by simply checking if the control point is outside of the square on each of its axes, and setting it back to the edge of the square if it is. Finally, we undefine the root `onEnterFrame` handler.

The last function to explain for the curve tool is the actual `drawCurve` function. This function very simply takes the positions of the three points, and draws the curve between them, setting it to the correct `lineStyle` as it goes:

```
drawCurve = function (clip1, control, clip2) {
    this.lineStyle
    ➥ (_root.mainButBrushSize.bSize,
    ➥ _root.col,
    ➥ _root.mainButBrushAlpha.bAlpha);
    this.moveTo(clip1._x, clip1._y);
    this.curveTo(control._x, control._y,
    ➥ clip2._x, clip2._y);
};
```

There is a glitch in the Flash curve drawing engine that you may see cropping up from time to time. If the anchor points and the control point are all in a straight line with both of the anchor points on one side, then the line drawn will often go a bit strange, like this:

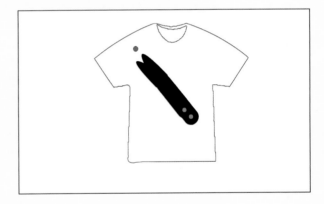

This shouldn't be too much of a problem though, as you'll normally be drawing straight lines with the line tool, not the curve tool.

Fill draw

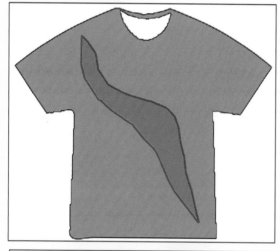

The fill draw tool is virtually the same as the pencil tool, with the added bonus of a lovely fill. The fill becomes cool when you change its alpha, so you can get a bit more depth.

During the planning stage, I came up with the following structure:

```
Press mouse button to begin drawing,
Do a beginFill declaration,
Draw a continuous line,
UNTIL....
The mouse button is released,
Stop drawing,
End the fill and close the shape.
```

The problem with this is when you call the `beginFill` method while Flash draws, it fills continuously and creates some bizarre and irrational shapes. The general rationale with the `beginFill` and `endFill` methods is that if the shape drawn with `lineTo` is unfinished – not a complete shape – then Flash finishes the shape as it sees best and fills it.

The problem with the live drawing attempt was that Flash was finishing and filling the shape at every interval, and this gave some crazy sharp geometric shapes, and loads of ugly extra lines where Flash finished the shape itself. The renditions this comes up with are bizarrely wireframe and 3Desque, and are fun to play with, but impossible to actually make anything of much use in a drawing app. Unless you make a totally irrational and random drawing app of course (a bit like Auto-Illustrator...!).

`SpecDraw_fill.fla` shows the general live fill drawing principle.

To get over this live filling, I decided to store the drawing routine in an array from the `onPress` and draw and fill the shape `onRelease`. The stored drawing is drawn in a temporary movie clip, and then cleared when the mouse button is released.

So the tool resembles the pencil tool, until the mouse button is released and the shape is redrawn and filled. By the way, rather than trust Flash's way of completing a shape, I stored the initial xmouse and ymouse positions and did a lineTo back to them after all the other strokes. Although Flash does this, sometimes it is best to leave nothing to chance. This method overrides any possible errors, and gives me peace of mind!

The first bit of code is very similar to the code for the pencil tool:

```
funcFillDraw = function (layerToDraw) {
    _root.penDown = 1;
    draw = function (layerToDraw) {
    if (_root._xmouse != oldX &&
    ➥ _root._ymouse != oldY) {
       if (_root.penDown == 1) {
         _root.moveX = _root._xmouse;
         _root.moveY = _root._ymouse;
         drawPad.moveTo(moveX, moveY);
         _root.penDown = 0;
```

The main addition here is the storage of the initial xmouse and ymouse positions in the variables moveX and moveY. As mentioned earlier, these variables are used when redrawing the lines, and we need to finish the shape correctly, and are also used to move to the start point before commencing the redraw.

The next lines set up the tempLayer movie clip, ready for drawing a preview shape:

```
tempLayer.lineStyle(_root.mainButBrushSize
➥ .bSize, _root.col,
➥ _root.mainButBrushAlpha.bAlpha);
    tempLayer.moveTo(_root.moveX, _root.moveY);
    } else {
```

The same brush styles are used here, to give the best and most authentic preview. The idea is to not let the user know that this is happening, as they might be annoyed by the thought that their creative strokes are being replicated by an automaton.

Then comes another section of code that should look familiar from studying the pencil tool:

```
    if (_root._xmouse>tabletleft &&
    ➥ _root._xmouse<tabletright) {
       oldX = _root._xmouse;
    }
    if (_root._ymouse>tablettop &&
    ➥ _root._ymouse<tabletbottom){
       oldY = _root._ymouse;
    }
    tempLayer.lineTo(oldX, oldY);
    _root.xStore[_root.count] =
    ➥ _root.oldX;
    _root.yStore[_root.count] =
    ➥ _root.oldY;
    _root.count++;
    }
  }
};
```

After the boundary checks, a line is drawn on the temporary layer, and then oldX and oldY are stored in the xStore and yStore arrays. These are the arrays used to store the co-ordinates ready to redraw the previewed strokes made by the user.

We then set what happens when the user presses the mouse button, putting the pen down:

```
drawPad.onPress = function() {
    _root.penDown = 1;
    _root.count = 0;
    _root.xStore = new Array ();
    _root.yStore = new Array ();

    layerToDraw.lineStyle
    ➥ (_root.mainButBrushSize.bSize,
    ➥ _root.col,
    ➥ _root.mainButBrushAlpha.bAlpha);
    fillInterval = setInterval(function ()
    ➥ { _root.draw(layerToDraw);}, 10);
};
```

Most of this will be familiar from the pencil tool, with the exception of the array declarations. Basically, each time the mouse button is pressed with this tool selected, the array is reinitiated, deleting the previous version of it. This wipes the slate clean of the last stored co-ordinates.

Next comes the code for when the mouse button is released:

```
drawPad.onRelease = drawPad.
➥ onReleaseOutside=function () {
    _root.penDown = 0;
    clearInterval(fillInterval);
    tempLayer.clear();
```

Again, this is old ground, with the exception of the clear method run on the temporary layer. This is run because the next piece of code reproduces the strokes from the stored arrays, so we no longer need the temporary layer.

Now for the interesting bit – this is the major difference between this tool and the pencil tool:

```
layerToDraw.beginFill(_root.fillcol,
➥ _root.mainButFillAlpha.fAlpha);
layerToDraw.lineStyle
➥ (_root.mainButBrushSize.bSize, _root.col,
➥ _root.mainButBrushAlpha.bAlpha);
layerToDraw.moveTo(_root.moveX,
➥ _root.moveY);
for (d=0; d<_root.xStore.length; d++) {
    layerToDraw.lineTo(_root.xStore[d],
    ➥ _root.yStore[d]);
}
layerToDraw.lineTo(_root.moveX, _root.moveY);
layerToDraw.endFill();
};
};
```

These lines of code take all the stored co-ordinates and draw the same shape that the user had previously drawn (but we had maliciously deleted with the clear method). There is nothing too complicated here, it's standard array storage, with values extracted with a for loop.

The first line sets up the fill style with the all-important beginFill method, taking the color and alpha from those set in the interface by the user. This is swiftly followed by the lineStyle setup, also captured from the interface text boxes.

The next line moves the drawing co-ordinates to the initial position defined at the press and stored with moveX and moveY.

Then a for loop is run, running the length of the xStore array. The loop could be run from the yStore array, as they would both give the same figure.

Within the loop is the drawing code, drawing a continuous line from the last position (initially defined with the moveTo to moveX and moveY) to the next position taken from the xStore and yStore arrays.

Once the loop is finished, a line is drawn to the initial position (moveX and moveY) to complete the shape, and the fill is ended with endFill.

Importing and masking a JPG

When I think back to why I thought of making this drawing app, I suppose the new JPG loading functionality of MX inspired me. Although I think the ability to load JPGs on the fly makes Flash MX 'mature', the way that it works with them leaves a lot to be desired. Of all the functionality of the application, the JPG took the most testing – at times the head was banging against the wall....

Load JPG tool

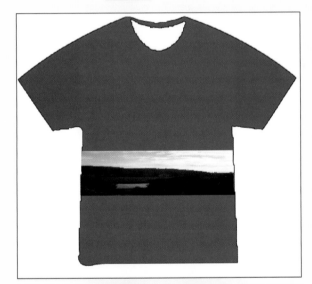

There isn't much to this tool on the face of things, but a great deal goes on here.

Issues with dynamic image loading

Before we get onto the code for the load JPG tool, it's worth looking at some of the issues with the dynamic image loading.

1. Flash MX will only load non-progressive JPGs.

That's right, Flash refuses to work with progressive JPGs – it will load them but not display them – and any other standard image formats such as GIF or PNG.

I know the reason behind this is down to the size of the Flash 6 plugin. The more formats supported, the bigger the plugin, and it is Macromedia's intention to keep it small. Great for the consumer, a little disappointing for Flash developers.

A way of getting around this is by using a server-side script to process the inputted JPG and re-export it as a non-progressive JPG image. This might involve some copyright issues though as you will have to fetch the image from the original URL location and place it on your server.

2. Flash MX dynamic JPG loading seems to have issues with browser cache.

During the testing phase of the application, I noticed that Flash seems to sometimes refuse to load JPGs when embedded in a browser.

Even though Flash's Test Movie mode and the Flash Player seem to work fine, when the Flash SWF is embedded in HTML and run in Internet Explorer, it seems to load one image and then refuses to load another image afterwards. Netscape seemed to work fine in tests though.

I think this might be down to a problem caused by Internet Explorer's caching system, and the fact that you can't turn off caching on a PC. The reason I say this is because I tested the SWF on Mac IE 5 with the cache set to 0MB, and the whole thing worked fine, any higher and the issue returns.

However, if an image is already in cache – say another browser window has it open – then the image will load in. With this in mind, a JavaScript pop-up solution would work fine, that is, if you like windows popping up everywhere...

As you can guess, this all makes for a pretty ugly situation. If you are testing the SWF in a browser, don't hold your breath for a second image.

A known way to get around this caching is to send a query string with a random number to a server-side script, preventing IE from caching it explicitly.

How it works

After all that evil, let's assess the functionality of the tool. The load JPG tool works by opening a dialog box, which requests the URL or location of a JPG image file. This location can be relative to the SWF's position, or absolute, with web prefixes.

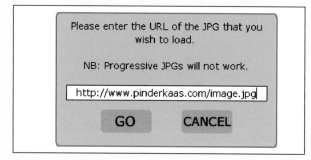

If you are testing the SWF offline, just stick a JPG in the same folder as the SWF and call that in. It will save a bit of typing and downloading.

Once the GO button has been clicked, the image is fetched (if it exists) and the percentage loaded is displayed and updated.

When the image has fully loaded, the dialog disappears and the image is resized to 200 x 200 pixels, and positioned at the center of the t-shirt, regardless of its original size. The JPG scale tool was included to allow the user to resize the image.

The code is made up of two primary functions – funcLoadJPG and loadImage. The former performs all the graphic and progress duties, whilst the loadImage function does the loading and completion tasks.

There is quite a lot of code here, but nothing that we can't handle.

First of all, we declare the function and call up the dialog box:

```
funcLoadJPG = function () {
   _root.attachMovie("loadJPGBox",
➥"loadJPGBox", 111111);
   _root.loadJPGBox._x = (Stage.width/2);
   _root.loadJPGBox._y = (Stage.height/2);
   Selection.setFocus
➥("_root.loadJPGBox.urlText");
```

loadJPGBox is pulled in from the Library and given the same name on the stage. It is then positioned on the screen.

The next line gives the urlText input field of the dialog box the text cursor's focus, using the Selection object. This object is pretty useful for any input situation, where normally the user would have to select a text box to proceed. This gives a degree of automation, and allows immediate typing from the user.

This next bit of code sets up the initial code for the GO button of the dialog box:

```
_root.loadJPGBox.goBut.onRelease = function() {
   JPG.unloadMovie();
   _root.loadImage
➥ (_root.loadJPGBox.urlText.text);
   _root.loadJPGBox.
➥ loadJPGBoxText.text = "Please
➥ wait... loading JPG\r\rIf nothing
➥ happens for a long time,\rplease
➥ hit Cancel and try another image";
   _root.loadJPGBox.goBut._visible =
➥ false;
```

The first thing that happens is that JPG is cleared. JPG is defined a little later, but is basically the container for our loadMovie calls. The next line calls the loadImage function – defined in a moment – sending the input of the dialog text box.

After this we set the text of the dialog box, informing the user of the current status. By the way, if you've every wondered what the \r is here, it is basically a line break, the equivalent of <br> in HTML or \n in numerous other scripting languages.

The last line disappears the GO button – as we don't need it any longer. It has fulfilled its aim and reason for existence.

This next bit of code checks every frame to see if the image has loaded before resetting the buttons, switching on the pencil tool and removing the dialog box:

```
_root.loadJPGBox.onEnterFrame =
➥ function () {
    if (JPG.getBytesLoaded() ==
    ➥ JPG.getBytesTotal() &&
    ➥ JPG.getBytesTotal() != 0) {
        _root.allButsOff();
        _root.mainButDraw.gotoAndStop(2);
        _root.funcFreeDraw();
        _root.help.text = "Click and drag
        ➥ to draw pencil lines";
        removeMovieClip(_root.loadJPGBox);
    }
};
};
```

We reset to the pencil tool simply because that's the default tool, you could easily change it so that it defaulted to another tool such as the JPG move tool if you'd prefer.

The reason the conditional is like this....

```
if (JPG.getBytesLoaded()==
➥ JPG.getBytesTotal() &&
➥ JPG.getBytesTotal()!= 0){
```

...is to check if the image has loaded and if getBytesTotal is not equal to zero. Flash is often likely to be a little slow on the uptake of the file coming in, and it might keep this value to zero for a while, until it realizes that a file is on its way.

We then need to set up the CANCEL button in the dialog box:

```
_root.loadJPGBox.cancelBut.onRelease
➥ = function() {
    _root.allButsOff();
    _root.mainButDraw.gotoAndStop(2);
    _root.funcFreeDraw();
    _root.help.text = "Click and drag to
    ➥ draw pencil lines";
    removeMovieClip(_root.loadJPGBox);
    JPG.unloadMovie();
};
};
```

If it's clicked, then the tools are reset, the pencil tool is activated, the dialog removed and the content of JPG is unloaded. Nothing too taxing here, but a necessary feature for the user.

Now we move on to the most important of the functions – the one that actually loads in the JPG:

```
loadImage = function (imageFileName) {
    JPG.loadMovie(imageFileName);
```

After the declaration here, the `JPG` global is told to load in an image with the argument `imageFileName`. When loading JPGs into Flash, the `loadMovie` command is used.

Then comes some code that will run every frame:

```
_root.onEnterFrame = function() {
  if (JPG.getBytesLoaded()>0) {
    _root.loadJPGBox.perc.text =
    ➥ (Math.floor((JPG.getBytesLoaded()/
    ➥ JPG.getBytesTotal())*100))+"%";
  }
  if (JPG.getBytesLoaded() ==
➥ JPG.getBytesTotal() &&
  ➥ JPG.getBytesTotal() != 0) {
```

It sets the percentage loaded text which appears in the dialog box, and checks if the image has fully loaded. The same conditional is performed here, to counteract Flash's slow pick up of files.

When the image is fully loaded, we then need some code to place it on the screen:

```
      JPG._width = 200;
      JPG._height = 200;
      JPG._x = -JPG._width/2;
      JPG._y = -JPG._height/2;
      JPG._visible = true;
      JPGContainer._x = _root.square._x;
      JPGContainer._y = _root.square._y;
      JPGContainer._xscale = 100;
      JPGContainer._yscale = 100;

      _root.onEnterFrame = undefined;
      duplicateMovieClip(_root.tshirt,
      ➥"newtee", 600);
      JPGContainer.setMask(_root.newtee);
    }
  };
};
```

The `JPG` movie clip is resized to the forced 200 x 200 pixels, and the image is repositioned so that it is centered on the registration point (when images are loaded they are positioned by default at an absolute position of (0,0)). It is repositioned so that the JPG scale tool can scale it from the center outwards.

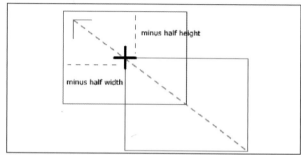

The next two lines of code position `JPGContainer` at the same position as `square`. `square` has a center registration point, so this action centers the JPG image in the middle of the t-shirt.

`JPGContainer` is then reset to a scale of 100%, to reset any previous manipulation.

The last couple of lines of code here set up a mask for the `JPGContainer`, so that the image doesn't cover the interface when it is moved around.

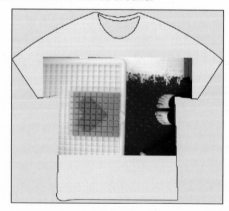

That's it for the JPG loading stuff.

The JPG element is extended later on in the chapter with the JPG scale tool and the dynamic masking....

JPG masking

The appeal of the JPG masking in this application extends past the standard square or shape mask. In this application, the user is able to draw his own mask shape and then apply it to the loaded JPG.

This part will be split into two sections – the first covers the drawing of the mask, and the second applies the mask to the JPG image.

Drawing the mask

You'll be glad to know that we have already covered the tool required to draw the mask. The mask drawing uses the fill draw tool code, but drawing to its own layer. The drawing movie clip for this tool is set-up in the initialization for the whole movie:

```
jamJar.createEmptyMovieClip("masker", 503);
```

This movie clip is made global there too:

```
_global.JPGM = jamJar.masker;
```

The reason the user is limited to using a fill draw-esque tool is because strokes cannot be used as masks, and therefore the line tool or pencil tool would be pretty useless, so I made the decision during development to limit the tool to this.

Not only did it save me some coding – making a new tool – but it also gets the user familiar with this and the fill draw tool at the same time. Neat deal.

Once you have a mask shape drawn, you'll need something for it to mask....

Applying the mask to the JPG

The application of the mask to the image is switched on or off through one simple function.

The general strategy here is to use the setMask method, and to switch the mask on or off, depending on the last state. Here's the first bit of code:

```
funcApplyMask = function () {
  _root.allButsOff();
  _root.mainButDraw.gotoAndStop(2);
  _root.funcFreeDraw();
  _root.help.text = "Click and drag to
➡ draw pencil lines";
```

No, this isn't a printing error. When this button is pressed, as well as the masking being done, the pencil tool is defaulted to. This is pretty much a standard action throughout the buttons.

In the next chunk of code, we actually do something in the way of masking:

```
if (_root.JPGMaskOn == false) {
    JPG.setMask(JPGM);
    _root.JPGMaskOn = true;
} else if (_root.JPGMaskOn == true) {
    JPG.setMask(null);
    _root.JPGMaskOn = false;
}
};
```

Now that is more like it – something relevant. The conditionals here check to see if the mask is already applied or not using the JPGMaskOn variable. JPGMaskOn is initialized as being off.

In either event, the mask is toggled on or off (using JPG.setMask (null) to remove it) and the JPGMaskOn variable is changed.

In case you missed it, JPG was defined in the previous section on loading a JPG.

As you can see, there is nothing fancy about this code, just toggling, and the superb setMask command.

JPG and mask move tools

These tools are both very similar, so they can be covered at the same time. Without further ado, let's take a look at the code. We first swap the depth of jamJar with the drawPad so that it's above the drawings and you can see what you're doing:

```
funcMoveJPG = function () {
    jamJar.swapDepths(drawPad);
```

We then set up a couple of event handlers. When you click, then you begin dragging the JPG or mask, and when you release, you stop dragging it. It's as simple as that:

```
jamJar.onPress = function() {
    JPGContainer.startDrag();
};
jamJar.onRelease =
➡jamJar.onReleaseOutside = function () {
    JPGContainer.stopDrag();
```

The last piece of code just swaps the depth back with the drawPad, and resets the drawing tools to use the free draw option:

```
    jamJar.swapDepths(drawPad);
    allButsOff();
    _root.mainButDraw.gotoAndStop(2);
    funcFreeDraw();
    };
};
```

JPG scale tool

The JPG scale tool contains quite a lot of code, but it can be easily broken down into more manageable pieces. First though, let's take a quick run though of what the tool actually does. When you click and drag a JPG with the scale tool, you get a freeform scaling effect. This means that if you drag along the x-axis, but not the y, then you'll scale the image only along the x-axis and vice versa:

A nice side-effect of the way this scaling is done is that you can also flip the image along either of its axes by simply dragging past the origin in the opposite direction:

If you don't want to deform the image though, you can hold the SHIFT key down to constrain the proportions of the image:

This will keep whatever proportions the image was in when you first clicked, so if it was in a pretty strange shape already, then it will remain in a shape of those proportions when you SHIFT-drag it.

OK, hopefully you know pretty much what effect we're trying to create – now we just need to code it.

The first thing to do, much like we did for the move tools, is to swap the depth of `jamJar` with `drawPad` to ensure that the image is visible and easy to scale. We then set up an `onPress` event handler:

```
funcScaleTool = function () {
    jamJar.swapDepths(drawPad);
    jamJar.onPress = function() {
```

Inside this, we store the mouse co-ordinates and the scale of the JPG container clip:

```
_root.origx = _xmouse;
_root.origy = _ymouse;
_root.oldxscale = JPGContainer._xscale;
_root.oldyscale = JPGContainer._yscale;
```

The reason that the JPG was nested in its own clip one layer deeper than the mask is purely so that we can scale it properly. When you create an empty movie clip using code, the registration point of that clip is automatically set to the top-left corner. This is fine for most things, but a nightmare when you want to scale that clip. Because you can only alter the movie clip that a JPG is loaded into rather than the JPG itself, you end up with an effect where the JPG appears to move away from you as it grows. This is due to the fact you're scaling it from its top-left corner rather than the center, and annoyingly there's no way to change the registration point of a movie clip using code. The way to get around this is to nest the JPG within another clip and center it within that clip. This means that you can scale the holding clip and give the effect of the JPG scaling smoothly from its center. It's a bit of a convoluted method, but it works in the end.

The next thing to do is to set an `onEnterFrame` event handler on the root. We'll use this to update the image scale every frame. First of all, we create variables to store the new `xmouse` and `ymouse` co-ordinates in the current frame, then we store the difference between these current co-ordinates, and the original co-ordinates:

```
_root.onEnterFrame = function() {
    _root.newx = _xmouse;
    _root.newy = _ymouse;
    _root.xdiff = _root.newx-_root.origx;
    _root.ydiff = _root.newy-_root.origy;
```

We now check the state of the `shiftTog` variable. We'll come to `shiftTog` in a minute, but basically it tells us if the SHIFT key is being pressed or not. If the SHIFT key isn't down, then we simply scale the image according to the difference between the original mouse position and the current mouse position. We also add the original image scale to this value. If we didn't do this, then the scale would immediately be set to 0 every time we clicked the mouse – it would still work, it just wouldn't be as nice an effect:

```
if (_root.shiftTog == false) {
    JPGContainer._xscale =
    ➥ _root.xdiff+_root.oldxscale;
    JPGContainer._yscale =
    ➥_root.ydiff+_root.oldyscale;
}
```

If the SHIFT key is held down, then we run through a slightly more difficult set of actions. To constrain the proportions, we check both axes to see which is the greater difference in mouse position – that is, which is currently the bigger scale – and then set the other axis to equal that one. Let's run through the code for the x-axis and see what happens:

```
if (_root.shiftTog == true) {
    if (_root.xdiff>_root.ydiff) {
        _root.newx = _root._xmouse;
        JPGContainer._xscale =
        ➥ _root.xdiff+_root.oldxscale;
        JPGContainer._yscale =
        ➥ _root.xdiff+_root.oldyscale;
    }
```

We first check to see if `xdiff` is greater than `ydiff`, and if it is then we only update the `newx` position, and we set both the x and the y-scale to equal the x difference. Basically then, whenever the x-scale grows, the y-scale is set to be exactly the same size. The code for the y-axis is exactly the same, but with the x-axis constrained:

```
else {
    _root.newy = _root._ymouse;
    JPGContainer._xscale =
    ➥_root.ydiff+_root.oldxscale;
    JPGContainer._yscale =
    ➥_root.ydiff+_root.oldyscale;
}
```

When you're happy with the scale, you release the mouse and the image is swapped back under the `drawPad`, and the draw tools are set back to the default pencil tool:

```
jamJar.onRelease = jamJar.onReleaseOutside
➥ = function () {
    jamJar.swapDepths(drawPad);
    _root.onEnterFrame = undefined;
    _root.allButsOff();
    _root.mainButDraw.gotoAndStop(2);
    funcFreeDraw();
    _root.help.text = "Click and drag to
    ➥draw pencil lines";
};
```

The last thing that we need to do is set up the `Listener` for the SHIFT key. The `Listener` is an object called `shiftList`. We perform two checks with the `shiftList` object. The first of these is to detect when a key is pressed, and if it is SHIFT (defined as constant `Key.SHIFT`) then `shiftTog` is set to true:

```
shiftList = new Object();
shiftList.onKeyDown = function() {
    if (Key.isDown(Key.SHIFT)) {
        _root.shiftTog = true;
    }
};
```

When a key up is detected, we also check to see if the SHIFT key is down. This may seem a little odd, but it is just an extra check to catch any keys that were pressed while the SHIFT key was down. If this check wasn't here then if you held down SHIFT, but then pressed and released another key whilst SHIFT was still down, `shiftTog` would be wrongly set to false:

```
shiftList.onKeyUp = function() {
    if (Key.isDown(Key.SHIFT)) {
    } else {
        _root.shiftTog = false;
    }
};
```

Here, we only act if the key is not down. We now just need to add the `Listener`, and initialize `shiftTog` to false:

```
Key.addListener(shiftList);
_root.shiftTog = false;
};
```

That's it, the scaling code is over, and I bet it wasn't that bad after all. One thing worth noting is that if you scale your images to massive proportions, then Flash may start to slow down quite a bit. If you're sensible with your scaling though, then this shouldn't be a problem.

General tools

t-shirt mask

One of the major delights about this application for me is the ability to preview the hard (or not so hard) work that I've put into making a t-shirt. If you're a little confused about what I mean by preview, I mean super-tidying it up – killing all unnecessary lines and presenting the colored t-shirt against a pristine white background.

If you can't see my enthusiasm and need convincing, then take a journey of cheese with Mr. Miyage:

"Mask on...":

"Mask off...":

I hope you can see that the masked article is luscious and ready to be printed.

Okay, enough excitement already! Now onto the technical stuff...

The masking process involves a number of masks and, above all these, a drawn outline to keep the shape. The outline is found on the stage and looks like this:

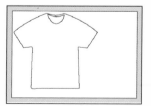

Now onto the actual masking.

Firstly, masking the main t-shirt is a little more complex than the JPG masking, simply because it has more things to mask. The main mask has to hide the content of `drawPad`, `square` and `jamJar`.

It might seem like overkill, but there are three masks working here. The reason for this is because Flash masks can only mask one item each. Of course, you can mask more items by nesting them, but it's not always possible and you do lose a little control.

Even though there are three masks, you'll be glad to know that one is reused. When we first loaded in a JPG (see the load JPG code), a mask was created for it called `newtee` to prevent it going outside the t-shirt area and engulfing the whole interface. When the main mask is applied, the `newtee` mask is told to mask the whole `jamJar` movie clip – this being the JPG mask (`_global.JPGM`) and the JPG (`_global.JPGContainer`).

The other two masks are hidden on the main stage, called `tshirt` and `tshirt2`. Both of these are instances of `tshirt_mask`:

Here is the code for the main mask:

```
funcMainMask = function () {
    if (_root.maskOn == false) {
        _root.square.setMask(_root.tshirt2);
        drawPad.setMask(_root.tshirt);
        jamJar.setMask(_root.newtee);
        _root.maskOn = true;
    } else if (_root.maskOn == true) {
        drawPad.setMask(drawPadMask);
        JPGContainer.setMask(_root.newtee);
        _root.square.setMask(null);
        _root.maskOn = false;
    }
};
```

A lot of this is quite simple and incredibly similar to the JPG mask script, using a toggle to switch the masks on or off, and check its current state. The only difference here is that some masking is changed depending on the states. Here are the actions that take place:

- The mask of `drawPad` is changed from `drawPadMask` – a square the size of the drawing area – to `tshirt` when the mask is on.

- `square` is masked by `tshirt2`, and is unmasked (`null`) when the mask is off.

- `newtee` is used as a mask for the parent of `jamJar` when the mask is on, and masks `JPGContainer` when it is off.

That's it for the masking code. There is nothing to it that we haven't seen before.

Clear tool

The clear tool is what you use when it all goes wrong. It deletes everything that you've done so far, and starts you off again with a blank canvas and a pencil. That sounds a bit drastic, and it is, so as with all drastic actions, you get a second chance to confirm if that was really what you wanted to do. This is done with an alert box that jumps to the center of the stage with the following options:

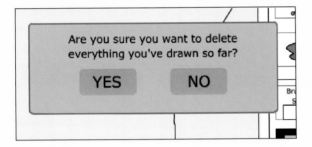

The first thing that happens when the button is pressed is that we attach the `clearCheck` alert box from the Library and position it in the center of the stage:

```
funcClearTool = function () {
    _root.attachMovie("clearCheck",
 ➥ "clearCheck", 111111);
    _root.clearCheck._x = (Stage.width/2);
    _root.clearCheck._y = (Stage.height/2);
```

We then set up the actions for each of the buttons. The "yes" button clears the `drawPad`, erasing all of the drawings, and also wipes the JPG mask layer, and unloads the JPG image as well. After this thorough bit of vacuuming, it then turns on the free draw tool, corrects the help text, and then deletes the alert box from the stage:

```
_root.clearCheck.yesBut.onRelease =
 ➥ function() {
    drawPad.clear();
    JPGM.clear();
    JPG.unloadMovie();
    _root.allButsOff();
    _root.mainButDraw.gotoAndStop(2);
    _root.funcFreeDraw();
    _root.help.text = "Click and drag to
 ➥ draw pencil lines";
    removeMovieClip(_root.clearCheck);
};
```

The "no" button skips the first three lines of erasing code, but then carries on exactly the same as the "yes" button. It just resets the drawing tools to free draw mode and deletes the alert box from the stage:

```
_root.clearCheck.noBut.onRelease =
 ➥ function() {
    _root.allButsOff();
    _root.mainButDraw.gotoAndStop(2);
    _root.funcFreeDraw();
    _root.help.text = "Click and drag to
 ➥ draw pencil lines";
    removeMovieClip(_root.clearCheck);
};
};
```

If you'd prefer, you could store the previous tool in a temporary variable so that if you chose to cancel the clear command, you'd be returned to your exact state before you pressed the clear button.

210

Outro

As much as this application is finished, it is still ripe for improvements. When I was showing this to various people, they all requested a tool that wasn't present, from the ubiquitous undo option to a text tool to a shape tool. The reality is, development of this application is never-ending...

The emphasis in my version is on creating basic designs and compositions. The limit on the tools encourages people to be more creative and resourceful.

Any news and updates to this application will be posted online at www.pinderkaas.com/foed_tshirt. If you do use this on your website, or make any amendments or improvements, please let me know through the contact on the website – I'd love to see other people's interpretations of it!

Enjoy...

INTERACTIVE VIDEO: KARATE!

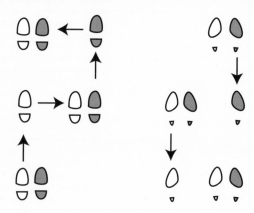

Having a working knowledge of Flash puts us in a fortunate position. When having one of those late night discussions about things you'd love to do but have never gotten round to, a friend mentioned his wish to demonstrate his adeptness at karate to others in some kind of instructional film. This got me thinking. Would it be possible to use Flash to help him realize this aim? Flash MX's new video capabilities have opened up endless possibilities, and my mind immediately started ticking over with ways to make this wish a reality. However, I knew the challenge would not simply be to get a video on the web. The site would have to be instructional, and what's more, it needed to be easily updateable. After all, he wanted to be ultimately in control. Would it be possible to create an expandable interface to which he could prepare and add additional content, with a minimum amount of effort once the groundwork had been done? Not one to baulk at a challenge, I set to work.

The basic techniques of karate include stances and methods of blocking, kicking, punching, and striking. These techniques are combined during practice in choreographed patterns called katas (pronounced KAH tahs). We have all seen diagrams illustrating dance moves using a multitude of feet symbols and arrows. Although Flash would be adequately equipped to deliver a how to dance movie, outside of the *Strictly Ballroom* or *Billy Elliot* movie hype driven fads, who wants to dance? However, this idea of diagrammatic representation seemed to lend itself very well to my challenge, finding an effective way of demonstrating karate.

Little foot position diagrams are all well and good, but of course we wanted to add an extra dimension to this technique through the addition of some hardcore karate video action. Using Flash MX's new capabilities to embed video into our Flash movies, combined with the traditional Flash techniques of vector based motion graphics, we can analyze video content and use Flash as an educational content producer, in this case to illustrate the performing of a kata. I set about this by creating two Flash movies. The first one would enable me to record a kata's movements, and the second would be designed to play back this captured information as a karate tutorial movie. Our first movie is called `kata_record.fla` and our second `kata_play.fla`.

So it happened that, one Friday night as the rest of the working world was winding down for the weekend, myself and a man dressed in white pajamas found ourselves in an abandoned kick boxing gym, armed only with a DV cam and a tripod.

We recorded the kata being performed a number of times, both from the front and side. It was decided that these were the two angles that gave most information to the viewer. We wanted to give the viewer a choice of views when watching the completed movie so it was important to think ahead and make sure that any footage that was going to be required was captured at this time.

Ideally, these two angles would have been recorded simultaneously using two DV cams – but we don't live in an ideal world, and as I'm a true professional I'm used to working round technological and financial restraints. We filmed the kata being performed both towards the camera and then across the field of view. (Incidentally for the purposes of this project the exercise being performed is the Pinan Yondan kata, but then I guess you would have spotted that yourself.)

iMovie was used to capture the footage. This has the advantage of being simple to use, plus of course it was freely available to us as it comes as standard with all current Macs. (It is Mac only software but Movie Maker for Windows XP would do the same job if you were planning a similar project and needed to use a PC.)

Once the footage of the kata being performed from each angle was imported into iMovie, (and the two clips imaginatively named `katafront` and `kataside`) a little editing was required, as we needed to check that our two clips began and ended at the same point along the timeline.

With the kata being an intricately choreographed routine the length of time it takes to perform each occasion is of a near identical duration. We needed to sync `kataside` with `katafront`. The first step in each kata is a bow, or rei, as it is known (educational, this, isn't it?). We needed to have the rei taking place at exactly the same position on the timeline in each of our movies.

In our movie `kataside` the rei takes place at 2.2 seconds.

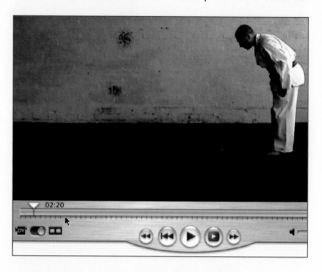

In `katafront` it takes place at 1.15 seconds

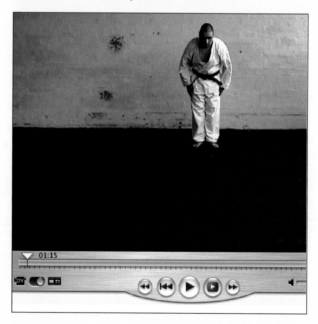

A little simple mathematics showed me that I needed to remove 2.2 minus 1.15 seconds from `kataside` – 1.05 seconds. To do this we position the playhead at 1.05 seconds and then split the video clip. Edit > Split Video Clip at Playhead or CMD / CTRL-T.

I now had two video clips starting at exactly the same time before the kata starts, and, due to the tight choreography, finishing within fractions of a second of each other. I then trimmed the ends of our video so that I had two clips of identical length, one minute and two seconds long.

I didn't want to over complicate the movie clips with effects, but in order to make our end product seem a bit more professional I applied a simple Fade In and Fade Out to the beginning and end of both clips. This means that the final movie won't have such a brutal change of appearance between being static and playing.

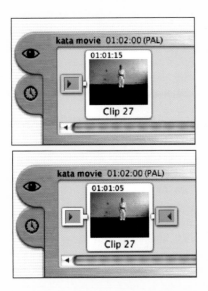

iMovie can export movies in a range of formats. I chose to export the two clips as QuickTime (.mov) clips. Macromedia Flash MX has an advanced method of compressing video, built-in in the form of Sorenson Spark. This means it's advantageous to keep movies at as high a quality as possible until they are imported into Flash.

It is worth noting here that the video was exported as 25 Frames per second. The relevance of this becomes apparent once we import our movies into Flash.

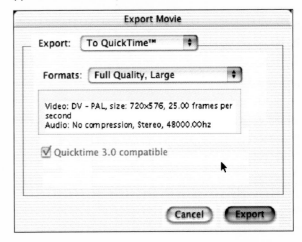

I now had my two movies, katafrontfql.mov and katasidefql.mov, each weighing in at a pretty hefty 224mb. (You can find lower quality versions of these clips in the download files, if you want to follow along with the development process.) Now obviously this is not the sort of file size we have come to associate with Flash design. Luckily Flash MX can help us to do something about this.

We can now start to piece together our first Flash movie, kata_record.fla.

With Flash launched the first thing to do is set our frame rate to match that of the video we are going to import. When we exported our QuickTime movie we made a point of noting that the frame rate was 25 fps, and we need to mirror this setting in the properties of our Flash movie. This can be done in the Properties palette, which should be visible by default when we launch Flash. We can also set the overall size of our Flash movie now. In order to have a nice big space to play with, go for a size of 700 x 420 pixels. Remember that Flash always resizes from the top left hand point of the stage – this can make it really important to think ahead when beginning Flash projects.

Let's finally get a video clip into the Flash environment. Go to **File > Import to Library** and navigate through your directories to find the QuickTime movies. As both clips are essentially the same footage, shot from different angles, we could select either one. Our first movie will make use of just one of the views that we shot. I have selected katafrontfql.mov. A window appears asking whether we wish to embed the video within our Flash movie or link to it externally. We want to embed it.

Sorenson Spark then launches from within Flash and the following window appears:

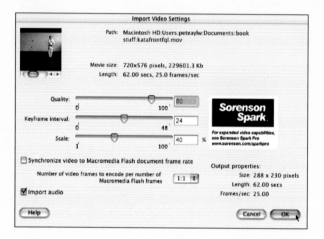

This is where we slim down our video content to a far more manageable size.

We can afford to lower the quality of our import to around the 80% mark, as this still gives us enough detail to analyze the video content.

Our video does contain a fair degree of movement, although it is movement within a static environment. We have therefore gone straight down the middle and selected a Keyframe interval of 24.

These two settings, Quality and Keyframe interval, do require a degree of trial and error to achieve results, as a little adjustment can give very different results.

The Scale slider is where we reduce the video size from the 'large' size that we exported from iMovie to the size we will eventually view it at. The video is going to make up approximately one third of our final movie's screen width, so thinking of a final screen resolution of 1024 x 768 pixels, a scale of 40% makes sense.

We don't need to synchronize the video to the document frame rate as we have already adjusted the document to match the video.

We can choose here whether or not to import the sound alongside our video. I have included the sound, as it is important to our end goal, the demonstration of karate. While performing the kata, sound plays an important part with the practitioner occasionally giving a yell called a kiai (pronounced KEE eye). However, as we know, sound is included at the expense of file size. Perhaps for Web presentation we should omit sound, but for this exercise I wanted to include it. You never know, this might end up being a best selling teach yourself karate CD-ROM.

Once we press the OK button we have a bit of a wait while Sorenson Spark works its magic. Probably a good time to work on developing that one–inch punch you so desire.

That should have stopped importing before you develop plans to take on Chuck Norris, and we can take a look at our new slimline video. Double clicking on my movie clip in the library shows me that Sorenson has managed to reduce my 224mb video to just 877k. Now that's impressive! Obviously if you are working with lower quality versions these figures will differ, but it should give you an idea of the power of Sorenson Spark's compression system.

Before we can do anything else we need to put that embedded video into a movie clip. Create a new movie clip called video and rename the layer Video too. Drag a copy of katafrontfql.mov from the library to the stage and a box will appear, asking whether to insert enough frames to display the whole video. We don't want to lose any of our video, so click yes.

Only three buttons to go now. Next we will sort out our slow motion button. Here's the ActionScript:

```
controls.slomoBut.onPress = function() {
  video.stop();
  count = 0;
  video.onEnterFrame = function() {
    count++;
    if ((count % 5) == 0) {
      video.nextFrame();
    }
  };
};
controls.slomoBut.onRelease = function() {
  video.onEnterFrame = null;
  video.stop();
  playing = false;
};
```

It's in two parts, as we are going to set it to function only when the button is actually pressed and held. The function is therefore set to run with an onPress event rather than the onRelease that the buttons have used up until now.

The first couple of lines tell the video to stop running, then set a variable called count to zero. Next the code attaches a function to the video movie clip. This function is the one that gets the video to play its next frame only every 5 frames. It does this by adding 1 to the variable count each frame then working out what's left over when dividing count by 5. If this equals zero it moves the video to the next frame. As a zero result can only be achieved when count is a multiple of 5, the video can only advance every 5th frame. Setting this to 5 works fine with our minute long movie but depending on the video being played an alternative value may be more appropriate.

When the button is released the second part of the ActionScript runs. This removes the function added to the video instance and stops the video at its current position. Again we have to remember to let the rest of the code know that the video is currently stopped with the playing = false line.

The code for the rewind and fast forward buttons is similar to the slow motion one, in that it is in two parts, one part for press and one for release.

```
controls.rewindBut.onPress = function() {
  video.onEnterFrame = function() {
    video.gotoAndStop(
    ➥ video._currentframe-10);
  };
};
controls.rewindBut.onRelease = function() {
  video.onEnterFrame = null;
  video.play();
  playing = true;
};
```

Once again the button press attaches, via an onEnterFrame, a function to every frame of the video instance. This function looks at the current frame, then goes to and stops 10 frames further back along the video clip's timeline, where the function is played through once more.

When the button is released the function is removed from the video instance and the video is left playing.

The code for fast forward is uncannily similar:

```
controls.ffwdBut.onPress = function() {
  video.onEnterFrame = function() {
    video.gotoAndStop
    ➥ (video._currentframe+10);
  };
};
controls.ffwdBut.onRelease = function() {
  video.onEnterFrame = null;
  video.play();
  playing = true;
};
```

It's the same as the rewind code but the `-10` is replaced with a `+10` and the button instance name changed from `rewindBut`, to, you guessed it, `ffwdBut`.

So there we have it, a nice body of ActionScript that has given us complete control over our video clip. Test it out and make sure that you are happy with the speed of slow motion, fast forward and rewind. If not the relevant code can be amended. We will need to add further elements to some of the button code as we progress, but the important thing at this stage is that the basic video control buttons work.

We want to have the ability to annotate our video clip with both graphics and text. The text will take the form of captions, which will be entered and recorded while reviewing our video and then played back in the correct order while watching our video back. To enter our captions we are going to need an input text box. This will be positioned close to our buttons inside the controller movie clip.

We will shortly require two further text boxes so create a new layer within the controller movie clip and name it textboxes. Below our row of buttons create an input text box, 200 x 25 pixels, and give it an instance name of caption. Set it to accept 14pt Arial typeface and ensure it is left aligned. We want to have our text box match the aesthetics of our movie. We can do this with a small block of code, entered at the foot of our existing code.

```
controls.caption.border = true;
controls.caption.borderColor = 0x3399CC;
controls.caption.textColor = 0x000000;
controls.caption.backgroundColor =
➡ 0x9CB5EF;
```

This code will give us an input text box with a border to match our other elements, black text and a background to complement our overall color scheme. These changes will not be visible until we preview our movie.

Now we'll look at how we can integrate our video with our initial idea of diagrammatic feet symbols. The reason that Flash is such a relevant tool for delivering web content is that it is vector based. This means that all elements within a Flash movie are determined by a series of numbers, in the form of co-ordinates and degrees of rotation for example. This mathematical approach keeps file size down, but in this case we will use the function to help us to both record and set the position of symbols simply using numbers.

Each stance requires the feet to be in a set position at a given point in time. What we therefore need to do is calculate the position and rotation of each foot during the kata and then be able to represent this data in diagrammatic form. We don't really want to have to deal with the co-ordinates and rotations themselves, that is, not the actual numbers involved anyway. We need a front end to provide an interface to help capture the information we require.

Create a new graphic symbol called foot and draw a stylized foot. (Or if you're not feeling very artistic, once again you could always steal it from the download files.) Karate takes place bare-footed so the shoe print graphic used in typical dance step diagrams has been replaced by a bare-footed version. The graphic needs keeping nice and small, the grid in our example is an 18 x 18px grid to give an idea of scale.

Use this graphic in two new movie clips, footleft and 'footright', footleft using the graphic as it was drawn and footright flipping it horizontally. We now have our pair of feet to use in our diagrams. Create a new layer, name it feet and drag an instance of each foot onto it.

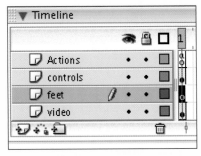

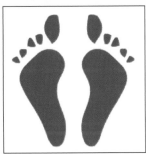

These feet need to be given an instance name each, so I've called them leftFoot and rightFoot respectively.

Our feet need somewhere to perform, a karate mat if you like, so we shall create that next. Create another new movie clip called square and in it draw a square 400 x 400 px. The feet movie clip will need to stand out against the color of the mat so choose a contrasting color for the fill. The mat should have its top left hand corner at the coordinate (0,0) as this will help when we come to position it on the main stage. As with corners on other graphics we have created, we have rounded the corners on our square, this time to 15px.

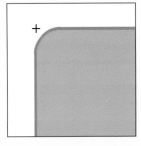

Our feet need to stand on the mat so create a layer below the feet layer, and drag the square onto it, and give it an instance name of mat. Your stage should now look something like this:

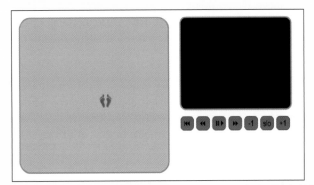

We need to be able to both move and rotate our feet symbols and switch between these two options. We are therefore going to add further buttons to our controller, a rotate button and a move button. These buttons will be movie clip symbols rather than the button symbols we used for our video controls. The two buttons will sit next to each other to give the impression of a single switch so we need to make sure they fit neatly together.

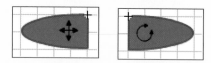

Open the controller symbol and drag an instance of the two new buttons onto the buttons layer. Move them into position and name the instances moveBut and rotateBut.

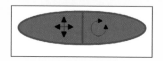

Before we add functionality to these buttons we need to think about how the end movie is going operate. We're going to use it to play back the video. When we decide that a stance needs adding we'll stop the video at the correct point. The feet will need to be dragged into their correct positions and rotated to face the right direction. This information will then be recorded, before the video is advanced to the point that another stance needs adding where the process will repeat itself. Once all stances have been recorded they will need to be exported, ready for use in the playable version of the movie.

Another two buttons are needed then, an insert instruction button and an export button. For these we can use the same buttons we used for our video controls. Add two of the generic button symbols to the buttons layer of controller. Name the instances recordBut and exportBut. The export button will only be used once in the recording process so to highlight its importance we have given it a red tint, and to make it harder to press accidentally it has been scaled down. A descriptive name has also been added.

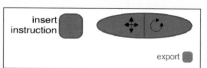

When our movie is being used, the video needs to be stopped, the feet positioned and any caption added before the insert instruction button is pressed. This could seem counter-intuitive, with the temptation to press the insert instruction button prematurely. To guide the user through the various steps in the correct order, (after all, the intention is to make this movie accessible to a relative novice) we will hide the insert instruction button till the video stops playing. This will be done with some code shortly.

In our controller movie clip add a dynamic text box to our textboxes layer. This should be called buttonText and positioned to the left of our insert instruction button. It should be set to multiline and be right aligned.

We will be able to keep track of the number of instructions recorded through monitoring a variable we will create shortly called i. This will be displayed as a counter in our controller movie clip. Add a dynamic text box with an instance name of countDigit to the textboxes layer. It should have a variable name of i, and be set to display 20pt Arial. This box will be positioned over our insert instruction button. They will not be visible simultaneously so they can happily occupy the same position on the stage.

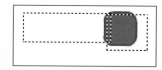

Positioning these boxes can be tricky until we start previewing the movie so we should be prepared to move things around slightly. As we develop the rest of the movie we should be thinking about how our buttons are positioned. The video controls will be used together, so they are grouped. The insert caption text field, move and rotate buttons are also used in conjunction with each other so are grouped too. The insert instruction and export button can be positioned near each other too.

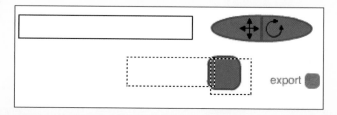

We need to add some code to make use of our text fields and also set the insert instruction button to hide when we don't want to see it. We will create two functions to do this – `setFocal` and `unsetFocal`. Here is the ActionScript, it should be added at the top of our code:

```
setFocal = function () {
   controls.buttonText.text = "Insert
   ➡ Instruction";
   controls.recordBut._visible = true;
   controls.countDigit._visible = false;
   controls.caption.text = "Insert Caption
   ➡ Here";
   Selection.setFocus(controls.caption);
   Selection.setSelection(0,
   ➡ controls.caption.length);
};
unsetFocal = function () {
   controls.ButtonText.text = "Number of
   ➡ Steps";
   controls.recordBut._visible = false;
   controls.countDigit._visible = true;
   controls.caption.text = "";
};
```

This code will be used to show or hide, as well as add, descriptive text to either the insert instruction button or instruction counter. It will also add and highlight some default text, Insert Caption Here, to the text input box. We should then add these functions to the code controlling our video. The new code is shown in bold.

```
//play and pause
controls.playBut.onRelease = function() {
  if (playing == false) {
    video.play();
    playing = true;
    unsetFocal();
  } else {
    video.stop();
    playing = false;
```

```
    setFocal();
  }
};
//back one frame
controls.backFrameBut.onRelease = function() {
   video.prevFrame();
   playing = false;
   setFocal();
};
//forward one frame
controls.forwardFrameBut.onRelease = function() {
   video.nextFrame();
   playing = false;
   setFocal();
};
//rewind to start
controls.homeBut.onRelease = function() {
   video.gotoAndStop(1);
   playing = false;
   unsetFocal();
};
//slow motion
controls.slomoBut.onPress = function() {
   video.stop();
   count = 0;
   video.onEnterFrame = function() {
     count++;
     if ((count%5) == 0) {
       video.nextFrame();
     }
   };
   unsetFocal();
};
controls.slomoBut.onRelease = function() {
   video.onEnterFrame = null;
   video.stop();
   playing = false;
   setFocal();
};
//rewind
controls.rewindBut.onPress = function() {
```

code continues overleaf...

```
    video.onEnterFrame = function() {
      video.gotoAndStop
      ➡ (video._currentframe-10);
    };
    unsetFocal();
};
controls.rewindBut.onRelease = function() {
    video.onEnterFrame = null;
    video.play();
    playing = true;
    unsetFocal();
};
//fastforward
controls.ffwdBut.onPress = function() {
    video.onEnterFrame = function() {
      video.gotoAndStop
      ➡ (video._currentframe+10);
    };
    unsetFocal();
};
controls.ffwdBut.onRelease = function() {
    video.onEnterFrame = null;
    video.play();
    playing = true;
    unsetFocal();
};
```

All the buttons are now in place to be able to set up our ActionScript to get the movie doing what it was designed to do; record information. The code will follow our button code attached to frame 1 of our actions layer. There is quite a bit of it but that is mainly because of the different variables that need recording. The first bit of the code lays this out. The co-ordinates, rotations and frame numbers where these occur will be written into an array that will be used in the playback movie.

First we define the function that gathers all the information that we require in our array:

```
recordCurrent = function () {
```

We then record the frame position where the instruction occurs:

```
changeFrame[controls.i] = video._currentframe;
```

Then comes some code to record the position of the right foot:

```
rightPosX[controls.i] =
➡ Math.round(rightFoot._x);
rightPosY[controls.i] =
➡ Math.round(rightFoot._y);
```

and then the left foot:

```
leftPosX[controls.i] =
➡ Math.round(leftFoot._x);
leftPosY[controls.i] =
➡ Math.round(leftFoot._y);
```

We then record the rotation of each foot:

```
rightRot[controls.i] =
➡ Math.round(rightFoot._rotation);
leftRot[controls.i] =
➡ Math.round(leftFoot._rotation);
```

and the caption from our input text box:

```
caption[controls.i] = controls.caption.text;
```

The next section of code adds to the array number and resets the button to the default move option:

```
    controls.i++;
    resetButtons.call(controls.moveBut);
    moveFoot.call(leftFoot);
    moveFoot.call(rightFoot);
};
```

We then add another line to define the function that will export our recorded details into the correct array format:

```
exportAll = function () {
```

and set our initial output string to be clear:

```
exportStr = "";
```

The `if` statement here makes sure that there is something to export. If there isn't, Flash jumps ahead to the code after the `else` command.

```
if (changeFrame.length>0) {
```

We then have a chunk of code that defines the format that the exported code will take:

```
exportStr += "\r// export code begins // \r";
exportStr += "changeFrame = new Array ();\r";
exportStr += "rightPosX = new Array ();\r";
exportStr += "rightPosY = new Array ();\r";
exportStr += "leftPosX = new Array ();\r";
exportStr += "leftPosY = new Array ();\r";
exportStr += "rightRot = new Array ();\r";
exportStr += "leftRot = new Array ();\r";
exportStr += "caption = new Array ();\r";
exportStr += "////////// \r";
```

`\r` gives us a new line, and the `+=` operator adds the new information to the end of the current value of the export string.

We then need some code that exports the data that has been recorded:

```
for (count=0; count<changeFrame.length;
 count++) {
```

We need to have the collection of different arrays exported for each instruction we have recorded. The `for` loop will do that by creating a `count` variable and comparing it to the length of the `changeFrame` array, exporting the arrays until `count` has the same value as the length of the array. We could have chosen any of our arrays to act as the indicator of the total length of arrays, but I've chosen `changeFrame`.

We then add some code that writes out the arrays from the details recorded:

```
exportStr += "changeFrame ["+count+"] =
 "+changeFrame[count]+";\r";
exportStr += "rightPosX ["+count+"] =
 "+rightPosX[count]+";\r";
exportStr += "rightPosY ["+count+"] =
 "+rightPosY[count]+";\r";
exportStr += "leftPosX ["+count+"] =
 "+leftPosX[count]+";\r";
exportStr += "leftPosY ["+count+"] =
 "+leftPosY[count]+";\r";
exportStr += "rightRot ["+count+"] =
 "+rightRot[count]+";\r";
exportStr += "leftRot ["+count+"] =
 "+leftRot[count]+";\r";
exportStr += "comment ["+count+"] =
 \""+caption[count]+"\";\r";
exportStr += "////////// \r";
}
}
```

The caption export string needs to have quotation marks surrounding its exported content, so escaped quotes are added to that line before and after `"+caption[count]+"`.

Then comes a section that tells the movie that if the export string has not changed from how it was initialized above, to send "No code" to the output window, but if there is code, to export it:

```
if (exportStr == "") {
  trace("No code.");
} else {
  trace(exportStr);
}
};
```

That is the majority of the code needed to record and export the information required to set our feet at the right place at the right time. We'll need some initialization code, but we'll firstly deal with the buttons we created to enable interaction with the recording and exporting functions.

First is the code to attach the record and export functions to the relevant button:

```
controls.exportBut.onRelease = function() {
  exportAll();
};
controls.recordBut.onRelease = function() {
  recordCurrent();
  video.stop();
};
```

Then comes some code to create a new function to leave our move and rotate buttons in a faded state when not active. The button that has called the function is then set to an alpha of 100 to indicate that it is the active one.

```
resetButtons = function () {
  controls.moveBut._alpha = 50;
  controls.rotateBut._alpha = 50;
  this._alpha = 100;
};
```

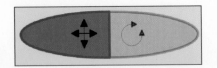

The initial state of moveBut will be set later in the code.

Once the move button is clicked it is highlighted through the resetButtons function:

```
controls.moveBut.onRelease = function() {
  resetButtons.call(this);
  moveFoot.call(leftFoot);
  moveFoot.call(rightFoot);
};
```

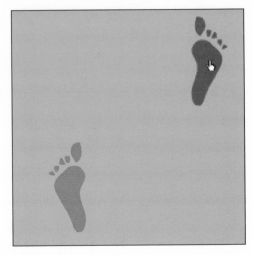

The ability to move the two feet is also activated through the next bit of code:

```
moveFoot = function () {
  this.onPress = function() {
    this.startDrag(true, mat._x, mat._y,
    ➥ (mat._x+mat._width),
    ➥ (mat._y+mat._height));
    this._alpha = 100;
  };
  this.onRelease = function() {
    this.stopDrag();
    this._alpha = 50;
  };
};
```

Once a foot is pressed it can be dragged around the mat – the code after the `startDrag` action constrains the feet to the mat. The alpha of each foot is increased while it is pressed. Once released the foot returns to its faded state.

The feet need the ability to rotate too – that is what this code is for:

```
controls.rotateBut.onRelease = function() {
    resetButtons.call(this);
    rotateFoot.call(leftFoot);
    rotateFoot.call(rightFoot);
};
```

The code is similar to that which gave the ability to move the feet, but this time gives the ability to rotate:

```
rotateFoot = function () {
    this.onPress = function() {
        this._alpha = 100;
        myX = this._x;
        this.onEnterFrame = function() {
            this._rotation +=
            ➥ Math.round(_xmouse-myX);
        };
    };
    this.onReleaseOutside =
    ➥ this.onRelease=function () {
    ➥ this._alpha = 50;this.onEnterFrame =
    ➥ undefined;};
};
```

Again the alpha is increased to 100 once a foot is pressed. The rotation function works through getting the position of the foot on the x axis, then rotating it depending on the mouse position from the foot. This can result in minus rotation if the mouse is moved to the left, and plus rotation if the mouse is to the right. As we will only see the static result of any rotation it does not matter if the foot rotates as a plus or minus.

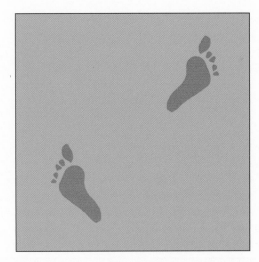

We then have the ActionScript that initializes the rest of the code through creating the empty arrays and setting the move and rotate controls to their default states:

```
video.stop();
playing = false;
unsetFocal();
changeFrame = new Array();
rightPosX = new Array();
leftPosX = new Array();
rightPosY = new Array();
leftPosY = new Array();
rightRot = new Array();
leftRot = new Array();
caption = new Array();
controls.i = 0;

leftFoot._alpha = rightFoot._alpha=50;
resetButtons.call(controls.moveBut);
moveFoot.call(leftFoot);
moveFoot.call(rightFoot);
gridvis = false;
grid._visible = false;
infovis = false;
info._visible = false;
```

There is some additional code here too. This will be required for the final stage of our preliminary Flash movie.

The final elements of this movie are aimed at making it simpler to use. The first is a grid, which we can turn on or off to help make it easier to position the feet in the correct position. This grid will be positioned over the mat.

Create a new movie clip symbol called grid and draw a basic grid on it. The simplest way is to draw a hairline weight line and duplicate it 20 times or so. Drag the last duplicate to a position that will form the outer grid line, at least 400 pixels distance from the first line. Use the Align tools to space them equally. Select all, duplicate once more and rotate this new set of lines through 90 degrees. (Alternatively you could use my grid from the library if you're feeling lazy.)

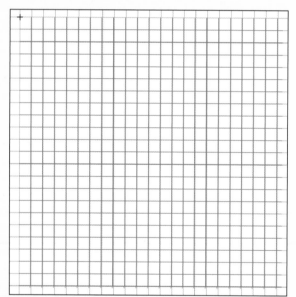

Drag this new clip onto the main stage, on a new layer above the mat layer, called, surprisingly, grid. Name the instance grid and then create a new layer above this one and drag an instance of square on to it. Position this instance of square exactly over the mat and then turn the layer into a mask, and the grid layer to a masked layer.

We now need to create a button to both activate and

deactivate this grid. Do this by adding another button to the controller movie clip, with some graphics on the text layer to indicate what it does. Name this button gridBut.

We need another bit of ActionScript to add functionality to this button. As it is associated with a button, I have placed it before the insert and record mode. This just keeps things neater. The code checks to see whether the grid is already visible – if it is it turns it off, and if it isn't it turns it on:

```
controls.gridBut.onRelease = function() {
    if (_root.gridvis == false) {
        grid._visible = true;
        gridvis = true;
    } else {
        grid._visible = false;
        _root.gridvis = false;
    }
};
```

We want it off to begin with which is why we have

```
gridvis = false;
grid._visible = false;
```

in the code that initializes everything at the foot of the ActionScript.

We want our karate expert to use this movie easily, so let's provide some basic instructions in the form of an information panel. We will do this in a similar way to the grid, by having a symbol that we can switch on and off. Create a new movie clip symbol called information, and within a box provide basic instructions on the use of this movie. Topics should include how to import a fresh video clip and how then to insert instructions and export them. We can also use another instance of the generic button to add a close button to the window. Scale it down, add a standard 'x' and give it an instance name of closeBut.

To Add Instructions

1. Whilst playing back the video press find position for first stance and stop the video.
2. Insert caption, then move feet into new position, press rotate and rotate feet.
3. Press Insert Instruction button.
4. Play video to next step and repeat process.
5. Once all instructions are entered press export, then copy code from the output window.
6. Paste code into text document and save as kata.as.

To Replace Video

1. Double click on the current .mov file in the library.
2. Select new video to import.
3. Open the video movie clip and drag the newly imported video to the stage. Extend the timeline if necessary.

Create a new layer on our main timeline and call it info. This should be our uppermost layer as it will appear on top of everything. On this layer we can position our info box where we please. Give it an instance name of info.

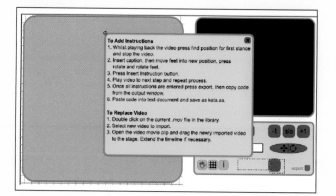

Add yet another generic button to the controller movie clip. Call this one infoBut and add an 'i' for information to the text layer. We then need to add a little more ActionScript to our body of code.

```
controls.infoBut.onRelease = function() {
    if (_root.infovis == false) {
        info._visible = true;
        infovis = true;
    } else {
        info._visible = false;
        _root.infovis = false;
    }
};
info.closeBut.onRelease = function() {
    info._visible = false;
    _root.infovis = false;
};
```

This code is essentially the same as the code to get the grid functioning, but with grid replaced with info. The second bit of the code activates the button on the info box itself.

One final addition to our movie is the function to make our controls and video clip draggable. This simply allows the user to position things where they want them. It's only a few lines of code and helps to make the interface customizable.

On the controller movie clip add yet another generic button, this time calling it dragBut. Create an icon for it too, as we need to know what all the buttons do.

This code simply allows the controller to be dragged around while the drag button is pressed until the button is released:

```
controls.drag.onPress = function() {
   startDrag(controls);
};
controls.drag.onRelease = function() {
   stopDrag();
};
```

This next code allows us to drag the video around. There is no need for a button as it is the only function the video clip needs to have.

```
video.onPress = function() {
   startDrag(video);
};
video.onRelease = function() {
   stopDrag();
};
```

Finally, we can make our controller look a little slicker, add a body to frame our buttons and generally neaten it up. I've scaled down and dropped the alpha on the less important buttons too.

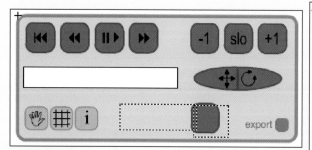

And there we have it. A Flash movie that we can use to generate an array containing all the information we need to produce an interactive karate tutorial. The playback movie will need creating next, but first we should use our recording movie to capture some karate stances to play back.

The recording movie is used in Flash's preview mode – if we published it and tried to play the resulting SWF, we would not have the output window we need to copy our code from.

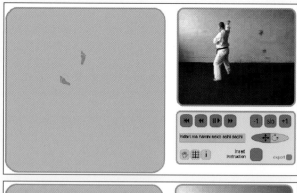

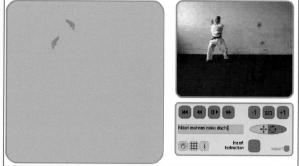

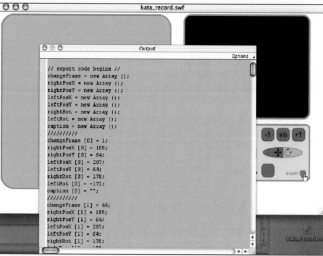

Once we have got to the end of our video clip, inserting instructions as we go, we can press the export button to have the array we need generated in the output window. This should then be copied to your clipboard. We need to create a file that includes this information that our playback movie will be able to make use of. The recommended file extension for saving ActionScript is `.as`. Using TextEdit on a Mac, or Notepad on a PC, paste the contents of the clipboard into an empty document and save this as `kata.as`. This should be in the same folder as the FLA and SWF files we are creating.

The playback movie can utilize some of the elements we created for the recording movie. The video movie clip, mat and feet all remain the same and the video control elements of the controller movie clip will still be needed to play back our now diagram-enhanced video.

There are a number of ways in which we can make constructing the playback movie simpler. Perhaps the easiest is to save our first movie, `kata_record` under a new name, `kata_play`, and then delete the aspects we no longer require and adapt the others. This is the technique we will document here.

We can safely delete the buttons that are linked to the record functions – that's insert code, move, rotate and export, plus all the code that accompanies them. The fast rewind and forward buttons will be superfluous too. We also don't need the info box or the ability to drag the video clip, so again any symbols or code associated with this can be removed.

What we do need are some new buttons in the controller movie clip. These are going to move us forward and back one step, and toggle between the side video we prepared earlier and the front video we have used until now. These buttons should have instance names of forwardBut, backwardsBut and toggleBut respectively. Our new slimmed down controller should look something like this.

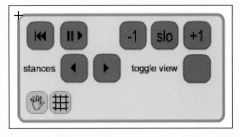

We need to import our side view video. We do this just as we did the original one, through the **File > Import to library** menu option. We should import this with identical settings to the first video we brought into Flash.

As with the front video, the side one needs to be housed in a symbol. If we duplicate our current video symbol, calling it video side, we can replace the video on the video layer with our freshly imported side view video.

Back on the main timeline, insert a new layer above the current video layer. Drag an instance of video side to the stage, aligning it exactly with the existing video clip. Call this instance videoside. We now need to add a function to our toggle button so as to see either one view or the other. This is the code:

```
controls.toggleBut.onRelease = function() {
  if (_root.fvvis == false) {
    video._visible = true;
    videoside._visible = false;
    fvvis = true;
  } else {
    video._visible = false;
    videoside._visible = true;
    _root.fvvis = false;
  }
};
```

It only allows one video view to be visible at a time, setting the alternative each time the toggle view button is pressed.

We can use the same video controls to control both video clips but we do need to add some extra lines to our existing control code. Each time the code refers to video, we need to add a line to ensure that the same action happens to videoside. If we did not do this, our video clips would run out of sync, with one continuing to play while the other was stopped.

Here is the code, which is essentially the same as before with the extra lines.

```
controls.playBut.onRelease = function() {
  if (playing == false) {
    video.play();
    videoside.play();
    playing = true;
  } else {
    video.stop();
    videoside.stop();
    playing = false;
  }
};

controls.backFrameBut.onRelease =
➡ function() {
  video.prevFrame();
  videoside.prevFrame();
  playing = false;
};

controls.forwardFrameBut.onRelease =
➡ function() {
  video.nextFrame();
  videoside.nextFrame();
  playing = false;
};
```

```
controls.homeBut.onRelease = function() {
  video.gotoAndStop(1);
  videoside.gotoAndStop(1);
  playing = false;
};

controls.slomoBut.onPress = function() {
  video.stop();
  count = 0;
  video.onEnterFrame = function() {
    count++;
    if ((count%5) == 0) {
      video.nextFrame();
    }
  };
  videoside.stop();
  count = 0;
  videoside.onEnterFrame = function() {
    count++;
    if ((count%5) == 0) {
      videoside.nextFrame();
    }
  };
};
controls.slomoBut.onRelease = function() {
  video.onEnterFrame = null;
  videoside.onEnterFrame = null;
  video.stop();
  videoside.stop();
  playing = false;
};
```

If we pick the play/pause button to look more closely at we can see that the line `videoside.play` has been added after `video.play();` and `videoside.stop();` after `video.stop ();`.

```
controls.playBut.onRelease = function() {
    if (playing == false) {
      video.play();
      videoside.play();
      playing = true;
    } else {
      video.stop();
      videoside.stop();
      playing = false;
    }
};
```

This method has been repeated throughout the code. We can now test the movie and see that using the toggle button flips us between the front and side view videos.

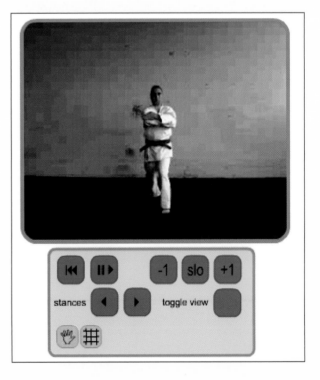

Next we need to make use of the arrays we created earlier. The first line of the ActionScript for this movie should import our arrays. Importing these arrays will ensure that they are in place for the rest of our code to refer to. We have called it `kata.as`, so add this code to line 1 of our code. Remember to ensure that the `.as` file is in the same directory as the Flash movie.

```
#include "kata.as"
```

The captions we recorded are going to be written to a dynamic text box at the lower edge of the mat. Add a new layer above the grid mask layer and call it text. Create a large dynamic text box with a variable name of captionText across the bottom of the mat. Center align the text in it.

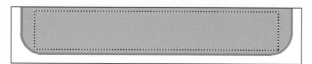

We can now add the code that will deliver the information recorded in our first movie and stored in `kata.as`. This will monitor the video movie clip and ensure that the feet graphics and captions are played back at the correct time. This code is added above the button code, and is similar to the recording code, in that it uses all the same variables for position and rotation, this time though it is setting these variables rather than recording them. Let's take a look.

This function sets the position and rotation of the feet at any recorded point and places the caption dynamically:

```
setFeetGraphic = function (changeNum) {
    rightFoot._x = rightPosX[changeNum];
    rightFoot._y = rightPosY[changeNum];
    leftFoot._x = leftPosX[changeNum];
    leftFoot._y = leftPosY[changeNum];
    rightFoot._rotation = rightRot[changeNum];
    leftFoot._rotation = leftRot[changeNum];
    caption = caption[changeNum];
```

It uses the same variables as the record movie.

We then have this code to call `positionLastFeet`, a function created in the next piece of code:

```
positionLastFeet(changeNum);
    };
```

We want to show the feet position immediately before the current one, which is known as change-1. This code creates these feet, with a low alpha so we know which are previous and which are current stances:

```
positionLastFeet = function (change) {
    if (change>0) {
        lastrightFoot._visible = true;
        lastleftFoot._visible = true;
        lastrightFoot._alpha = 20;
        lastleftFoot._alpha = 20;
        lastrightFoot._x = rightPosX[change-1];
        lastrightFoot._y = rightPosY[change-1];
        lastleftFoot._x = leftPosX[change-1];
        lastleftFoot._y = leftPosY[change-1];
        lastrightFoot._rotation =
➡ rightRot[change-1];
        lastleftFoot._rotation =
➡ leftRot[change-1];
    } else {
        lastrightFoot._visible = false;
        lastleftFoot._visible = false;
    }
};
```

This will enable us to see where our feet are going to move from and to, in relation to each other, rather than just giving us a disembodied pair of feet with no reference to position. If there is no previous incarnation of the feet, it makes the instance lastrightFoot and lastleftFoot invisible. There is no need to know the last caption so this instruction is omitted from this function.

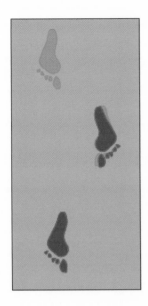

Then come the functions `singleCheck` and `playChecks`, which work hand in hand monitoring the current frame number of the video movie clip and if necessary change the feet position using the `setFeetGraphic` function and then add one to `currentInstruction`.

```
singleCheck = function (added) {
    toCheck = currentInstruction+added;
    if (video._currentframe ==
➡ changeFrame[_root.toCheck]) {
        setFeetGraphic(toCheck);
        _root.currentInstruction += added;
    }
};

playChecks = function () {
        _root.onEnterFrame = function() {
        singleCheck(1);
        };
    };
```

To save a little on processor usage this function stops the `onEnterFrame` script from running. It also lets Flash know that video has stopped playing:

```
stopPlayChecks = function () {
    _root.onEnterFrame = undefined;
    playing = false;
};
```

The following functions are those that our backBut and forwardBut buttons will call. `previousInstruction` checks to see that the current instruction is not the first, calls the `stopPlayChecks` function, then removes 1 from `currentInstruction`. It then positions the feet according to this instruction and moves both video clips to the correct frame.

```
previousInstruction = function () {
    if (currentInstruction>0) {
        stopPlayChecks();
        currentInstruction— —;
        setFeetGraphic(currentInstruction);
        video.gotoAndStop
        ➡ (changeFrame[currentInstruction]);
        videoside.gotoAndStop
        ➡ (changeFrame[currentInstruction]);
    }
};
```

We want `playCheck` to be functioning when the video is playing so we need to attach an extra line of code to PlayBut.

```
controls.playBut.onRelease = function() {
    if (playing == false) {
        video.play();
        videoside.play();
        playChecks();
        playing = true;
    } else {
        video.stop();
        videoside.stop();
        playing = false;
        stopPlayChecks();
    }
};
```

The second function, `nextInstruction`, will act as the `previousInstruction` function yet in reverse. We have to use a -1 with the `currentInstruction` if action, this is due to arrays starting at zero rather than one. The other difference is that the `currentInstruction` is added to rather than subtracted from.

```
nextInstruction = function () {
  if (currentInstruction
  ➥ <changeFrame.length-1) {
    stopPlayChecks();
    currentInstruction++;
    setFeetGraphic(currentInstruction);
    video.gotoAndStop
    ➥ (changeFrame[currentInstruction]);
    videoside.gotoAndStop
    ➥ (changeFrame[currentInstruction]);
  }
};
```

Then we need the code that attaches our previously defined functions to the buttons that we added to the controller earlier.

```
controls.forwardBut.onRelease = function() {
  nextInstruction();
};
controls.backBut.onRelease = function() {
  previousInstruction();
};
```

We need to add some final code to initialize the movie.

We also need to initialize the movie to set one of the videos to visible and one to invisible, so this code needs to be the foot of the ActionScript.

First we set the initial video to be the front view:

```
fvvis = true;
video._visible = true;
videoside._visible = false;
```

`currentInstruction` is set at -1, to act as our counter:

```
currentInstruction = -1;
```

The movie starts to check each frame for instructions with the `playChecks` function:

```
playChecks();
```

We tell Flash that the video is playing:

```
playing == true;
```

Finally, four lines of code make sure that the previous stance is set to a lower depth than the current ones:

```
rightFoot.swapDepths(3);
leftFoot.swapDepths(4);
duplicateMovieClip("rightFoot",
➥ "lastrightFoot", 1);
duplicateMovieClip("leftFoot",
➥ "lastleftFoot", 2);
```

This gives some added prominence to the current feet. We don't want to trip ourselves up whilst trying to follow the steps.

We then need to add the `singlecheck` function to our single frame forward and back button code.

```
controls.backFrameBut.onRelease =
➥ function() {
  video.prevFrame();
  videoside.prevFrame();
  playing = false;
  singleCheck(-1);
};
controls.forwardFrameBut.onRelease =
➥ function() {
  video.nextFrame();
  videoside.nextFrame();
  playing = false;
  singleCheck(1);
};
```

The movie is now ready to be published and we are ready for our next lesson – learning our first kata, but that's another book altogether.

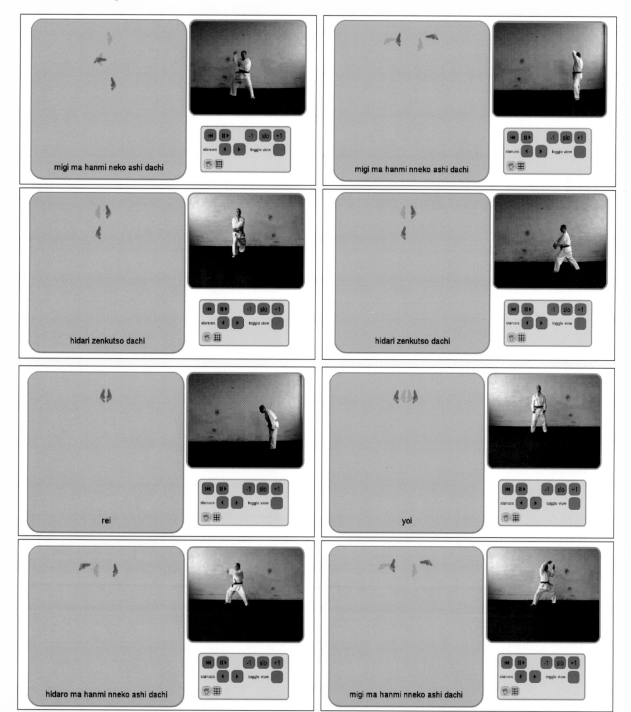

So what next? The movies are modular enough to allow further kata movies to be imported and have the same techniques applied. This could be built up into a whole library of kata videos with diagrammatic foot sequences to accompany them. The Flash movies themselves can be pretty hefty, as even compressed video can take up quite a lot of file size, depending on the quality of the video, but these Flash movies could be run from a CD, or saved as a projector file and downloaded by the user to run as a stand-alone application.

The techniques used in this exercise could be expanded endlessly, with the addition of more variables in the recording movie. We could add another set of symbols to indicate hand movements or have English translations of the named stances.

There are many activities that could be treated in a similar way to this. Many sports that involve a technique based approach could be video taped and imported into Flash for analysis and visual annotation.

Golf swings could be recorded and analyzed to improve technique.

Key moves from football games could have 'expert opinion' style scribbles added to them.

Outside the world of sports Flash could be used as a subtitling application, to translate foreign video clips perhaps as a language teaching aid.

The concept could even be expanded to add animated characters to video clips, in a Mary Poppins or Scooby Doo style.

As with so much in Flash, it is easy to see how you could continue to adapt and expand the techniques here for a wide variety of different uses.

The index is arranged hierarchically, in alphabetical order, with symbols preceding the letter A. Many second-level entries also occur as first-level entries. This is to ensure that you will find the information you require however you choose to search for it.
Download files are listed at the beginning of the index.

friends of Ed particularly welcomes feedback on the layout and structure of this index. If you have any comments or criticisms, please contact:
feedback@friendsofed.com

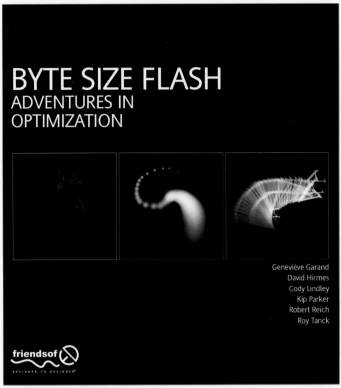

BYTE SIZE FLASH
ADVENTURES IN
OPTIMIZATION

Geneviève Garand
David Hirmes
Cody Lindley
Kip Parker
Robert Reich
Roy Tanck

friendsof
DESIGNER TO DESIGNER®

isbn: 1-904344-09-7
price: $29.99
publication date: december 2002

This collection shows you just exactly what can be done with **tiny** Flash files, using some of the **hottest** Flash designers around. These authors pull designs out of the top drawer and show you exactly how you can go about creating great SWFs with the smallest amount of download pain.

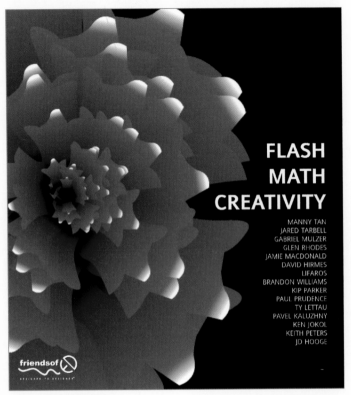

isbn: 1-903450-50-0
price: $49.99
publication date: january 2002

Forget school math class, **Flash Math** is about fun. It's what you do in your spare time - messing around with little ideas until the design takes over and you end up with something **beautiful**, **bizarre**, or just downright **brilliant**. It's a book of iterative experiments, generative design; a book of inspiration, beautiful enough to leave on the coffee table, but **addictive** enough to keep by your computer and sneak out while no-one's looking so you can go back to that Flash movie that you were tinkering with 'til 3 o'clock this morning.

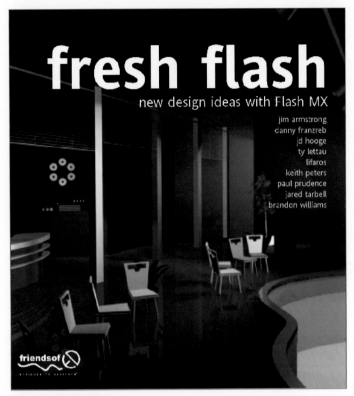

isbn: 1-903450-99-3
price: $49.99
publication date: september 2002

From the acclaimed team that brought you **Flash Math Creativity** comes this inspiring volume, full of brand new effects and discussion on what Flash MX is going to do for designers -- and where we go from here.

isbn: 1-903450-58-6
price: $49.99
publication date: september 2002

This title provides the **Flash MX designer** with a rich reference for all things ActionScript-related. It features a designer-oriented A-Z reference of the ActionScript language, all appropriately demonstrated in FLAs on the accompanying CD. These examples illustrate **ActionScript** in context - that is, in the combinations that you're likely to encounter them in the real world. The book also has substantial narrative sections that cover global approaches to solving common design problems with ActionScript. This book is designer-focused, and aims to be the richest and most practical ActionScript **reference** ever created.